The Honshu PIONEER

The U.S. Occupation of Japan
and the First G.I. Newspaper

TOM THOMAS

Copyright © 2013 by Arthur DeLong Thomas III
All rights reserved, including the right to reproduce
this book, or portions thereof, in any form.

ISBN: 1489523669
ISBN 13: 9781489523662

Library of Congress Number: 2013909645
CreateSpace Independent Publishing Platform
North Charleston, South Carolina

The Honshu PIONEER

The U.S. Occupation of Japan
and the First G.I. Newspaper

EDITED BY

TOM THOMAS

FOREWORD

My late father, Arthur DeLong Thomas, Jr., served in the U.S. Army during World War II. He was in the OSS, which later became the CIA, and his military career was more interesting than most, I would imagine. A very brief summary: He served in both theaters of the war, and was involved in secret operations behind enemy lines in Germany, where he was wounded. He was sent to England for medical repairs, came home on furlough for a bit, and was then posted to Japan in the very early days of the U.S. Occupation.

It is this last phase of his service that is of interest to us here, because he helped found the first daily newspaper for American servicemen in Japan – the aptly named Honshu Pioneer. Dad did not talk a great deal about his Army days when I was growing up, other than a few humorous anecdotes, but I did hear about the Honshu Pioneer a few times. He and my mother had both worked on the yearbook at Dearborn High School, which was called the Pioneer, and she was of the opinion that Dad had named the newspaper in its honor. (Perhaps, but there are other theories on this.)

Dad died in November, 2004, but it was not until after my mother passed away in June, 2012 that I discovered the existence of a large collection of Honshu Pioneer issues that Dad had brought home from Japan with him. These were printed by mimeograph on the lowest quality paper imaginable, but had survived in surprisingly good condition. They start in late September, 1945 and end in February, 1946. I assume that Dad returned home after that date, or the Honshu Pioneer ceased publication altogether.

I started reading through these papers in a kind of random fashion, focusing mainly on things written by my father, but to say they were fascinating and educational from a historical perspective would be an understatement. Naturally, the most compelling aspect of them for me personally was hearing my father speak "from beyond the grave", as it were, in his daily column. To my surprise, I discovered that his column usually had little to do with world politics, the occupation itself, or even local news and current events. I would characterize it as a humor column, dealing primarily with the issues faced by servicemen in a foreign land who want nothing more than to go home, but instead must deal with all manner of privations and the absurdity of military life. Some, though, were just pure (often zany) entertainment.

My father was well known for his sense of humor in later years, so I suppose I should not have been surprised that it was so evident in his columns. In my childhood, he often regaled us at bedtime with extemporaneous stories about the outrageous exploits of Eunice and Ephraim (or "U" and "F") – two incorrigible children who left a trail of havoc wherever they went. He was also quite good at composing ridiculous nonsense songs and verse. Nevertheless, I found his courage in poking fun at just about everybody and everything, in the aftermath of a war, while living in the homeland of a defeated enemy, and under military supervision, to be pretty remarkable.

I think Dad got away with his irreverent humor in part because a casual or dull reader might not even realize that he was being funny. There was a dry, deadpan, almost British quality to his wit. You have to read carefully and think, at times, to get the joke, or to even realize he is kidding you. His publisher, in the letter of recommendation that he wrote for Dad (reproduced on the next page), mentioned that he was "called on the carpet" by the top brass more often for Dad's columns than for any other cause, which in his opinion was very high praise. My guess is that the top brass actually missed the joke more times than not.

```
                                        1020 Shasta Avenue
                                        Dunsmuir, California
                                        March 24, 1946

To: Whom it may concern:

The bearer of this letter, Mr. A. D. Thomas, was a member of the
staff of the GI newspaper HONSHU PIONEER from September 1945
until January 1946. During that time Mr. Thomas contributed a
daily column and wrote other original material for the Sunday
Supplement of the PIONEER. In addition to these duties he wrote
news articles and covered many special events as a representative
of the paper.

Although the PIONEER was, at its best, only a memeographed
facsimile of of our larger dailies, it gained fame as the "First
GI Daily in Japan". It was later described by the Pacific
Stars and Stripes as 'One of the best, and undoubtedly the cockiest,
GI publication we've read---'.

Naturally Army newspapers don't enjoy full freedom of the press.
I was called 'on the carpet' concerning Mr. Thomas' writings
more often than for any other feature of the newspaper. I consider
that to be a great compliment indeed.

Mr. Thomas' experiences in counter-intelligence work in Germany--
where he made a narrow escape from death in a patrol behind the
enemy lines---and later his firsthand glimpse of Japan shortly
after the surrender have afforded him with an excellent background.

I have known Mr. Thomas since the early part of 1944 when he
was assigned to K Company of the 303d Infantry Regiment, 97th
Division.

I consider it a privilIege to recommend him most highly.

                                    Sincerely yours,

                                    James P. Hanratty

                                    JAMES P. HANRATTY
                                    (Former Editor, HONSHU PIONEER)
```

    Interestingly, I was exactly three days old when that letter was written.

That this merry band of scribes was able to publish a 4-page newspaper every day (with a special insert on Sunday) was a near-miracle in its own right. I don't know if you are old enough to remember what a mimeograph machine was, but it was like a repetitive silkscreen process, where ink was squeezed through a master stencil that had been cut by a manual typewriter and stretched over a rotating drum. Corrections could only be made by over-striking with the typewriter or manually scratching the stencil with a stylus. Any letters bigger than the standard typewriter font had to be hand-drawn with a stylus and perhaps a standard alphabet stencil, and, of course, all illustrations were drawn by hand.

I have selected the very first issue to use the name Honshu Pioneer (the first few issues used the name Kazo Kurier, until relocation made that obsolete) as one of the more legible examples to scan in its entirety, to give you an idea of what the Honshu Pioneer looked like. Pages were 7 inches wide by 10 inches high, so if we shrink the images a bit, they should fit pretty well on this format. The paper color reflects about 67 years of oxidation, achieving a shade I would call "pale pumpkin". It's not the original shade, but I doubt that the original paper was lily-white, anyway. These pages were scanned as color JPEG files, but knowing they would be printed in black and white, I bleached them electronically as best I could.

As luck would have it, a very prophetic editorial appeared on Page 2 of this particular issue. It was called "WHY STRIKES!", describing the attacks on American unions that were already under way at that time, and continue to this day. It not-so-subtly points out that Hitler and Tojo both banned unions in their countries, but American unions were instrumental in supporting the war effort. In the interest of fair play, the Pioneer presented both sides of the union debate on this page. The opposing opinion, called "THE STRIKE MENACE" is also interesting, because it only questions the behavior of unions at that time, while still agreeing that "organized labor is necessary". If this debate were held again in 2013, I wonder whether either side would make that claim. This was my first clue that I ought to be paying more attention to the editorial content of the paper, regardless of who wrote it.

This sample issue also happens to contain my father's very first daily column, "FROM A 2-SEATER", although not yet under his byline. This same column will be included again in the transcribed section later in this book. As it always did, Dad's column appears in the upper left corner of Page 3.

HONSHU PIONEER

THE FIRST G.I. DAILY IN JAPAN

UNIFORM STILL | DUFFLE BAGS

VOL. I NO. 11   KAZO   * * *   JAPAN   OCT. 9, 1945

CHINESE TAKE OVER FORMOSA

An advance party of Chinese landed at Kilung to make preparations for the formal entry of troops into Formosa.

The Island has been in Japanese hands since 1898 when they took it from a weak Chinese government.

EUROPE NEEDS FOOD - TRUMAN

President Truman asked Congress today that 550 millions be appropriated to UNRRA to alleviate Europe's food shortage.

NAVY RELEASES SPEEDED-UP

While the Senate was trying to decide on a committee to investigate Army demobilization, the Navy revealed its critical point score will be lowered by November first.

KAZO KURIER BOWS OUT

At 2400 yesterday the roar of the mighty presses ceased momentarily, the staff bowed their heads for a few seconds silence, and the Kazo Kurier solemnly took its place among the great publications of the past.

Simultaneously, not unlike the Phoenix rising out of the ashes, the Honshu Pioneer materialized.

Our movement to Kagohara Airfield necessitated a change in the name of the paper to one which would not denote our geographical location in such a strict manner.

Anticipating our transfer, the paper sponsored a Pick-A-Name Contest among our readers, several days ago. Over a hundred entrants were considered before the name suggested by Pfc Jean Tartter was selected.

41ST & 25TH DIVS HIT JAPLAND

After several days of bad weather, the veteran 41st and 25th Infantry Divisions, landed yesterday on the Islands of Honshu and Hokkaido.

The 41st landed at Otaru, Hokkaido, to swell the Ninth Army.

The Eighth Army was joined by the 25th, which came ashore at Hiroshima and Nagoya.

STUDENTS PACK JAILS IN B. AIRES

The spirit of an awakening democracy put in a tragic appearance in Buenos Aires Monday.

The funeral of a student killed by the terror developed into a demonstration by the thousands of attending youth. Arrests were so great criminals were let go to empty cells.

HONSHU PIONEER
Published daily for
the members of K Co,
303 Infantry, APO 445
at Kagohara, Honshu

Publisher................Capt. F. Arthur
Editor..................J. P. Hanratty
Sunday Editor...........H.H. Owen
Features...............F.W. Stark
News Editors...........A.D. Thomas
                      Myron Adler
Sports Editor..........D.E. Anderson
Art Editors............T.W. Sibbitt
                      R.M. Allen
Business Mgr...........R.D. Andrews
Circ. Mgr..............J.E. Rich
Columnist..............A. Hamburger
Printer................E.J. Zapp

Formerly publ'd as the KAZO KURIER.

EDITORIAL

THE LABOR QUESTION:
(Editor's note:...Two Pioneer staff members have disturbed their fellow workers several times by heated arguments on the subject of unions, strikes, and labor in general. It was unanimously agreed to let them air their opinions below.)

THE STRIKE MENACE:
It's very true that the World Charter may end all World Wars, but what guarantee is there against a revolution in the United States? The ultimate in the disputes between labor and management if they are to continue is something more than strikes.

The unions have turned down every proposal that has been made toward any solution. They say that strikes are only used as a last resort. They seem to have forgotten what the laborer is to subsist on while he is on strike.

Organized labor is necessary, but the present methods that are used to reach their ends aren't.

Our government at present is trying to form a federal commission, consisting of six men, that would have the final say in all labor disputes. The members would be completely impartial, and if at any time one of the members is undesirable to either party they can ask to have him replaced----unions object. What are they afraid of?

One must choose the sole leader—government or unions. Who thinks that he would be better off under the rule of a few men not elected?

WHY STRIKES!
Hitler in Germany and Tojo in Japan abolished all labor unions.

In the U.S. the C.I.O. and AFL called for increased production; condemned even the 1/10 of one percent of all workers who were on strike at any one time.

Why the present wave of strikes today in the nation?

The campaign to discredit the unions with the public and servicemen that was carried on during the conflict has now been intensified. Unemployment is expected to reach 8,000,000. Wages are being cut. Hours are lowered. Anti-union laws are being passed. Wartime improvements in conditions and higher standard of living are disappearing.

The unions have a job. Their weapon is the strike. It is used as a last resort when all mediation and arbitration prove futile. It is dreaded by all. Men receive no pay, risk their security; funds are depleted by legal battles. Better for all are gains without strikes.

Unions have given the 8 hour day, safety devices, better conditions, - etc. to progress. Future holds more.

FROM A 2-SEATER

Sitting here wetly, thinking dank thoughts, my interest is arrested by the "2 1/2" in front of Guard Post #5. Now that we've spent two weeks guarding $800,000 worth of signed-for equipment, Division Salvage takes it away; nothing left for our next tenants to guard. Now, K, 386 will have nothing to do, but favorably compare Camp Arthur to their old home.

* * *

Now that the war is over and Sunday drivers are cluttering up the highways, accidents in the states are mounting mercurially.

Cpt. Arthur excited camp traffic yesterday, when he plowed up a sturdy Japanese oak with Jerry White's jeep.

The tree won't be missed. It might be the accident was done with an appreciative eye for landscape.

* * *

I've seen some darn attractive kimonos that have really been gifts for as little a price as a carton of cigarettes. Hey Mac will you pass that butt this way after the next drag?

* * *

"It is a pleasure and an honor to be placed in command of a unit which has a record as outstanding as that of the 97th Infantry Div."
——Major General H.F. Kramer on assuming command of the 97th Div.

"It is indeed an honor to assume command of the 3rd Army whose breakthrough in France and Germany wrote so glowing a chapter in the annals of military history." said Lt General L.K. Truscott on assuming command of the 3rd Army.

DEPARTMENTAL SUMMARIES

WAR: Advanced ROTC was reactivated today, after a lapse two years. Veterans wishing to enroll in advanced RO will receive monetary allowances in addition to those provided by the G.I. Bill of Rights.

NAVY: Admiral Daniels led 5 cruisers into the Chinese-Communist controlled port of Chefoo.

STATE: Portugal was making preparations to enter the war against Japan to recoup their loss of Portugese Timor when the war ended.

* * *

PVT. H. B. TWILL — CAMP ARTHUR

"THERE'S A YEN, CHERRY B. IT'S YER 10% CUT FER BRING-IN' ME LUCK IN THE CRAP GAME LAST NIGHT."

SPORTS

HOLY CROSS

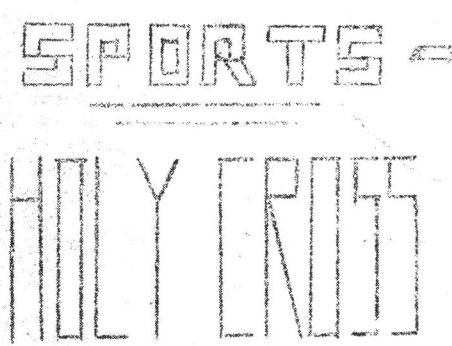

In the pre season forecasts it was agreed by the experts that the greatest teams in the East were, of course, Army and Navy. The first two weeks of the season have certainly proved this without a shadow of a doubt.

The writers went on to say that the third most powerful eleven was the "Red and Blue" of Penn. This, to be sure, is partially true because Penn romped over Brown and won a close one from Dartmouth, but it is quite evident now that the experts overlooked the Holy Cross Crusaders from Worchester, Mass.

The unheralded Holy Cross delegation was equal to Penn. in beating Dartmouth but looked far superior to the "Red and Blue" when they bowl over a strong Yale last Saturday.

The Crusaders' schedule of remaining games contain nothing better than second-rate teams so you can expect and undefeated, untied season for Holy Cross.

Apologies to —
Doug Jackson!!!

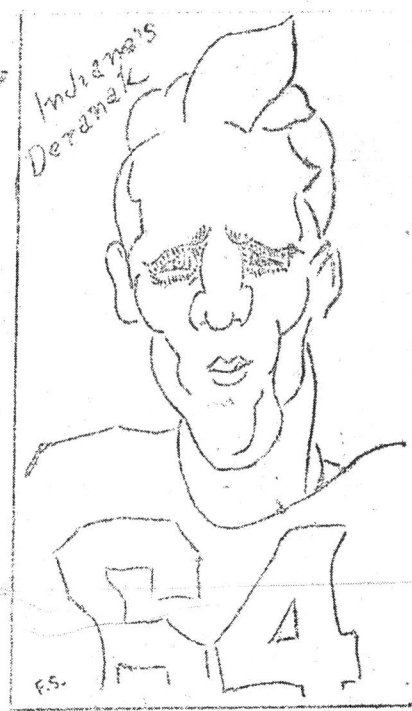

Indiana's Deramax

f.s.

BIG TEN CONFERENCE STANDINGS

	Won	Lost	Tied	Pct.
Indiana	2	0	1	1000
Ohio State	1	0	0	1000
Purdue	1	0	0	1000
Michigan	1	1	0	.500
Northwestern	0	1	1	.000
Wisconsin	0	1	0	.000
Iowa	0	1	0	.000
Illinois	0	1	0	.000
Minnesota	0	0	0	.000

SATURDAY'S CONFERENCE TILTS:
Ohio State at Wisconsin
Purdue at Iowa

When I say that this was one of the more legible specimens, I am not joking, so you should get some idea of the overall print quality we are dealing with. (Actually, I am the one dealing with it. You will be able to read the transcribed versions.) Print quality did start to improve over time, but typos, spacing problems and spelling errors never really disappeared.

I decided that Dad's Honshu Pioneer columns really ought to be collected, published and preserved for future generations of our family, and anyone else who might be interested. It would have been nice (and a lot less work) to just scan each issue digitally and publish those images, but the print quality is so poor on many them that this would not have produced worthwhile results. Consequently, I have transcribed them all, sometimes using a magnifying glass, and often guessing at missing or illegible words from the surrounding context. I have also taken the liberty of correcting some spelling and punctuation errors (Dad's was almost always abominable – how did he get through Harvard?).

To provide some historical context, I have included the headlines and brief news summaries from each issue, and again, I learned a great deal about this particular period of history in the process. It is hard to imagine that another half-year could have been chosen out of the 20th Century that would have included more major (and far-reaching) events unfolding on the world stage than this one.

As I read through the papers in chronological sequence, my interest in the events described and the editorial opinions expressed began to equal my interest in my father's columns, so I started including more and more of this material. These writings were as remarkable as anything offered up by my father in their fearless criticism of both Army decisions and U.S. foreign policy. They also maintained almost incredibly high moral standards, and clearly they wanted their sacrifices during the war to result in a better world for everyone. Some of their expectations may seem pretty naïve by today's standards, but they were nearly always standing on moral high ground.

Finally, I started to pay more attention to the cartoons in each issue – most of them drawn by Fred Stark. I slowly came to the realization that Fred was communicating the experience of the GI's stationed in Japan far better than anything else in the paper, and that he was much more than just a gifted graphic artist. Actually, his work is really worthy of its own book, so I collected all his output and attached to the end of this book as a sort of appendix, which for some readers might be the best part of the whole thing.

Now that the transcribing, scanning, editing and publishing tasks are complete, my intention is to donate the Honshu Pioneer originals to the University of Michigan History Department, provided they have any interest in them. The U of M is where Dad received his Masters Degree in History after graduating from Harvard when the war was over. It is also the alma mater of both his father and his son (me), not to mention quite a few other family members, and he actually taught at their Dearborn Campus, so I think it is what he would have wanted.

HISTORICAL NOTES

To better understand the Honshu Pioneer, I wanted to find some background information on the U.S. Occupation of Japan – timing, goals, guidelines, etc. – so I went to the most authoritative source I could think of – Wikipedia. (Plus all their content is free to reproduce, which is very friendly.) Here's what I learned:

Japan surrendered to the Allies on August 14, 1945, when the Japanese government notified the Allies that it had accepted the Potsdam Declaration. On the following day, Emperor Hirohito announced Japan's unconditional surrender on the radio (the Gyokuon-hōsō). The announcement was the emperor's first ever radio broadcast and the first time most citizens of Japan ever heard their sovereign's voice. This date is known as Victory Over Japan, or V-J Day, and marked the end of World War II and the beginning of a long road to recovery for a shattered Japan.

On V-J Day, United States President Harry Truman appointed General Douglas MacArthur as Supreme Commander for the Allied Powers (SCAP), to supervise the occupation of Japan. During the war, the Allied Powers had planned to divide Japan amongst themselves for the purposes of occupation, as was done for the occupation of Germany. Under the final plan, however, SCAP was given direct control over the main islands of Japan (Honshū, Hokkaido, Shikoku and Kyūshū) and the immediately surrounding islands, while outlying possessions were divided between the Allied Powers as follows:

- Soviet Union: North Korea (not a full occupation), Sakhalin, and the Kuril Islands
- United States: South Korea (not a full occupation), Okinawa, the Amami Islands, the Ogasawara Islands and Japanese possessions in Micronesia
- Republic of China: Taiwan and Penghu

It is unclear why the occupation plan was changed. Common theories include the increased power of the United States following development of the atomic bomb, Truman's greater distrust of the Soviet Union when compared with Roosevelt, and an increased desire to contain Soviet expansion in the Far East after the Yalta Conference.

The Soviet Union had some intentions of occupying Hokkaidō. Had this occurred, there might have been the foundation of a communist "Democratic People's Republic of Japan" in the Soviet zone of occupation. However, unlike the Soviet occupations of East Germany and North Korea, these plans were frustrated by the opposition of U.S. President Harry S. Truman.

The Far Eastern Commission and Allied Council for Japan were also established to supervise the occupation of Japan.

Japanese officials left for Manila on August 19 to meet MacArthur and to be briefed on his plans for the occupation. On August 28, 150 U.S. personnel flew to Atsugi, Kanagawa Prefecture. They were followed by USS Missouri, whose accompanying vessels landed the 4th Marine Division on the southern coast of Kanagawa. Other Allied personnel followed.

MacArthur arrived in Tokyo on August 30, and immediately decreed several laws: No Allied personnel were to assault Japanese people. No Allied personnel were to eat the scarce Japanese food. Flying the Hinomaru or "Rising Sun" flag was initially severely restricted (although individuals and prefectural offices could apply for permission to fly it). The restriction was partially lifted in 1948 and completely lifted the following year.

On September 2, Japan formally surrendered with the signing of the Japanese Instrument of Surrender. On September 6, U.S. President Truman approved a document titled "US Initial Post-Surrender Policy for Japan". The document set two main objectives for the occupation: (1) eliminating Japan's war potential and (2) turning Japan into a western style nation with pro-American orientation. Allied (primarily American) forces were set up to supervise the country, and "for eighty months following its surrender in 1945, Japan was at the mercy of an army of occupation, its people subject to foreign military control." At the head of the Occupation administration was General MacArthur who was technically supposed to defer to an advisory council set up by the Allied powers, but in practice did everything himself. As a result, this period was one of significant American influence, having been already identified in 1951, that "for six years the United States has had a freer hand to experiment with Japan than any other country in Asia, or indeed in the entire world."

MacArthur's first priority was to set up a food distribution network; following the collapse of the ruling government and the wholesale destruction of most major cities, virtually everyone was starving. Even with these measures, millions of people were still on the brink of starvation for several years after the surrender. As expressed by Kawai Kazuo, "Democracy cannot be taught to a starving people," and while the US government encouraged democratic reform in Japan, it also sent billions of dollars in aid.

By the end of 1945, more than 350,000 U.S. personnel were stationed throughout Japan. By the beginning of 1946, replacement troops began to arrive in the country in large numbers and were assigned to MacArthur's Eighth Army, headquartered in Tokyo's Dai-Ichi building. Of the main Japanese islands, Kyūshū was occupied by the 24th Infantry Division, with some responsibility for Shikoku. Honshū was occupied by the First Cavalry Division. Hokkaido was occupied by the 11th Airborne Division.

I also checked on the World War II record of the 97th Infantry Division, which was home to the Honshu Pioneer staff. Their accomplishments were pretty remarkable. The 303rd Regiment, which these guys belonged to, is actually mentioned in the saga below:

> The 97th Infantry Division landed at Le Havre, France, 2 March 1945, and moved to Camp Lucky Strike. On 28 March, the division crossed the German border west of Aache and took up a defensive position along the west bank of the Rhine River opposite Düsseldorf, engaging in patrolling. The 97th entered the battle of the Ruhr pocket crossing the Rhine near Bonn, 3 April, and taking up a position on the southern bank of the Sieg River. It crossed that river, 7 April, with the troops suffering 80% casualties in wounded and dead. However, many of the survivors credit their lives to Pfc. John Hedrick, who took control of an abandoned boat and made sure the survivors crossed the river safely. He received the Silver Star for his valiant efforts. There was a building marked by a red cross which the 97th assumed was a hospital and therefore, did not attack it. In fact, it was a factory that made German 88's. The Germans had tunnels dug there and after the troops got up on land, past the river, the Germans came up behind them. They then shot at the Americans from both directions. It fought a street-to-street engagement in Siegburg on 10 April.
>
> After Siegburg, they captured Cologne (Koeln) Germany. Pushing on toward Düsseldorf through difficult terrain and heavy resistance in densely wooded areas, the division captured Solingen on 17 April. The Germans cut down trees to impede the infantry's

advance, thus blocking the roads in the woods. Düsseldorf fell on the next day and the Ruhr pocket was eliminated. The infantry drove through Düsseldorf, waiting for the Germans to shoot at them; then they would find the pockets of Germans and shoot at them to flush them out.

On 23 April elements of the 97th, together with members of the 90th Infantry Division, liberated Flossenbürg concentration camp near Floß in Bavaria. A Military Police patrol from the 303rd Infantry Regiment may have been the first U.S. Army unit to reach the camp, although the 2nd Cavalry Group, Mechanized, as well as a colonel from the 90th later took credit for liberating the camp. Members of the 97th Division treated sick and dying prisoners and buried the several hundred corpses discovered in the camp. Brigadier General Halsey inspected the camp as did General Sherman V. Hasbrouck, the commanding officer of the division artillery. Members of the Counter Intelligence Corps, which included Robie Macauley, Ib Melchior and Anthony Hecht, interviewed former prisoners and gathered evidence for trials of former camp officers and guards. The 97th also liberated Helmbrechts concentration camp, a sub-camp of Flossenbürg for female prisoners.

On 25 April the division entered Ash, Czechoslovakia. Moving to protect the left flank of the Third Army on its southern drive, the 97th took Cheb, Czechoslovakia, on 25 April 1945 and attacked the Czechoslovak pocket near Weiden, Germany, on 29 April. It had advanced to Konstantinovy Lázně, Czechoslovakia, when it received the cease-fire order on 7 May. Part of the division was in Teplá where the German 2nd Panzer Division had surrendered. The troops used the monastery there as a POW camp for the Germans.

The division left for Le Havre, 16 June 1945, for redeployment to the Pacific, arriving at Cebu, Philippine Islands, 16 September, and then sailed to Japan for occupation duty, arriving at Yokohama on 23 September 1945.

97th Infantry Division was credited with firing the last official shot in the European Theater of Operations during World War II. This shot was fired by PFC Domenic Mozzetta of Company B, 387th Infantry Regiment, 97th Division, at a German sniper near Klenovice, Czechoslovakia shortly before midnight, 7 May 1945.

The Division was made inactive in March, 1946 in Japan.

It is fair to say that my father must have been involved in a good deal of this. I do remember one story of him paddling a canoe across the Rhine River in the dark of night, to do some reconnaissance, and shooting out a German searchlight with his M-1, so he was probably present from the beginning of the above account. I also know that he used his German language skills to interview a number of prisoners and local people, but I have no details. After reading this description of their exploits, I would have to say that any member of this Division should be extremely proud of its achievements.

The Honshu Pioneer's unit – K Company of the 303rd Infantry Regiment, 97th Infantry Division – arrived in Kazo, Japan on the island of Honshu on September 26, 1945, just over three weeks after the surrender was signed.

BIOGRAPHICAL NOTES – MY FATHER

Arthur DeLong Thomas, Jr. was born August 20, 1923 and grew up in Dearborn, Michigan. He met Mary Jean Armstrong (always known as "Sarge", even back then) in Latin class at Dearborn High School, where both of them were also in the marching band (She played clarinet. He played bassoon.) and worked together on the school paper and yearbook. They graduated in June, 1941, and both left for college the following fall. Art went to Harvard, where he majored in sociology. He struggled mightily in his freshman year, primarily because he chose to study Greek and German at the same time. (Who would do that?) Sarge matriculated at Michigan State, where she majored in advanced calculus and eventually graduated second in her class. (She was a woman of exceptional intelligence, skills and beauty, but that, as they say, is another story.)

Art was in the Harvard class of 1945, but did not graduate that year, because World War II intervened. When the Army discovered that he spoke German (sort of), he was sent off for more intensive language training and then assigned to the OSS for intelligence work. He was posted to Germany, where he was involved in a number of "cloak and dagger" episodes, the most famous and dangerous of which was a behind-the-lines patrol to capture a certain German rocket scientist. (I only heard this tale a couple of times, and the last was over 50 years ago, so some details might be muddled, but I will try to recount it here.)

> Four OSS men got behind the German lines at night, driving a Jeep with no lights, to avoid detection. The Germans had conveniently dug a large pit in the road, to guard against just such enemy activity. The Jeep crashed into the pit at a considerable

rate of speed and all occupants were thrown from the vehicle. One was killed, while Art had his face bashed in and was unconscious. The other two were shaken, but not seriously injured. They stashed their unfortunate comrades in the woods, after wrapping up Art's bleeding face as best they could. They then extricated the Jeep from the pit somehow, completed their mission successfully, came back and collected Art, and then went door to door in search of a German doctor. They found one soon enough, and Art, having regained consciousness, said to him, "Es ist sehr oberflächlich." (It is very superficial.) The doctor was quite surprised to be addressed in his native tongue by an American G.I., but the injuries were actually not all that superficial. Most of the bones in his face were broken, and it took a fair amount of surgery in England to put his visage back together.

The two successful members of this patrol both received the Silver Star for their efforts, but Art never even got a Purple Heart. He wrote a famous (or infamous) letter to Sarge from England, describing the nice view from his London hospital room. It began, "From what I can see out of one eye…" with no further description of his injuries, leaving Sarge to speculate on what pieces of her husband still remained intact. Fortunately, the English doctors did a fine job of reassembling his face.

Before Art was shipped to Germany, he and Sarge were married on December 28, 1944 in the Martha Mary Chapel at Greenfield Village in Dearborn. (See photo next page.)

After returning from the English hospital and spending some time back home, Art was sent to San Luis Obispo, California for additional training, in preparation for his next assignment – the occupation of Japan. His experiences in Japan can be pretty well inferred from his writings in the Honshu Pioneer, which form the main body of this book.

After the war, he returned to Harvard, this time with his wife and infant son (me), and completed his undergraduate degree. He then moved his family to Willow Run, Michigan, where we lived in some tiny Quonset hut apartments that were left over from some wartime activity in the area, I think. Thanks to the GI Bill, Art enrolled in the Masters program at the University of Michigan, studying history, and supported us by working on the assembly line at Ford Motor Company, and also by building ships at the Great Lakes Shipyard. (One of my earliest memories is watching a huge ore freighter that Dad had worked on slide down the ways at its initial launching.) Art and Sarge also added a daughter, Abbie, to the family during this time.

After receiving his Masters degree, Art embarked on a teaching career, which would consume his entire working life. He started in a rural one-room school in eastern Michigan, then landed a job at a junior high school in Dearborn, and then moved up to teach at Dearborn High School, where he had been a student only a few years earlier. After two years at DHS, however, he got the opportunity to teach American history at Henry Ford Community College, which was the crown jewel of the Dearborn Public School system.

He taught history there for over 30 years, and held a number of additional posts, including Dean of Academic Education, which are summarized in a few pages. However, he loved teaching and disliked administration, so he requested a return to the classroom full-time, which was eventually granted. His classes were considered among the toughest at HFCC. He lectured at a terrific pace, and covered a lot of ground, but even worse (in some opinions) he did not believe in grading on a curve. He had absolute standards, and if one or two students in the class managed to meet them (about the usual number, I think), they might get an A. (It should be borne in mind that the admission policy at HFCC was such that any graduate of any Dearborn high school would be admitted, so grading on a curve might have been a questionable idea, anyway.)

After a few years, Art also began teaching history classes at the University of Michigan, Dearborn Campus, which was practically next door to HFCC, since both were built on land that had been part of Henry Ford's Fairlane estate. Art was also known as an expert on the pre-Revolutionary period of American history, and often received manuscripts from publishers to review, for books pertaining to that period. In the summer he worked for the Dearborn Department of Recreation as a tennis instructor and playground supervisor. He was a good athlete and had absolutely classic tennis strokes, although he wasn't very successful as a tournament player. Sarge, on the other hand, actually won the Detroit News Novice Tournament one year – a testament to Art's coaching skill.

After her children reached a certain age, Sarge also started teaching for the Dearborn Public School system, first as a high school math teacher, but later she also joined the faculty of HFCC, teaching math and logic. Her teaching career was interrupted in 1963 by the arrival of a third child – Amy. Art and Sarge remained at HFCC until their retirement in 1985. They joined Elderhostel and took educational trips all over the world, usually with groups that included other bridge players. Bridge was a lifelong passion for both of them.

Art was contacted by HFCC as their 50th anniversary was approaching. The school was founded in 1938 and had grown almost incredibly in size and reputation in the ensuing half-century. They asked Art to write a history of the college, to be published as part of the anniversary celebration. This was not a trivial task, at least not the way Art went at it. Sarge was also deeply involved as editor and contributor, since she could type about three times as fast as Art, and also had a better grasp of little grammatical details like punctuation.

After more than a year of work by both of them, the book was published by HFCC in 1988, right on schedule. It was entitled <u>For the Good of All – A Pledge Respected</u>, 347 pages, including indexes, appendices and eight pages of footnotes. (Library of Congress Catalog Card Number 88-80703) The title was taken in part from the school's Latin motto: "Pro Bono Omnium", which means "For the Good of All". This was a very thorough scholarly work, but, of course, my father managed to cram in every humorous anecdote he knew of, as well as some of the political power struggles and policy battles that took place over the years.

Near the end of the book, the college provided a photo of Art in the classroom, with a brief summary of his contributions to HFCC. It has been included on the next page.

Arthur D. Thomas, Jr. acted in many roles at Henry Ford Community College prior to his retirement in 1985. He joined the College History Faculty in 1954 and at various times has been Social Science Division Head, Chair of the Faculty Senate, Chapter President of the American Association of University Professors and interim Dean of Academic Education. In addition to these major posts his services in such diverse activities as tennis coach, Faculty Sponsor of the Air Force ROTC and numerous other committee posts have given him insight into College operation and history. Mr. Thomas took his Baccalaureate at Harvard College and his Master of Arts in History at the University of Michigan. He is a member of numerous professional associations.

Somewhere in the 1990's, Art had a stroke that left him weak on his left side, and pretty much put an end to their world travel. However, he and Sarge still made it up to Ipperwash Beach in Canada every summer for family vacations, and down to Cincinnati to visit their grandchildren at the holidays for several more years. Eventually, though, he started to become confused, and would wander off if not watched closely. His conversation also started to drift off, and he couldn't follow a train of thought for long. At one point he told Sarge that he couldn't concentrate well enough to play bridge any more – a huge blow for her. Sarge finally had to place him in the nursing home section of the retirement community they were living in, where she visited him every day for the rest of his life.

Art died on November 22, 2004, after a few more years of decline into dementia. The death certificate listed Alzheimer's Disease as the cause that gradually rendered him mute and insensible – a sad end for such a clever and entertaining man, but he had a great life.

TRANSCRIBED COLUMNS, EDITORIALS, DAILY HEADLINES

EDITOR'S NOTE: From here on, it's all transcriptions of daily headlines and brief news summaries, columns, some of the more interesting editorials, and other odds and ends from the newspapers themselves, including an appendix of cartoons drawn by Fred Stark. I have sprinkled in some [quite a few, actually] explanatory comments and thoughts of my own, in the form of "editor's notes", which are always in italics and parentheses. I will not be explaining my father's jokes, however, unless I happen to be in possession of "inside information" that might help you understand them, but if you assume that everything he writes is meant to be funny at some level, you won't be far off.

All material directly transcribed from the <u>Honshu Pioneer</u> is printed in the closest font I could find to the original 1945 manual typewriter keys:

```
Courier New
```

KAZO KURIER – VOL I, NO 1 – KAZO, HONSHU – SEPT. 29, 1945

HEADLINES:
1. A NEWSPAPER IS BORN – KAY COMPANY INITIATES FIRST G.I. DAILY NEWS IN HONSHU
2. HIROHITO BOWS TO MACARTHUR (The bow took place yesterday at the American Embassy. Rumors of Hirohito's abdication are still prevalent.)
3. NEWS BULLETIN (Secretary Patterson predicts that 7,000,000 of the 8,000,000 men in the U.S. Army will be civilians by July 1, 1946.)

(EDITOR'S NOTE: This paper was printed only 2 days after K Company landed in Japan, and there was not much to it.)

I. KAZO KURIER – VOL I, NO 4 – KAZO, HONSHU – OCT. 2, 1945

HEADLINES:
1. EICHELBERGER TOURS ALL 8TH ARMY UNITS – (The General will make an inspection tour of all units under his command - No mention of the 97th, though)
2. K CO. COMMANDER DISSATISFIED WITH GUARD (Capt. Arthur to K Co.: Wear weapons, stand up, know special and general orders, and BE ALERT!)
3. LEATHERNECKS GO WADING (In China, 1st Marines waded ashore "in full battle dress, met by joyous Chinks firing firecrackers. Casualties were slight.")

(EDITOR'S NOTE: That last item sure sounds like my father, but who knows?)

EDITORIAL:

```
                  PERISH FORBID
   The Dodo bird is extinct, pure-blooded South
Sea Islanders are becoming extinct, and so are
whales, walruses, sea otters, and the Greater
Manchurian White Mink. And so are buck privates.

   Now the Army, which never does anything with-
out a good reason, must have had something pret-
ty sharp in mind when they created this rank,
yet there are fewer privates than General Staff
Officers.

   To be sure, a lot of PFC's try to look like
privates by not sewing on their stripes and by
trying to give the impression that they, too,
have been digging latrines and sumps. In combat,
this is practiced by all ranks. But deep down all
```

these soldiers impersonating something which they are not, know that they are only has-beens.

I personally have done my best to keep the rank flourishing and have received official recognition of my efforts in the restoration of my privacy. But I am one of an all too small number which will soon overtake the whales, walruses, sea otters, and the pure-blooded South Sea Islanders, Greater Manchurian White Mink on the lonely path of gradual extinction, a number which must ultimately, like the clumsy Dodo bird, slip unheralded over the brink into the dark abyss of non-existence.

(EDITOR'S NOTE: I do know, positively, that my father wrote this. His own column will not start for a few more days, but after you read through this book [if you do], you will have no doubts about the author of this little gem. After a few more doses of his humor I will not need to inform you that the Greater Manchurian White Mink never existed anywhere except in his imagination.)

KAZO KURIER – VOL I, NO 5 – KAZO, HONSHU – OCT. 3, 1945

HEADLINES:
1. MAGIC CARPET SPEEDS VETS HOME (War Department: 20 escort carriers and 200 transports to be used to take men home, including carriers Hornet, Bunker Hill, Saratoga and Ticonderoga – 400,000 men to be home by Jan. 1, 1946.)
2. KURIER FORECASTS (All men with 60 points will be home by Christmas – those with 2 years of service by "the first swimming of next summer".)
3. STALIN REVEALS RUSSIA'S PLANS (In meetings with Senator Claude Pepper, Stalin expects friendly relations with the U.S. to continue while they rebuild from the war.)

EDITORIAL:
DANGER! MARINES AT WORK

Oh frabjous day! Calooh! Calay! The hard-living, keen-eyed, bronze-bodied Apollos of the "Fightingest force of all" have done it again. That gripping aura of "Do or Die" which has so captured the imagination of the civilian populace of the United States is not to be escaped in time of peace. The lights have gone on again all over the world, but the United States Marine Corps is still leading with its battered, clean-cut chin.

With combat photographers grinding bullet-riddled cameras and combat correspondents pounding shrapnel-shattered typewriters, hell-bent-for-leathernecks splashed grimly ashore near Tinsen, China. All present wore faded H.B.T. fatigues, full field packs, heavy helmets and carried weapons of attractive blue steel. The exciting panorama must have caused a reminiscent tear or three to dribble down the cheeks of any Army doughboys there who had witnessed these spectacles from other beaches in other days.

Coinciding with this front page news comes a world-shaking announcement from Gismofuhrer Vandergrift: An elite body of hand-picked volunteer "Minute Men" is being formed to enforce peace throughout the globe. It's a man-sized assignment, but these are indeed the men to handle it.

Poor simple old Woodrow Wilson - people would have adhered to his 14 points, if only he had a Point 15 with provisions for such an organization, but Vandergrift, with that same perception which carried him to the top in the corps, realizes it's not yet too late. In times to come, the magic phrase "Beware the Marines Minute Men" will strike terror into the hearts of all nations. For how can naughty boys grow to be naughty men, when they are told from the cradle: "Respect the San Francisco Conference, my child, or the big bad Minute Men will get you!" Although startled "Goo" from the little would-be trouble maker may be the only proof he has heard this maternal advice, we can be sure he'll never forget.

And while the Marines dash about the world casting oil on the turbulent waters of the ocean of world peace, rear echelon troops, such as those "Soldiers" who have frittered away the war in the Infantry Divisions, will carry on in well-deserved obscurity, hiding from scornful eyes in the rice paddies of Honshu and the forests of

Bavaria. Our own wistful eyes, surviving piles of fish-heads and frozen bean curds, will often conjure visions of ourselves – clothed in the shiny-white armor of U.S.M.C. Minute Men.

(EDITOR'S NOTE: OK, this piece has no byline, but I know positively that it was written by my father. The infinite sarcasm, the quote from "Jabberwocky" [his favorite poem], the disdain for Marines, and the complete lack of respect for Generals could only have come from one man. Calling the Commandant of the U.S. Marine Corps "Gismofuhrer"? Oh... My... God... Furthermore, I would bet that this "editorial" is what caused the staff of the <u>Honshu Pioneer</u> to give Dad his own column a few days later, so they could separate his sarcastic humor from "serious" editorial commentary. It is well that Dad overcame his antipathy for the Marine Corps [or learned to suppress it] in later years, because his only sister, Betty, married a guy who ended up as a bird Colonel in the Marine Reserves, and he would have had no sense of humor about the Corps being made fun of like this.)

KAZO KURIER – VOL I, NO 6 – KAZO, HONSHU – OCT. 4, 1945

HEADLINES:
1. PATTON OUSTED (His remark comparing Bavarian politics to American was deemed inappropriate – demoted to Commander of the depleted 15th Army.)
2. SECOND AMERICAN DAILY HITS JAPAN (<u>Stars and Stripes</u> to start publication in Tokyo – ETO version was excellent – no impact expected on <u>Kazo Kurier</u> circulation.)

(EDITOR'S NOTE: At this point the paper was still struggling for news and other content, and looking pretty shabby, as you can on the next page, but Fred Stark's farewell drawing is nice.)

KAZO KURIER – VOL I, EXTRA – KAZO, HONSHU – OCT. 4, 1945

HEADLINE:
1. KAY-CO C.O. LEAVES! (Captain F. W. Arthur has received orders from Lt. Col. Victor E. Wallace to sign over all company property to 1st Lt. James D. Warn, Executive Officer. Capt. Arthur intends return to the States, take a 90-day terminal leave, and then decide whether or not to leave the Army.)

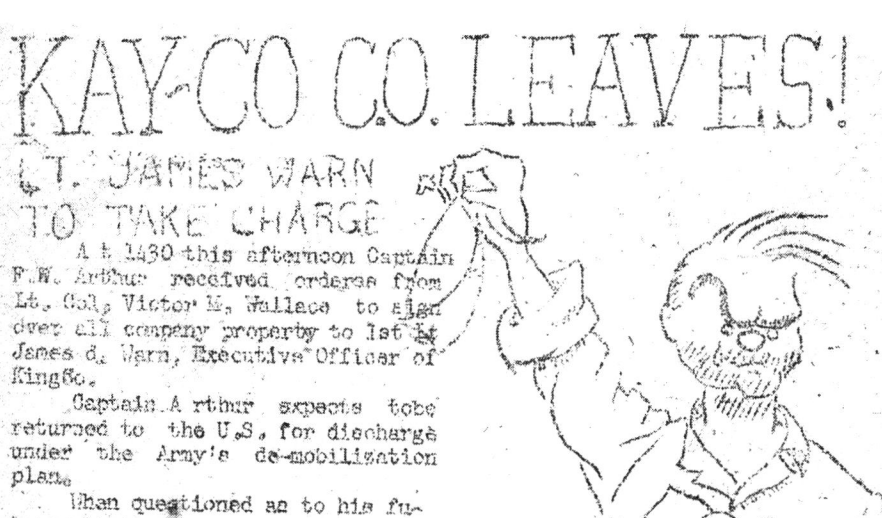

KAY-CO C.O. LEAVES!

LT. JAMES WARN TO TAKE CHARGE

At 1430 this afternoon Captain F.W. Arthur received orders from Lt. Col. Victor M. Wallace to sign over all company property to 1st Lt. James d. Warn, Executive Officer of King Co.

Captain Arthur expects to be returned to the U.S. for discharge under the Army's de-mobilization plan.

When questioned as to his future plans, the man who has been KayCo's C.O. for over thirteen mos., stated that he wasn't sure whether or not he would leave the Army. At present he intends to take a 90-day terminal leave and decide then.

He will remain in command until further orders are received.

LATE SPORTS RESULT

The Chicago Cubs defeated the Detroit Tigers in the first game of the World Series, 9 to 0.

KAZO KURIER – VOL I, NO 7 – KAZO, HONSHU – OCT. 5, 1945

HEADLINES:
1. BIG 5 MEETING CLOSES ON NOTE OF DISCORD (London: Russia unhappy with occupation plans – US wants China & France included in discussions, but Russia does not – no agreements reached.)
2. "THANK YOU" AMERICAN SOLDIER (Local artists and musicians performed folk dances for US troops last night in the Arthur Memorial Auditorium.)
3. UNIT GRIPE COUNCIL MEETS (Chief gripes included fleas, bedbugs, food, USAFI courses, and souvenir policy. Steps to address these will be taken.)

EDITORIAL:

ASIA FOR THE ASIATICS?

If the renaissance was peculiar to the Western World, a matter of the West catching up with the East, the recent risorgimento among the countries is peculiarly oriental.

Every popular democratic movement seems to have had its inception in an essentially fascistic beginning. The Italians threw off Austrian oppression after they had seen how successful the French people and Napoleon were.

The present Japanese government, although defeated, was in a far greater sense extremely successful – unwittingly so, of course. The propaganda of the Japanese sank in. Their Asiatic Co-Prosperity Sphere, their Asia for the Asiatics, found an appreciative audience with the people of Asia. That the Japanese government was fighting purely a war of aggression seems conclusively proved. It was the countries who were overrun by Japan: Siam, French Indochina, the Dutch East Indies, the Malay States that changed the whole character of the war.

The Asiatics have watched the Western Nations for over a century. The Brown races realized the import of these imperialistic grabs and rebelled more than once. Under the Boxers, a popular movement in China, there was an attempt to thwart Western exploitation. The Japanese served notice to would-be imperialists that Japan was for the Japanese when they defeated Russia in 1905.

The attempt of the Boxers was premature, but there has never been a time like the present for the people of Asia to get their necks out of the yoke. And they're trying. It's only a matter of time until the people of Asia are completely free of their European lords.

(EDITOR'S NOTE: Once again, there is no byline here, but I submit that my father was the likely author of this historical analysis of the post-war political situation. For those readers unfamiliar with the term "risorgimento", it refers to the 19th-century movement for Italian unification that culminated in the establishment of the Kingdom of Italy in 1861. I strongly suspect that my father was only member of the staff that would have used that word. What's surprising to me is the revolutionary political tone of this piece. Dad was a lifelong Republican, even though he was very active in his union - The American Association of University Professors.)

KAZO KURIER – VOL I, NO 10 – KAZO, HONSHU – OCT. 8, 1945

HEADLINES:
1. TOKYO AWAITS ANNOUNCEMENT OF NEW PREMIER (Following the mass resignation of the temporary Higoshi-Kuni cabinet formed just after surrender, a new Premier is about to be named. MacArthur recently ordered the abolition of all orders prohibiting free speech or mention of the Emperor.)
2. SOVIET SLAMS U.S. POLICY (Stalin: "The U.S. must realize that one government cannot rule the world.")
3. U.S. IRONCLAD SINKS JAP JUNKS (Ambushed without provocation in the Straits of Malacca, a U.S. ship defended itself successfully against a lateen-rigged junk.
4. LATE BULLETIN JUST RECEIVED (Long-time liberal leader Kijuro Shidehara was sworn in as Japanese Premier in a solemn ceremony.)

EDITORIAL:

WAR PROPHYLAXIS

Of the best of recent war stories is one of a father and son. This young man, on his way overseas, is accompanied to the station by his father, who, after saying a silent goodbye, retreats slowly homeward. He berates himself for his ignorance of world conditions and their interpretation with the view toward war prevention.

What does this mean to you?

We now know that had we not sent Japan tons of scrap iron and in other ways helped her build a formidable military machine; nor appeased Germany at the time of Munich, that the catastrophe now ended might have been prevented.

History is dynamic and there are constant new developments, but there are similarities at which we point and say that history repeats itself.

We must face the future and realize that if we are to make sure our sons are not drafted into a far bloodier holocaust then it is on our shoulders that the burden of peace rests.

It has been repeated so often that it is almost the consensus of the company that the greatest wish is to go home and never again deal with politics or world events and see to it that our sons are trained so they will all be rear echelon.

If we but take our heads out of the sand for a moment we see that this is impossible. But what can we do?

We must take an even greater interest in world affairs than ever before. We must know the meaning of the peace treaties. We must follow the actions of our representatives in Congress carefully, and actively impress on them our wishes. We must elect those who will do our bidding. We must carefully scrutinize our foreign policy.

In brief, we must know what is going on all the time and take a part in it, or we and our sons may find ourselves in khaki all too soon.

(EDITOR'S NOTE: This is the first of many anti-war editorials, which seem to share the idea that the sacrifice we have just endured must be made to mean something – world peace.)

KAZO KURIER – VOL I, NO 10 – KAZO, HONSHU – OCT. 8, 1945

HEADLINES:
1. STATESIDE TWO-YEAR MEN GOING HOME (All men in the US with 2 years of service & not fit for overseas duty will be discharged, except those in the Regular Army or "essential jobs".)
2. USS ATOULIN ODYSSEY FINIS (USS Atoulin, 36 days out of Seattle, has arrived with more men of the 97th aboard – passengers got 18-hour passes in Honolulu en route.)
3. AN APPEAL TO WARM-CLOTHED KAY COMPANY ("Tropically clothed" veterans of the 43rd are in desperate need of warmer clothing – any contributions welcome.)

EDITORIAL:

A ROLLING STONE

Putting out a daily newspaper in conjunction with regular tours on guard duty is no easy task. The members of this staff have proven in the past ten days that the job is not impossible.

The fact that we have no typewriter of our own has made it difficult at times for us, and working into the wee small hours has become SOP.

The first few editions of the Kurier were a test of our ability to work together and make the best with what we had.

Our combined efforts have produced what we believe to be (contrary to opinion in some quarters) a reasonable facsimile of a daily newspaper, whose aim is to supplement the meager reading material of our company, to present the news in a lively manner, and by those copies which are circulated without the unit, to keep the rest of the Division informed about one of their better companies.

(EDITOR'S NOTE: I worked on my high school paper briefly, so I had already pictured in my mind how difficult it must be to lay this paper out into columns, combining contributions from a dozen reporters and editors, fill all the space, and get only one chance to type it onto the stencil correctly. I was already in awe of these guys, but then to learn that they had to do it all on a borrowed typewriter after normal working hours leaves me speechless.)

GETTING, GIVING AND GEISHAS

We are members of a conquering Army. You possibly have many good ideas about how to treat a beaten nation – a nation whose ex-Premier asked, "Aren't you Americans ever going to forget Pearl Harbor?"

However, our attitude has undergone a national change. Japan is vastly different than we expected. Certain fundamentals are important. We respect the traditions and ways of other peoples, and here in Japan we are using their ways in accomplishing our tasks. Briefly, we must use common sense. Obviously, therefore, we do not destroy property, rape, steal or encroach on Jap customs.

Women here are held to be inferior. They are subservient to the men, are quiet, and rarely display emotion.

Their understanding of sex is alien to us. Here it is simple direct and brutal. Romance is a western conception, kissing in public obscene, and a pass made at a Japanese woman means classifying her as a prostitute.

Geisha houses do not exist in Japan. The name is used, but they're not actually brothels. The Geisha is not essentially a prostitute. She is a specially trained entertainer for "clubs" where the men do not take their wives, yet want female company. The Geisha may entertain horizontally, but only if she likes the man, and then is not paid, but rather "tipped".

We are already cognizant of the high disease rate in Japan, especially V.D. and malaria.

One last tip: There are no "one price" stores in Japan. You must bargain shrewdly or be cheated.

(EDITOR'S NOTE: The explanation and advice about Geishas and sex in Japan seems amazingly well-informed for a group of young men that been in the country less than 2 weeks at this point. I would guess that very few of the Americans spoke any Japanese, although there must have been interpreters around. Where did this valuable information come from? Perhaps their training in San Luis Obispo?)

EDITORIAL:

HOW MUCH A LOSER?

Is Japan a conquered nation? Consider – many of her cities have been left fairly intact, and now that the war is over, she won't have an employment problem as acute as other powers.

Nearly 70% of her peace-time population was engaged in fishing or farming, and our bombing has made no noticeable change in either. Germany was two-thirds industrial, and in comparison, a great number of her people were displaced, even more killed, and her cities were hard hit.

The Japs now seem to be biding their time until we leave. Is this cordial attitude an outgrowth of this, and do they hope to hasten our departure by doing so?

All this is very good, as the sooner the defeated nations reach economic stability, the easier it will be for them to forget war hatreds and provide a united world, but – is Japan a conquered nation?

(EDITOR'S NOTE: Not the most cogent piece of writing to grace these pages, but the author does mention a couple of considerations that I had not thought of. The disparity between Germany and Japan's prewar levels of industrialization [if true] was a total shock to me, and would certainly have had a major impact on their economic recovery from the war, as the author suggests. However, I can't figure out what point he is trying to make. He seems suspicious that the Japanese are insincere in their actions, in an effort to get the Allies to leave, and maybe that things are not as bad in Japan as one might expect in a "conquered nation". My reaction to the former is, "So what?" and to the latter, "Maybe it could have been worse, but it was bad enough to satisfy all but the most vindictive.")

HONSHU PIONEER – VOL I, NO. 11 – JAPAN – OCT. 9, 1945

HEADLINES:
1. CHINESE TAKE OVER FORMOSA (The island had been in Japanese hands since 1898.)
2. KAZO KURIER BOWS OUT (Relocation to Kagohara Airfield made the old name obsolete. The new name – <u>Honshu Pioneer</u> - was chosen from over 100 entrants in the Pick-A-Name Contest.)
3. NAVY RELEASES SPEEDED UP (Navy reveals its critical point score will be lowered by November 1, but the Senate is still working on an Army demobilization plan.)

(EDITOR'S NOTE: The following is the earliest example I have of my father's daily column. Having seen the actual documents, I believe his choice of title must have been inspired by the quality of the paper that was used to publish the <u>Honshu Pioneer</u>. His hand-drawn logo featuring a roll of toilet paper would seem to support my theory.)

FROM A 2-SEATER:

Sitting here wetly, thinking dank thoughts, my interest is arrested by the "2 ½" in front of Guard Post #5. Now that we've spent two weeks guarding $800,000 worth of equipment, Division Salvage takes it away; nothing left for our next tenants to guard. Now K, 386 will have nothing to do, but favorably compare Camp Arthur to their old home.

★ ★ ★

Now that the war is over and Sunday drivers are cluttering up the highways, accidents in the States are mounting mercurially. Cpt. Arthur excited camp traffic yesterday, when he plowed up a sturdy Japanese oak with Jerry White's Jeep. The tree won't be missed. It might be the accident was done with an appreciative eye for landscape.

★ ★ ★

I've seen some darn attractive kimonos that have really been gifts for as little a price as a carton of cigarettes. Hey Mac, will you pass that butt this way after the next drag?

★ ★ ★

"It is a pleasure and an honor to be placed in command of a unit which has a record as outstanding as that of the 97th Infantry Div," – Major General H. F. Kramer, on assuming command of the 97th Div.

"It is indeed an honor to assume command of the 3rd Army, whose breakthrough in France and Germany wrote so glowing a chapter in the annals of military history." said Lt. General L. K. Truscott on assuming command of the 3rd Army.

HONSHU PIONEER – VOL I, NO. 12 – KAGOHARA, JAPAN – OCT. 10, 1945

HEADLINES:
1. REVISE G.I. BILL – BRADLEY (General Bradley proposes changes to the G.I. Bill to lengthen the 2-year period for applications. 80,000 veterans are now receiving $20 per week unemployment benefits,)
2. WIVES TO VISIT ETO HUSBANDS (Steps to be taken soon to allow wives and families of occupation forces in Europe to visit. Voluntary re-enlistments are at 10%.)

FROM A 6-HOLER:

Sitting on a wooden refuge in a morass of mud, grimly looking at the saturated world floating around me, my sad heart goes back to the bright world of Kazo. There was mud at Kazo, but there was humus earth to sop it up, and what is more – there was a reason you can get a hold of for your being there. You can't get a hold of mud; it only sticks to you.

✱ ✱ ✱

It was two weeks ago that a dusty cavalcade of K Company men rode along the backwoods road that runs from Kumagaya to Kazo. On that trip pedestrians viewed the procession with a dignified hauteur, curt bows and very correct salutes. Today, "INSCRUTABLE ORIENTALS" beamed and bowed, yelled and helloed and carried on as if we were a vaudeville troupe. Everyone was demonstrative in their greeting, even those whose backs were turned.

✱ ✱ ✱

While reading last month's articles in last week's "Yank" in one of our comfort stations, I was interrupted by a committee of Jap homemakers enjoying an unescorted visit to our area. I'm not proud, but I do think definite visiting hours should be established.

(EDITOR'S NOTE: During my own rather brief visit to Japan [late 90's], I also noticed that the American idea of privacy in bathrooms still did not exist there. I was a bit unnerved at first [as I suspect Dad was in the above incident] to have a cleaning woman mopping the floor around my feet as I stood at the urinal.)

HONSHU PIONEER – VOL I, NO. 13 – KAGOHARA, JAPAN – OCT. 11, 1945

HEADLINES:
1. TOKYO MOVE IS RUMORED (We might be going to relieve the 1st Cavalry in Tokyo, or we might be moving 100 miles north into previously unoccupied territory.)
2. CHINESE RED SLAIN – GREEK GOV'T FALLS (Danger of civil war in China, which was thought to have been averted, now seems greatly enlarged, due to the killing of a Communist leader.)
3. EUROPEAN HIGHLIGHTS – ITALY (Outbreaks of sabotage in Milan – underground Fascists blamed.) – RUSSIA (Moscow radio: U.S. and England conspiring to aid Germany rebuild her industry.)

FROM A 6-HOLER:

A look at any of Kagohara's airy hangars suggests a view of a county fair. It's all there: the roped-off concessions, the heavy odors of hot dog stands; and the perennial sawing and carpentry that's always needed to trim off the frayed edges of old fairground buildings. The two things that go as much toward setting the picture off are the little knots of spectators around the games of chance, and the way in which the concessionaires and exhibitors string out their personal effects and clothes with a view toward willful abandon.

★★★

It's easy enough to see that K of the 303rd Inf. hasn't been around Kagohara long. They still have reveille and police-up, and a fine little aquatic show it must be for the other companies, too.

★ ★ ★

The 97th has a combat-training complex. Everything is still marked "Top Secret, officers only, for troop dissemination, get control of your men, blah, blah, blah." It's good, then, to find someone who's willing to shed his steel and forget for a while we were fighting in Europe five months ago. Such a man is Lt. Omer Houle, of 3rd Bn. Hdq. Co. The lieutenant plans to inaugurate a streamlined college math course on a discussion group level. He said that improving your minds now won't any longer jeopardize our winning the war.

EDITORIAL:

RED CHINA:

Through a constant propaganda barrage beginning after the first World War the name "Red" has achieved a connotation linking it with beards and bombs.

However, information regarding the Chinese Communists has been slowly gathered by many reporters of various newspapers and Life Magazine. These visits to North China or the Borderland, as it is sometimes called, have revealed that this area is a far cry from Communism as it is properly defined.

The Yenan group, rather than collectivize industry, wants to eradicate feudalism and thereby institute the first phase of a virile capitalism.

Instruction in farming methods, government-sponsored private business and education for all, are a part of the program.

These ideas sound more like "New Dealism" than Communism.

(EDITOR'S NOTE: You may smile at the author's willingness to believe Communist press releases if you like, but hindsight is 20-20, as they say. Surprising to me is that this editor felt empowered to take a pro-Communist position in print, and in an Army paper. It helps to remember that Chiang Kai Shek was the only viable alternative at the time, and to men who had recently incurred heavy casualties fighting fascism, he could not have looked like much of a bargain, either.)

HONSHU PIONEER – VOL I, NO. 14 – KAGOHARA, JAPAN – OCT. 12, 1945

HEADLINES:
1. CONGRESS LAMENTS DISCHARGE RATE (Congress unleashes "a broad indictment of the slowness in Army and Navy discharges.")
2. "MAC" CLOSES GEISHA SPOTS (MacArthur orders the closing of 211 geisha houses and over 300 other spots "to protect occupation troops from alcohol poisoning and disease.")
3. OFFICIAL RAPS VETS LOW PAY (Maj. A. McDermott decries the substandard wages being offered to returning veterans – often as low as $25 per week.)
4. TIGERS WIN '45 WORLD SERIES (over the Cubs)

FROM A 6-HOLER:

```
  This "6-Holer" is just a holdover from Kazo. I
discovered yesterday much to my discomfort that
it's only a 4-holer; and what's more it's not even
ours. We only share it. We don't even have our
own stove pipes. If they ever did give us stove
pipes, I think a better use could be made of them
on these wet, cold mornings; the idea of smoke
coming out of them is somehow more attractive.
```

✯ ✯ ✯

```
            It used to be,
      We were shoved like cattle
         From camp to camp
        And from camp to battle.
```

> Now is seems
> We're more like geese
> From mudhole to mudhole
> In spite of world peace.

SOCIAL NOTE: Friends of K Co. were entertained yesterday in the spacious hall of number 4 hangar. Those present were members of M Co. who left yesterday for a brief sojourn in the South. The menu was attractively planned and included Vienna sausages, potatoes au dehydrate, green beans, peach halves. Coffee was served in the drawing room.

(EDITOR'S NOTE: Vienna sausages were the mainstay of the GI diet at this time, and were not all that popular, I believe.)

HONSHU PIONEER – VOL I, NO. 15 – KAGOHARA, JAPAN – OCT. 13, 1945

HEADLINES:
1. PEACE TIME DRAFT AIRED (Senate debates number of conscripts required, or whether a draft is necessary at all, now that the war is over.)
2. ALL NAZIS WAR GUILTY (N.Y Post: Death to all Nazis of certain organizations, regardless of other charges, is a possibility in the German war crime trials.)
3. IS IT SAFE TO GRIPE? (A griper of K Co. was arraigned before his Platoon Leader. Since griping is officially endorsed [by reason of our Gripe Council], discrimination against "wildcat" griping seems contradictory.)

(EDITOR'S NOTE: Unfortunately, my copy of this issue did not make it through the mimeograph machine the second time, so Pages 2 and 3, which would have contained the editorial and my father's column, are missing.)

HONSHU PIONEER – VOL I, NO. 16 – KAGOHARA, JAPAN – OCT. 14, 1945

HEADLINES:
1. JAPS PLAN CONST'L MONARCHY (Emperor losing ground – democracy gaining.)
2. DANNY KAYE HERE WED. (with Leo Durocher.)

FROM A 6-HOLER:
One of the few men who has been fortunate enough to receive a letter felt as if he were a miser. To appease his conscience he asked us to publish his letter for the benefit of the whole company, so...

September 27, 1945
Thursday
Tacoma, Wash.

Dearest Jim,

How's my little "big wheel" today? I miss you like the very dickens. It gets worse each day, what's it going to be like by the time you get back? Umm – just think what kind of reception you'll get! I hope I'll be here, if not I'll probably be in California.

Those five days we had just <u>can't</u> be the end of it. I want so much to see you again. Do you think it can be arranged?

Oh, what a beautiful day! It would be perfect for a picnic (not indoors either).

I went downtown shopping today, bought a few new things. Wish you were here. I feel like stepping out and doing things. Don't worry though I'm going to stay home. I haven't been anywhere except a few shows since you left. I've been a very good girl since you left and intend to continue this way. I love you so much Jim.

Am going to close now. I know this is just a short letter, but have got quite a bit of work to do. I'll write again tomorrow.

Always,
Irene

(EDITOR'S NOTE: *In case you were wondering, my father certainly composed this letter himself, and did not actually publish some guy's letter from his girlfriend.*)

EDITORIAL:

TOKYO ROSE:

According to our Tokyo correspondent who attended the grand opening of the American Red Cross Canteen, "Tokyo Rose" was back at her old job of entertaining our boys. This time she was serving doughnuts and coffee to the gaping GI's.

Miss Iva Taguri, whose western appearance and oriental demeanor indicate her California education and Japanese background, is well-known to Pacific vets for her program of popular songs and chit-chat designed to make them feel homesick.

No doubt she will soon be receiving offers from Hollywood.

(EDITOR'S NOTE: *You can probably detect the sarcasm in this piece, wondering how this famous "war criminal" could be walking around free and serving doughnuts, but that didn't last long. You have probably heard of this woman, who was one of the most famous figures to emerge from the Pacific war, thanks largely to*

American war movies. She was born in Los Angeles, California, on Independence Day, July 4, 1916. Her father was a Japanese-American who owned an import shop. Iva aspired to be like all American teenagers. She wanted to become a doctor and attended UCLA, graduating in 1941, but then was sent to Japan to visit her sick aunt. After Pearl Harbor, the last ship bound for America left without her and she was stranded in Japan. Letters from home stopped coming, because her family was placed in an Internment Camp in California. Japanese secret police came to demand that she renounce her U.S. citizenship and pledge loyalty to the Japanese emperor. She refused. She got a job with a Tokyo radio station transcribing English language shortwave broadcasts, and eventually went on the air herself. She never dispersed much propaganda, as was the main goal of the broadcasts, but she did make G.I.'s homesick. Iva never called herself Tokyo Rose on the air. That name was given to her by American troops. The irony was that Iva wished desperately to return to the U.S. She worked as a radio personality for three years. After the war, the Army began to investigate her as a traitor, having committed treason for broadcasting Japanese propaganda. She was imprisoned for one year but was released for lack of evidence. In 1948, President Truman felt moved to act by public outcry, stirred up partly by radio personality Walter Winchell, and she was eventually charged with treason and brought back to the U.S. as a prisoner. On July 5, 1949, Iva's treason trial was officially opened. The actual transcriptions of her broadcasts were never shared with the jury. She was found guilty and sentenced to 10 years in prison. After prison, she lived in Chicago as a state-less citizen. In 1976, President Gerald Ford wrote an executive pardon for Iva Taguri. She died in 2006.

A pretty sad story, don't you think?)

HONSHU PIONEER – VOL I, NO. 17 – KAGOHARA, JAPAN – OCT. 15, 1945

HEADLINES:
1. ASIA WAR DEATHS MOUNT – INDONESIANS DECLARE WAR; ANAMITES CONTINUE FIGHT (Indonesian People's Army is fighting the Dutch with bows and poison arrows. French attack Anamite stronghold, killing 100.)
2. JAPS ERASE VOTING BARS (Japan grants women suffrage and lowers the voting age from 25 to 20.)
3. ENLISTED MEN AREN'T RE-ENLISTING TSK TCH (Senate disappointed that their newly passed re-enlistment bill is obtaining 2 officers for every 1 enlisted man.)

FROM A 6-HOLER:

It remains to be seen whether we're through playing hide-and-seek with the mosquito menace. The Medical Corps isn't sure it wants to adopt an entirely worldly view of our Japanese occupation or go on with its playful, romantic view of the situation.

We are in the Orient, and there are mosquitoes in the Orient; and every movie romance I've seen with a 19th century Oriental outpost, theme has had swaths of mosquito nets in every reel. So why not keep our mosquito bars.

That medieval scourge, the Bubonic Plague is, however, a bug with a different squirm. Rats and lice did write history before Waterloo, but since 1815 rats have gone materialistic and kept their nose pretty much to cheese. The Medics should forget all about scourges and Black Deaths; shots and needles spoil the whole theme.

DREW PEARSON – EDITORIAL:

The Admirals and Generals couldn't say so publicly, but they are boiling mad at Secretary of State Jimmy Byrnes over giving Russia the Korile Islands – the strip of island stepping stones extending from Japan north to Siberia. Of course, the brass hats boil easily, but they say the Koriles are the best Pacific site for launching rocket bombs against the U.S.A.

There are strong winds that blow constantly from them toward Washington and Oregon. It was from here that the Japs launched their balloons to the U.S. Northwest.

(EDITOR'S NOTE: It seems that the Cold War is being planned, even as we work together with our Russian allies on occupation plans and boundary changes.)

HONSHU PIONEER – VOL I, NO. 18 – KAGOHARA, JAPAN – OCT. 16, 1945

HEADLINES:
1. ORDER RESTORED IN ARGENTINA – MILITARY REGIME OUSTS PRO-NAZI GOVT.
2. JAPS STILL BEAR ARMS (Jap troops repulsed an attack by the Indonesian Peoples Army on Bandevong Airfield in Indonesia.)

FROM A 6-HOLER:

NEWS ITEM: Washington (AP) – The Senate Mil. Affairs Committee announced that enlistees under the new re-enlistment bill were running much under Gen. George C. Marshall's proposed figure. Answering the call were 300,000 officers and 168,000 Enlisted Men.

It would seem from the above news that some do like the Army and that it makes a difference whether you're an officer or an EM: To utilize all voluntary enlistments, here is a suggested platoon T.O.:

Platoon Ldr – Brig Gen'l; Plt Sgt. - Col.; Plt. Guide – Lt. Col.; Squad Ldrs – Major; Ass't Sqd Ldr. - Captain; BAR men - 1st Lieuts.; 1st scouts – Second lieutenants.

The success of this plan will depend on whether a Major General will think keeping duty rosters beneath his dignity.

(EDITOR'S NOTE: This satirical plan for an all-officer Army never got the recognition it deserved, in my opinion.)

HONSHU PIONEER – VOL I, NO. 19 – URAWA, JAPAN – OCT. 17, 1945

HEADLINES:
1. "STRATEGY BEAT JAPS" – MACARTHUR (In his first radio address since arriving in Japan, the general stated that Japan's defeat was inevitable, due to strategy and tactics.)
2. CANUCKS STRANDED, DUTCH GET SHIPS (Britain sends ships to transport Dutch troops to fight in Indonesia, while Canadian troops stranded in England riot in protest.)
3. HUTCHINS WANTS SMALL ARMY (Pres. Robert Hutchins of Chicago University stated that the atom bomb has made armies as we know them obsolete.)

FROM A 6-HOLER:
Six holes is much more conducive to prolonged sitting and prolonged meditation than six trenches.

★ ★ ★

While everyone is asking what our duties here will be a directive from G-3 goes a little way toward clearing up the question. You may be relieved to know that you won't have to fight hand to hand, – with bolo knives or crawl through an infiltration course. No mention was made of problems involving the use of live ammo, but then what the hell. Time hangs pretty heavy here anyway.

General Lucien Clay demands that troops in Europe be given more to eat.

We mustn't let Gen. Clay's heart-rending appeal play on our sympathies too much. Those guys with 41 points who are putting up with salmon now will be eating turkey at home by New Years.

Field Manual Personal Hygiene suffers from Oriental exposure. Our newest dilemma: whether we want the dreaded Honshu Water Pox, (it leaves little holes, awfully unbecoming ones) or whether we want to go around dust-caked and insect ridden for the lack of water to wash them off.

✯ ✯ ✯

When we left Kagohara Airbase, we also left some of K Company's more accomplished performers. Eddie Zapp, typewriter speed merchant; Houston Bumgardner, guitar man from the hills; Leo Jones, recent transfer from the 43rd who cut hair, all went to Service Company.

(EDITOR'S NOTE: What I know about the "putting up with salmon" remark above is that for an extended period the occupation forces in this part of Japan could not obtain any substantial quantities of food other than canned salmon. My father steadfastly refused to eat salmon for the rest of his life. There also seems to be a recurring theme of "What is it that we're supposed to be doing over here?" in case you hadn't noticed.)

EDITORIAL:

WHAT COOKS?

Many of the Company noticed a strange thing shortly after our arrival.

The Japs at the factory across the street were being dismissed for the day.

They all fell into formation and, after what resembled a report in a strictly GI manner, were given a speech by what would be the equivalent of our 1st Sgt.

These men were not soldiers, but ordinary factory workers. This military business is also being handed out in schools.

We would like to know why such a situation exists two months after surrender. If the aim of American occupation is to pacify Japan we are wasting our time.

If the Nips are taught basic drills and military courtesy under the very noses of their conquerors, we're wondering what is going on in more obscure spots.

We'd also like to know what our policy is toward that which enabled them to grow strong enough to challenge us.

(EDITOR'S NOTE: I do not admire this editorial, but it is quite revealing on certain issues. It has been less than three weeks since these guys arrived in Japan, and they still have a lot to learn about Japanese culture, obviously. Things have changed a lot in the six or seven decades since then, but some Americans still find the Japanese tendency toward conformity, regimentation, and respect for authority baffling. That this author also found it militaristic and threatening should not surprise us, so soon after the end of hostilities.

After reading this, I remembered one of my most fascinating and delightful experiences in Japan in the late 90's. My boss and I were riding the shinkansen [bullet train] back from Kobe to Tokyo, and were amazed to have an entire passenger car to ourselves. Then the train stopped in Kyoto and 600 Japanese high school students came aboard, filling the entire train. All were dressed in identical very neat dark blue uniforms, but otherwise they seemed to act pretty much like [rather well-behaved] American kids would have. We had a group of six girls right across the aisle, and we managed to strike up a very entertaining conversation, as they were eager to show off their English. The noise level in the car was considerable, as kids were chattering everywhere. Very suddenly there was dead silence, and every face was focused on the front of the car, motionless. My boss and I looked at each other, bewildered. After a few seconds, one of the girls whispered to me in a very low voice, "Teacher is speaking." All similarity to American high school kids vanished right there. The editorial writer above had observed similar behavior in the factory across the street and interpreted it as militaristic and ominous, but I imagine after a few more weeks or months he would have understood it differently.)

HONSHU PIONEER – VOL I, NO. 20 – URAWA, JAPAN – OCT. 18, 1945

HEADLINES:
1. NEHRU, NETHERLANDS CRITICIZE BRITISH (Dutch: Ships should have been available months ago to transport troops to the East Indies, preventing the present crisis. Nehru: England shouldn't use Indian troops to fight "our Asiatic brothers".)
2. NAVY POINTS DROP (AGAIN) (On Nov. 1 the points needed for discharge from the Navy will drop from 44 to 41, and on Jan. 1 will drop further.)

FROM A 6-HOLER:

Dreaded Honshu Pox (habitat: Urawa well water) must have been licked. Our medics have scored again. Within 24 hours after announcing the dreaded disease, the medics found a way out of our difficulty and now we have running water horse troughs in which to wash and which might even serve as a bathtub for those of you who don't like Gracie's showers.

✯ ✯ ✯

A week ago the press featured Dutch Indonesians as a popular movement beating with tiny fists and poison arrows against the tyrannical Netherlands. Today, they're no better than a bunch of brigands, who run around killing Dutch women and children.

It looks like the World press takes its note from the way the British view the world (the same way American foreign policy takes its cue.)

✯ ✯ ✯

Old Commodore B--- Halsey's personal medic couldn't have spent all his time aboard the 3rd Fleet's flagship, doctoring up erstwhile-equestrian Halsey's sniffles and gout, because he summed up Japan as accurately as any Brass yet so far. Commodore B--- on Japan: "Japan is a land of fish, fleas, vermin and rodents – all the factors which promote disease. She has been and is a stench in the nostril of the world."

★ ★ ★

We think the cooks overdid it. Steaks would have been enough without showing off the chickens.

EDITORIAL:

THE PIONEER FURRY FRIENDS:

We have a cozy office for the Honshu Pioneer. It is crowded, but cozy. We suppose it's only natural that Urawa rats should think it a pretty good deal.

They do.

It's not easy to resent these rats, because they haven't attacked us yet and because they're such beautiful physical specimens.

If the Pied Piper had been commissioned to pipe rats like these out of Hamlin, he would have refused the Mayor and the Hamlinites would have kept their squawking brats.

Fine physical specimens.

Big strapping fellows with muscles strong supple as a mt. cat, with eyes fierce and alert as a jungle panther.

```
Active, too.

The thundering of their massive pawpads fills
the office every evening. Their hoarse voices drown
the printing press' roar.

But they haven't bothered us yet.

We don't bother them.
```

(EDITOR'S NOTE: There is no way to prove it, but this HAD to be written by my father. I can find no evidence that anyone else on the paper had quite his screwball sense of humor or his propensity for absurdly flowery language. If anyone else wants to claim authorship of this gem, please contact me.)

HONSHU PIONEER – VOL I, NO. 21 – URAWA, JAPAN – OCT. 19, 1945

HEADLINES:
1. W.D. DEALT BLOW BY BUDGET SLASH (Congress demands a speedup of demobilization as they slash $52 billion from the War Department budget. "Points or no points, the men must be released.")
2. ATLEE TALKS FAST ON INDIES (Responding to widespread criticism, British Prime Minister Clement Atlee defended their intervention in the East Indies, and insisted that the Netherlands should be shown every consideration, in light of the devastation there during the war.)

FROM A 6-HOLER:

The Japs have a certain Oriental, reverential precision for things G.I. Instead of our own six slit trenches we have a fine wooden box with six ornate holes (I'm glad to get back to six holes) and six symmetrical mounds that look as if they were freshly dug graves.

★ ★ ★

Blue King's company front is small. It's not small as a result of G-3's wanting it small, but as a result of seclusive neighbors, who don't want their inscrutability scrutinized at too close a range.

Now me, I'm from a small midwestern town and like to know what my neighbors are doing, or at least would like to know what they're doing when they make such a point of finding out what I'm doing. Our neighbors always turn up when we're eating, or out behind.

The Japs are excellent copyists. They've had opportunities to look at U.S, machines and duplicate them; now, maybe, they'll get down to fundamentals and use forks and porcelain toilet bowls, or at least wooden ones.

★ ★ ★

The 3% pass to Tokyo policy did not sound like much to us either. But resourceful K Co. must have unearthed retreats near at hand, if the absence of so many of our playboys is any indication.

★ ★ ★

The washing machine is about to start operations and we can hardly wait to get our waterproof field pants, suspenders and field cap into the tub.

(EDITOR'S NOTE: I would imagine that the comments above about the Japanese being excellent copyists and their interest in U.S. machinery did not excite much concern at the time, but 40 years later, when they had taken a large part of the auto market and nearly all of the machine tool and consumer electronics markets, Dad would have looked like a real prophet.)

EDITORIAL:

NO NIP BASEBALL:

An order from higher echelon forbids all athletic contests between American soldiers and the Japanese.

This helps to confuse us a little more on the Army's policy toward our former enemies.

Under the present circumstances, many unit baseball teams are unable to find competition among other outfits because of lack of transportation.

Their only alternative is to play Jap teams or not play at all.

Maybe higher-ups are afraid that the Americans will lose a game and lose face with our present hosts.

The ordinary soldier doesn't have much of a chance to be in contact with these people. Our relations with them now may have a great deal to do with their ideas on democracy, and change their minds about "white devils".

What could be a more common ground on which to meet than a game which we both love?

(EDITOR'S NOTE: The author makes perfect sense here, but I suspect that the real reason for such a stupid rule was the fear that a rhubarb over a bad call would result in a full-scale brawl and an international incident.)

HONSHU PIONEER – VOL I, NO. 22 – URAWA, JAPAN – OCT. 20, 1945

HEADLINES:
1. MAGIC CARPET GETS NEW SHIPS (To increase ship space to get the 2,100,000 Pacific troops home, 20 cruisers and 10 aircraft carriers are being added.)
2. INDIAN TROOPS FIGHT IN JAVA (Over Nehru's protests, Britain sends Ghurkas to aid Dutch troops in Java. The threat of protests against this action "casts an ominous shadow over all colonial Asia".)
3. A-BOMB MEANS LARGE ARMY (Responding to Pres. Hutchins' remarks, Gen. Marshall said a large Army was required to defend the U.S. against atomic threats.)
4. T. O. CHANGES DUE ("Latest news on the re-enlistment front was that the number of 1st graders desiring an Army career is nearly equal to that of privates who want to re-enlist.")
5. ORCHIDS FROM S & S "Yesterday's Stars and Stripes carried a short article on the Honshu Pioneer. No doubt the staff hasn't read Mauldin, or they wouldn't call us 'doggies'".

(EDITOR'S NOTE: Bill Mauldin was a popular Stars and Stripes cartoonist who covered the war in Europe from an enlisted man's point of view. My father had his wonderful book, Up Front, which he and I both admired greatly. I assume Dad wrote this blurb and probably #4.)

FROM A 6-HOLER:
Many more nights like the one before last, and the T. O. of this outfit will look like a unit of the regular army.

⭐ ⭐ ⭐

Every night just after dark
An angel comes aroun'
With lil' book, in which to mark
The good n' bad'ns down.

Just like Abou Ben Adam,
I trouble in my cot,
For my buddy's in a jam,
Even if I'm not.

He stayed in town,
When I came back,
Just to look aroun'
'fore hitting the sack.

But like basic training,
There's a NCO to see
That we ain't misbehaving,
By staying out 'til three.

⭐ ⭐ ⭐

The Army Air Corps training program is the first to feel the War Department ax. Judging from Air Corps men we've known, a college education has always seemed grossly extravagant.

EDITORIAL:

CONGRESS ACTS:

We see that Congress get down to business the other day and slashed the Army's budget for the fiscal year. It takes our representatives a little time to make their speeches and appoint their committees, but sooner or later the will of the people prevails.

During the past few years the Navy and Army got just about anything they wanted from Capitol Hill, because it was necessary for them to have free rein in prosecuting the war. With the '46 elections in the offing, the boys had to do something and do it fast. Regardless of the motives, we feel that it was a good idea to tighten the purse strings and force the hand of the brass.

Let us only hope that this move will result in a cut in personnel and not in rations and supplies. This does not apply to Vienna sausage or canned salmon.

SPORTS:

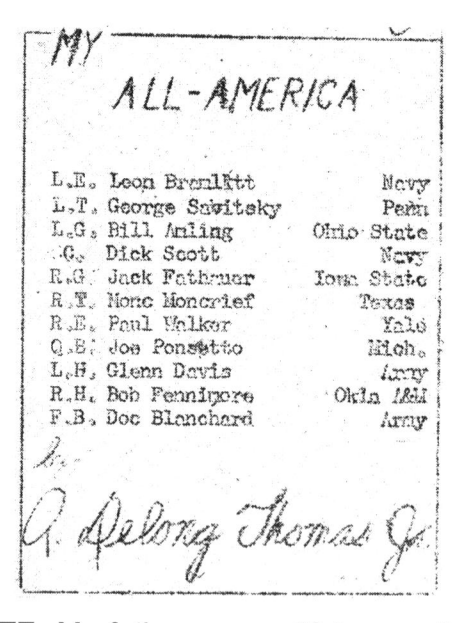

MY ALL-AMERICA

Pos.	Name	School
L.E.	Leon Bramlett	Navy
L.T.	George Savitsky	Penn
L.G.	Bill Amling	Ohio State
C.	Dick Scott	Navy
R.G.	Jack Fathauer	Iowa State
R.T.	Monc Moncrief	Texas
R.E.	Paul Walker	Yale
Q.B.	Joe Ponsetto	Mich.
L.H.	Glenn Davis	Army
R.H.	Bob Fenimore	Okla. A&M
F.B.	Doc Blanchard	Army

G. Delong Thomas Jr.

(EDITOR'S NOTE: My father was a lifelong college football fan, like most of the Thomas men, and considered himself something of an expert. Apparently he couldn't resist this opportunity to share his wisdom with his readers, and get in a plug for Michigan.)

HONSHU PIONEER – VOL I, NO. 23 – URAWA, JAPAN – OCT. 21, 1945

HEADLINES:
1. JAP FATE IN DOUBT – ALLIED COMMISSION POSTPONES MEET (meeting of the Allied Advisory Commission on Japan postponed from Oct. 30 to Nov. 30, in order to include Russia)
2. GHQ ADOPTS FRAT POLICY – DANCES BANNED (soldiers forbidden to accompany Japanese women to pubs; Red Cross dance canceled) – BLACK MARKET THWARTED (money orders home to be signed by an officer and come only from pay)

FROM A 6-HOLER:

Teacher, teacher I declare I see the color of your underwear. It's O.D.

(EDITOR'S NOTE: For non-military types, that's "Olive Drab".)

The 6th Army announced an ambitious education program, their goal: every man with a 5th grade education. It's a lot, but if the number of men K Co. has that profess an interest in USAFI we might even attain a 6th grade level.

★ ★ ★

Windows smashed, bottles broken,
Frequent trips out in the open,
Foaming froth down the gullet,
Beer, ah beer the GI's love it.

> From 3 point 2 to Japanesey;
> Drink, Drank, Drunk; gee it's easy;
> Let's get loaded, let's get bloated
> Staying sober is outmoded.

> Army men are drunk all over,
> From Tokyo to the Straits of Dover;
> Some drunk there, and some drunk here,
> Where the hell is my goddam beer.

✯ ✯ ✯

Take me out to the volleyball game. Take me out to the volleyball game, so I can star Capt. Frederick (Hotshot) Arthur perform his feats on the court. Although Capt. Arthur's prowess is unquestionable, his game would improve tremendously if instead of waiting for the ball to come to him he'd break down and make the effort of going to it.

✯ ✯ ✯

Garrison soldiery is a thing at which we've always excelled. Here's our chance. Yea 97th.

(EDITOR'S NOTE: *of all the surprises I have found in these papers, the biggest one for me personally is the amount of "poetry" that my father produced in his column. In later life, he was known to compose goofy songs and even cheers for sports teams, but nothing on this scale. I don't think Robert Frost has anything to worry about, but most of them do rhyme, and some are pretty funny.)*

HONSHU PIONEER – VOL I, NO. 24 – URAWA, JAPAN – OCT. 22, 1945

HEADLINES:
1. U.S. MINES CLOG JAP WATERS (15,000 unexploded mines are to be exploded, and 150,000 smaller mines are to be swept up. The U.S. Strategic Bombing Survey will determine the extent of industrial damage to Japan.)
2. ALL TROOPS HOME BY JUNE (Troops in Europe to be home by February.)
3. U.S. CLARIFIES FAR EAST POSITION (State Dept. states that French and Dutch sovereignty will be recognized first, but is prepared to arbitrate both conflicts.)

FROM A 6-HOLER:

"Line up men and draw your saber." Souvenirs, souvenirs get your souvenirs! Take something home and impress the kiddies. There's nothing quite so good to make a story of than a real, knocked-out Japanese Samurai sword.

★ ★ ★

K Co. is goofing off. The 97th Infantry Division has the biggest job (whatever it should turn out to be) in Japan. They've had to spread Trident men out over an area of 9,139 square miles (as big a job as we'll probably do). For all the territory the 97th has had to go into, K Co. should have wound up with a bigger portion than they did. We're closeted in an area of 20,000 square yards,

Some outfit is really taking a licking. One such outfit is Easy Co. Their squads are ten miles apart; their platoons 50 miles apart. They've had to give each platoon a kitchen, and what their C. O. has done, nobody seems to know.

The natives are mean when aroused.

★ ★ ★

Our big commander Lt. Gen. Eichelberger went out to see how things were going at the going-home part of Zama. (Zama is coming-here part as well).

Eichelberger told the men going home that they weren't going to be forgotten. Most of the men did not give a darn one way or the other. He also had a word for those coming here (Bless 'em). He said that the men could expect a pretty good time until they were assigned.

(EDITOR'S NOTE: The name "Trident men" used above refers to the insignia worn by the 97th Infantry Division, which was, in fact, a trident. At the right is a photo of my father in uniform, showing the trident patch.)

GUEST EDITORIAL – Pfc Jean R. Tartter

HERE WE GO AGAIN:

From one of Japan's most aristocratic families comes Prince Fuminaro Konoye. Through his entire political career partial to the militarists, Konoye became premier soon after Saito, a less ambitious minister, was murdered in a coup. The war with China began in July, 1937 while Konoye held office. During his second premiership, friendship with Germany was fostered, culminating in the Treaty of Alliance between Italy, Germany and Japan, which lined up the Axis against the world. Five months before Pearl Harbor, the infamous Tojo entered into Konoye's cabinet as head of the War Office, then took over as premier himself to direct the war effort.

Has the Prince committed harakiri? Has he been indicted as a war criminal? Is he in hiding? To the contrary, our friend is now Hirohito's chief adviser, a leader in Jap Constitutional Reform, and a big wheel in Japanese-American relations. Curious indeed are American methods of ridding the country of militarism.

(EDITOR'S NOTE: We have still been in Japan less than a month, but this eager beaver has his hanging rope ready and wonders what is holding things up. As we shall soon see, answers to his three questions will not be long in coming, and the outcome for the Prince will not be a happy one, but I find it a bit unseemly for a Pfc to be hurling brickbats at MacArthur and his team already, based on his own [totally wrong] assumptions about what is going on.)

HONSHU PIONEER – VOL I, NO. 25 – URAWA, JAPAN – OCT. 23, 1945

HEADLINES:
1. FRANCE SPURNS U.S. OFFER (As French troops were landing at Saigon, France "politely refused" the U.S. Offer to help settle the situation in French Indochina.)
2. JAP STUDENTS STRIKE (Students at four schools walked out to protest continued military training, and call for the dismissal of reactionary instructors.)
3. PENTAGON POWWOW PLEA (Soldiers going bats from Pentagon facts & figures – 6 million men home by May? – from where, since when? - please make things clear.)
4. FREE ASIA – N.Y. TIMES (The Times appealed to President Truman to look into the Asiatic uprisings, saying "White supremacy in Asia is approaching an end.")

(EDITOR'S NOTE: That last item makes me want to scream. If Truman and the State Department had heeded this plea from the Times, instead of continuing their support of the French, how many lives would have been saved in Vietnam?)

FROM A 6-HOLER:

HI-HO SILVER! Shades of Pony Express and Silvercup Bread are with us at night. Fast flying Jeeps and stern faced vigilanti spread fear into the hearts of the Japanese criminal.

No implements of war are going to be made under the watchful eye of K Company.

For those of you who didn't know, K Co. maintains a patrol (1 officer and 1 NCO) who ride out in the spirit of democracy to impress upon the Jap the futility of resistance, now and in the time to come.

✯ ✯ ✯

The Japs must be expecting us to stay a long time. They're certainly taking enough pains with the cement floor in the 4th Platoon Barracks to see to its indestructibility in our generation.

✯ ✯ ✯

Miss Japanesy is losing her coyness. Her appearance is less Oriental, more cordial and more in evidence. She washes her teacups while eight or ten guys are shaving in the same basin. There was a time when the only opportunity a GI ever saw a feminine Jap she was moving on the double, head lowered with the fear of the Mikado speeding her onward. The Oriental demeanor is giving way in the face of handsome GI's and their yens (all kinds of yens).

✯ ✯ ✯

Yesterday, we saw what a difference the end of the war made in one of our humbler Army institutions. A "short arm" isn't enough now. The new twist is we're getting foppishly dusted with talc.

HONSHU PIONEER – VOL I, NO. 26 – URAWA, JAPAN – OCT. 24, 1945

HEADLINES:
1. GHQ REVISES SCHOOLS – MILITARY TRAINING OUT; AIM AT U.S. VIEWS (Following student strikes, GHQ is overhauling Japanese schools to eliminate military training and "Fascistic teachings".)
2. NIP FINANCE MENACED (Col. Kramer working to break up immense Japanese companies. Minister Shibusawa refused to discuss anti-trust laws – thinks these firms will begin to break up of themselves.) (*EDITOR'S NOTE: Don't bet on it.*)
3. CHINESE GO VIA A.P.A. (Lt. Gen Wedemyer agrees to transport 20 Chinese divisions to Manchuria in American ships, but does not explain why they couldn't go overland, thus saving scarce shipping space for high-point GI's waiting in Zama and Nagoya for transport home.)

FROM A 6-HOLER:

Rather than put them in cosmoline, it has been decided to keep our rifles handy for cloak room work, obviously. The rifles that were toted through Germany and Czechoslovakia are nothing more now than material on which to lecture for two hours. It's a little late for classes on the functioning of the M1.

★★★

The clouds of DDT have settled, the soap and brush are back in the niche. Whatever lice, gnats and fleas there were have left for greener pastures. It's another triumph for the Medics.

We've been here a week and in that time the Medics haven't had any personal delousings. There have been no flea bites, no lice bites, and to our knowledge, no rat bites. On rats, we have only to say that their scamperings have become more furtive and their working hours aren't as long as they were.

★ ★ ★

There once was a Jap in Urawa,
Who found out much to his sorrowa
    That flat-chested Geishas
    Are willing to fleece yez
Down to your last hard-earned dollowa.

(EDITOR'S NOTE: Sorry about that. I was going to delete it, but I decided that historical accuracy was more important than taste.)

SPORTS: (verbatim)

Heavyweight Champion Joe Louis says that he will beat Billy Conn next June. "I've gained self-confidence in the Army", said Joe. The Brown Bomber is more fortunate than most.

(EDITOR'S NOTE: No byline on the above tidbit, but it's quite possible that my dad wrote it, considering the sarcasm.)

HONSHU PIONEER – VOL I, NO. 27 – URAWA, JAPAN – OCT. 25, 1945

HEADLINES:
1. HST ASKS CONSCRIPTION (President Truman asks Congress to continue compulsory military service in peacetime. "The United States cannot survive unless she remains a military power.")
2. FRENCH JAIL NATIVE CHILDREN (400 Anamite youths, 15 to 17 years old, sentenced to 15 to 20 years hard labor for their part in the Indochina uprisings.)
3. JAP YENMEN TAKE COVER – MITSUBISHI FIRM DISSOLVES ITSELF (Mitsubishi announces plans to close its books.)

FROM A 6-HOLER:

Everybody should have an opportunity to go to Tokyo and see Generals and Colonels and things. If the 386th is spread pretty thinly in this prefecture, not so the Brass in Tokyo. Tokyo is a veritable galaxy of stars and chickens.

★ ★ ★

Japanesy don't trouble yourselves,
If winter food stocks are low;
Hershey bars are lining your shelves
Even tho there's rice no mo'.

★ ★ ★

Such permanency! My duffel bag is almost empty, I know where the latrine is and I've learned the name of the town; and still we haven't moved. Division transportation must be pretty well tied up for K Co. not to have moved in a week's time.

It hardly seems possible they could have run out of factory sites.

✮ ✮ ✮

Straightening out a general misconception: Any picture of Japan as a story-book land of pagodas and wispy pines, ravaged by typhoons and earthquakes is stuff.

Two weeks ago meteorologists told us to "batten down" for a typhoon that did nothing more than get the ground a little more wet than it had been since the sun last shone. Yesterday an earthquake wiggled the ground for a few seconds, which makes us wonder if the Tokyo quake of '23 was anything more than a hoax on the part of the sympathy-mongering Japanese.

(EDITOR'S NOTE: You do realize that he's kidding, right?)

HONSHU PIONEER – VOL I, NO. 28 – URAWA, JAPAN – OCT. 26, 1945

HEADLINES:
1. INDIES NAT'LS COMPROMISE – DUTCH MAY KEEP HOLDINGS (Movement Leader Karno: "No power on earth can stop the Indonesian Movement for Independence." However, they want none off the Dutch holdings in the East Indies.)
2. CONGRESS DIVIDED ON PEACETIME CONSCRIPTION (Mixed response to Truman's request to extend the draft.)
3. BYRNES WARNS ON USE OF LEND-LEASE (Secretary of State Byrnes recommends to Britain that Lend-Lease not be used in the war against Karno's forces in Indonesia.)
4. RADIO HEADLINES (Washington: Problem of Japanese starvation has been solved – they can pay for food with textiles.) (Tokyo: MacArthur orders confiscation of all Japanese State Dept. archives to be investigated for "Jap perpetrated tricks".)

FROM A 6-HOLER:

In the first bit of entertainment for leisure-starved K Company we watched suave, soft-spoken Alan Ladd get the best of old meany Bruce Cabot.

Next time, the 386th A and R department breaks down with a movie let's hope it comes at night. Matinees are too civilian for our shot-in-the-arm-with-military GI's and not well adapted to our light-struck post amphitheater. Of course, if they keep us waiting for the next one as long as they did this one, we'll look at it by holding the film up to the sunlight. If we can't be lit during training hours we don't see why the amphitheater is permitted to be.

★ ★ ★

The way everybody goes to the aid of the poor little Netherlands in their Indonesian fight, it might not be long before we add another ribbon to our already colorful array. "The most traveled division" could add another 5,000 miles, and the Army could grab another laurel to take its place with the Mexican, Boxer and Nicaragua Campaigns.

★ ★ ★

The 97th has a mania for charts. At Leonard Wood it was POE charts; in California it was POM charts; in Europe it was casualty reports and ASR charts; and now in Japan it's TRAINING PROFICIENCY CHARTS.

The first charts were meant to find out how qualified we were for the job the infantry does; the Europe charts are self-explanatory; the Japanese charts are a complete puzzle. If we must have charts, let's have one on PROFICIENCY FOR CIVILIAN ADJUSTMENT.

EDITORIAL:

PEACETIME CONSCRIPTION?

The main topic of discussion at home concerns the question of a peacetime draft.

The re-opening of this question seems to prove that the Army is not attractive enough for volunteers, so now we're going to put everyone in.

One of the things for which we soldiers were fighting was so that our sons wouldn't have to waste the best portion of their lives in learning the fine art of military drill.

We don't think that they would enjoy a soldier's life any more than we do.

The main argument for the draft is that it is necessary for the safety of the nation.

Lately we have been hearing that the next war will last only a few days, and that large armies would never become engaged.

Just why we would need a large army under those conditions is not known.

It seems that a great deal more discussion should be given to ways of speeding up our research.

(EDITOR'S NOTE: The anti-war theme continues on the editorial page. Is anybody noticing at higher levels?)

SPORTS:

MONTREAL SIGNS NEGRO

The Brooklyn Baseball Club made Sports history yesterday when it signed on a negro, Jack Robinson, to play with its International League farm team, Montreal. Robinson, who attended U.C.L.A. and played semipro ball for the Kansas City Monarchs last year, is the first colored player to enter pro baseball.

Brooklyn big-wig Branch Rickey, Jr. was reported as saying that some Southern white players might refuse to go on the field with Robinson. He went on to say, though, that "After a few years in the cotton patches, they will be only too happy to get back into the game."

Robinson, when interviewed, said he will try his best to make a go of it, and that he is very happy to be given the opportunity to play big time baseball.

TUNNEY BLOWS HIS TOP

Former heavyweight champion Gene Tunney has been quite outspoken about the coming Louis-Conn fight. He said, "It's an outrage for promoter Mike Jacobs to permit Conn to meet Louis without first having a series of elimination bouts to determine the man who should meet the champ". Tunney further roared, "I'd be willing to bet $10,000.00 that Leo Robinson can beat Conn. Joe Louis and Conn can't fight their way out of a paper bag."

HONSHU PIONEER – VOL I, NO. 29 – URAWA, JAPAN – OCT. 27, 1945

HEADLINES:
1. OCCUPATION DETAILS AWAIT GOV'T MOVE – PREPARATIONS LACKING FOR ALLIED OCCUPATION (A previously announced plan for occupation duties in Japan to also be shared by China, Britain and the Soviet Union seems not to have been converted to action.)
2. LANDON HITS HST POLICIES (Alf Landon criticizes Pres. Truman, saying that atomic power should be internationalized, foreign bases should be abandoned, and that Russia was a new aggressor on the prowl.) (*EDITOR'S NOTE: Something seems a bit inconsistent about Mr. Landon's positions, doesn't it?*)
3. TRIDENT MEN HIT JACKPOT ($3,000,000 worth of silver bullion found in the hills of central Honshu, bringing the total of Japanese treasure to fall into American hands up to $250,000,000. $10,000,000 worth of Radium also discovered.)
4. NO. 4 NAZI TAKES LIFE (Robert Ley, former Nazi Labor Front leader, found hanging in his Nuremberg cell, with a towel that he should not have had.)

FROM A 6-HOLER:

Love is getting booted around a great deal in the United States.

Stateside tabloids, who owe their existence to sensationalism (unidentified youths and unclothed bodies of suburban girls, emotional slayings and Hollywood divorces) are having a change in "good copy". The best story now seems to run as follows: Ensign A is missing in Pacific action; wife of Ensign A is enamored of war worker Mr. B, who subsequently marries Ensign's wife. At a most inopportune moment Ensign A enters wife's bedroom (after drifting around on a rubber boat for 6 or 10 weeks) and there's a happy reconciliation (not so good copy), or an annulment (better copy), or a mud-slinging divorce case (best copy).

★ ★ ★

Uh huh. A few people didn't figure that Congress had made the re-enlistment bill in the regular army a good enough deal. One of these was Brig, General W. X. F. Heavey, who offered a Crackerjack of a prize to any regular army aspirants in his 2nd Eng, Supply Base outfit, by giving them a Samurai sword as they signed on the line. Good going men, that ole sword will look fine hanging on the wall of your squad room back in some barracks in the States.

★ ★ ★

There was an old soldier of K,
Who tried supplementing is pay
By selling soap,
By which the dope
Went dirty from August to May.

EDITORIAL:

AFTER YOU'RE OUT

Every legend has its truth. The "Magic Carpet" will soon carry, carry us back to civvies.

As a GI we may have been able to offer suggestions or gripe, but that was the extent of our contribution towards the running of the Army.

As a civilian our responsibility will be far greater. Our gripes can be translated into action. Our vote will be sought after.

The war was fought against a system which would have discarded all these expressions of democratic life with which we are familiar.

It might be said that in great part the responsibility of World War II was that of our parents and their generation. This was due to a lack of interest in their personal duties towards our democracy.

Are we going to repeat that mistake?

This is written as a reminder that none of us want our kids to go through another war period.

Such a situation will not occur unless we participate actively in the affairs of our democracy.

(EDITOR'S NOTE: We are hearing this again and again: We fought hard for world peace, but unless we continue to work for it in civilian life, it may have been in vain. If only it were that simple.)

HONSHU PIONEER – VOL I, NO. 30 – URAWA, JAPAN – OCT. 28, 1945

HEADLINES:
1. SHIPS RETURN TO U.S. WITH EMPTY BUNKS – ARMY OFFICER REVEALS LATEST WAR DEPT. SNAFU (300 empty bunks on a returning ship – accusations by maritime unions that ships are being returned to civilian use – general discontent with the pace of demobilization.)
2. CHINA RESUMES NORMAL RELATIONS (U.S. And China to resume normal relations on Nov. 1, after 8 years of upheaval.)
3. GUERILLA BANDS ACTIVE IN P.I. (The guerillas who fought the Japanese in the Philippines are now "roving bandits who steal anything and everything".)
4. LUXURIES EASE URAWA BOREDOM (Showers now have hot and cold water, a barber chair has been installed, and soon there will be a ball field, day-room and a post chapel.)

FROM A 6-HOLER:

Heartening news to all K Co. movie fans was the announcement by AFL that film makers would have to give up their strike and go back to grinding cameras, putting gilt on Dietrich's legs and shooing visitors away from the set when the little red light is on.

Allowing two years for production, K cinema addicts may take a long distance view toward getting movies – and go on hoping.

★ ★ ★

Cousin Larry writes that the new basic isn't what it was at old Camp Blanding. Since the end of the war the rookies have been cut back to the

40-hour week. The War Dept. must figure there's less for them to do now.

If things in Urawa are indicative of occupation all over, I wonder what they do for even 40 hours. Probably the same sort of things we've done for 45 for the last three years and continue to do now.

★ ★ ★

Joe and Wally have just left K Co.'s library.

"Hey, whatcha readin, Joe?"

"I just finished Canterbury Tales".

"Yeah, that was pretty solid, but wait til ya read the Complete Works of Milton".

"You miss a helluvalot by not readin it in Eyetalian, y'know."

"I heard the chaplain talkin about bringin over a mystery one of these weeks".

"You don't say – TSK TCH. It's going to be hard going back to that sort of stuff."

HONSHU PIONEER – VOL I, NO. 31 – URAWA, JAPAN – OCT. 29, 1945

HEADLINES:
1. TRUMAN STATES U.S. POLICY – 12 POINT RECIPE FOR PEACE OUTLINED IN NAVY DAY SPEECH (1. We will not shirk our role – 2. Return of sovereignty to all nations – 3. No territorial changes, except by plebiscite – 4. Self-determination – 5. Cooperation toward democracy – 6. No recognition of regimes imposed by force – 7. Freedom of the seas – 8. Trade and raw materials for all countries – 9. Monroe Doctrine & Good Neighbor Policy – 10. Bretton Woods agreement – 11. Freedom of speech & religion – 12. United Nations)
2. KOREANS WANT TROOPS WITHDRAWN – KOREA CRITICIZES US, SOVIET RULE (The U.S. And Russia are impeding, rather than promoting a popular government.)

FROM A 6-HOLER:

```
Time: The near future

Setting: A knotty-pine paneled booth in the Parnassus Room of the Hotel Olympus

2 GI's are seated left front, sipping watered brandy and sake.

Mac: (moodily) In all that time we were in Japan I sure as hell did not expect to come to Greece.

Doc: (gleefully) But gee whiz, you wouldn't a thought the Greeks on Cyprus would've wanted to be under Greek rule rather than British.

Mac: (credulously) Oh, is that why we're here?
```

Doc: (authoritatively) Yea. The United Nations were afraid Greece would take advantage of the Greeks wanting to be ruled by Greece.

Mac: (wonderingly) Hoe do you find time to keep posted on that junk when you spend all your time doing close order drill, M1 nomenclature, map reading, military courtesy...

Mars: (martially) Hello there fellows. How are you fixed for points?

Mac and Doc: (in unison) We're waiting to hear about our second battle star, but we should leave by September.

Mars: (recklessly) Hmm. I suppose you're still wasting your time as you did in Japan by puttering around with war stuff that will be outmoded by the time I decide there should be another one.

Mac: (querying) Well, what would you expect?

Mars: Hmpf … well, excuse me. I've got a date with a dream from deMilo.

(EDITOR'S NOTE: There's no way to know, of course, but I would wager that the little drama above got Mr. Hanratty one of his sessions "on the carpet".)

EDITORIAL:

ALLIES?

Our Chinese and Russian allies have both requested that they be permitted to send token occupation forces to Japan.

Thus far, no good reasons why they shouldn't be admitted have been given.

Our government seems to be beating around the diplomatic bush and no reply has been given.

If the American Army of Occupation is bolstered by several Allied troops, it means that some of our low point men can get home a few months sooner.

Russia has hated Japan since 1904, and Chinese enmity is centuries old.

The Nips are frankly worried by the thought of a Sino-Russian occupational army. The armies of other nations aren't as well supplied as ours, and they might be tempted to steal back some of their lost property.

Maybe the State Department is afraid that the friends and families of the veterans of the Pearl Harbor maneuvers would be molested.

(EDITOR'S NOTE: We have seen some pretty good editorials from these guys up to now, but this one is embarrassing [in my humble opinion]. Can the author think of no other reasons why it might be counterproductive to have a bunch of Russian and Chinese troops running around Japan? What was it that we were trying to accomplish there? Didn't it have something to do with establishing a western-style democracy? Would either Russian or Chinese troops have any idea what that should mean? The author seems to be so fixated on the idea of getting home as soon as possible that he can think of nothing else, with the possible exception of maximizing any punitive measures against Japan.)

HONSHU PIONEER – VOL I, NO. 32 – URAWA, JAPAN – OCT. 30, 1945

HEADLINES:
1. OPEN WAR IN CHINA! - GOVERNMENT TROOPS ATTACK AS NEGOTIATIONS COLLAPSE (Battles rage in north China – Chiang Kai Shek gives no reason for attack – Mao says negotiations broke down because Yenan group would not agree to separation of the areas now under Communist control.)
2. DOMEI AGENCY LAUDS KONOYE (Prince Konoye, it was claimed, had disagreed with Tojo about starting a war with the U.S. While China remained unconquered.)
3. UAW DENOUNCES G. MOTORS OFFER (Walter Reuther said a 45-hour work week would be unfair to returning servicemen and would cause great unemployment.)

FROM A 6-HOLER – BY A. DELONG THOMAS:

DANCE MACABRE

Tonight at midnight the departed ancestors come out of their Shinto Shrines and carry on in the light of the moon in the best Halloween tradition of Yankee ghosts.

That is, we can count on a performance, if the ghosts are as willing to put on as good a show as the government and people seem to be doing.

CIGARETTE LAB

With the new boom in education and English courses making considerable progress, there's been an increasing demand for courses in rolling your own. Any interested people should send to USAFI for texts and materials.

Those of you who haven't the patience to roll'em should contact the Jap in Urawa who was selling Luckies at 40 yen a pack. The fact that 40 is a little over ceiling bothers no one, OPA the least.

SHAVE AND A HAIRCUT TWO BITS

The only things missing from the community's barber shop is a black boot boy, a striped pole, a Varga calendar and a brass spittoon. On hand, however, are electric snippers and a moveable leather chair, making everything professional to the point of being civilized.

Esquire's on the carpet again. Same trouble, inflammatory stuff. Varga's too hot for the US MALE.

(EDITOR'S NOTE: I was a bit jolted by that "black boot boy" line, which would be completely out of character for the guy I knew, but I guess you have to remember time, place and community. This is the first column with a byline, which seems to make Dad unique on the paper. The Sunday Supplements often had signed items, but not the normal daily issues. Also interesting to me is that he used his father's name – not his own – although they are technically the same [mine too]. My grandfather was known as A. DeLong Thomas, and my father was always Arthur D. Thomas.)

HONSHU PIONEER – VOL I, NO. 33 – URAWA, JAPAN – OCT. 31, 1945

HEADLINES:

1. CHINESE BATTLE RAGES – HEAVY FIGHTING CONTINUES ON PEIPING SUIYAN R.R. (Yenan forces in control of 12 cities and inflicting heavy casualties – Chiang's troops to be flown [n American planes] to 11 provinces where fighting is raging.)
2. WHITE FLAG IN INDONESIA (Indonesian President Karno intervenes to stop the fighting, but the insurgents still have large supplies of ammunition.)
3. TROOPS FOR WORLD COUNCIL (U.S. State Dept. proposes a U.S. Ambassador to the U.N., and a "sizable force" to be available to the newly-formed Security Council.)

FROM A 6-HOLER:

> IN MEMORIAM
>
> In the hushed hours of early morn, there transpired a scene of stark horror, of tragic death. Death, that grim master of mammal's destiny, snuffed out the life of one of our fellow creatures. The earth still turned, voices still clattered on happily, yet hearts were sad and heads bowed in more than one Urawa cave-home or attic nook.
>
> Willie was a difficult fellow to get to know. He liked best to be off by himself, silent, thoughtful, contemplative, modestly keeping to himself his thoughts, his hopes and his views on life.

> It must be said: Willie purposely avoided people, Willie's seclusion, however, was not one of contempt for his fellow earth dwellers, but if the truth were known, Willie suffered from an inferiority complex. Not that Willie didn't try to be loved and respected, mind you. On the eve of Willie's demise, Willie tried. Willie had long watched and even unobtrusively visited the editorial offices of the <u>Honshu Pioneer</u>. Willie's leading desire was to gain the respect of the world as a Pioneer writer. It was indeed unfortunate that on the way to the typewriter he should have encountered a piece of cheese on a wooden slab. Willie now lies forgotten by a world that was never to know him, unsorrowed by an alien world.

(EDITOR'S NOTE: This is <u>exactly</u> the kind of inspired silliness that my father would come up with throughout his life and part of what made him such a unique person.)

EDITORIAL:

NO CIGARETTES!

The tobacco shortage in this Regiment is no longer a subject for amusement.

At the present time it is practically impossible to find a man in possession of any cigarettes, much less smoking one in the presence of his buddies.

Last week's standard question of "Have you got a cigarette?" has been changed to "How about a draw, buddy?"

The reason for this unprecedented lack of tobacco in any form can be traced quite easily.

It seems that our enemies of a few short months ago are rationed to two cigarettes a day and are willing to pay for more at the rate of 30 Yen a pack.

Reports indicate that an ample supply of tobacco is reaching Japan, but by the time the supplies reach lower levels, the week's ration is cut to nearly one-half of that to which we are entitled.

In other words, there is something VERY, VERY rotten on the Island of Honshu.

(EDITOR'S NOTE: as a reminder, 30 Yen = $2 at this time, but that's over $25 in 2013 currency. Other sources confirm that black marketing of cigarettes [and other goods] by American troops was a huge industry in Japan at this time, and officers were often involved. The author seems to know this, but doesn't want to spell it out for us. Check out Fred Stark's related cartoons for October 29 and 31, included at the back of the book.)

HONSHU PIONEER – VOL I, NO. 34 – URAWA, JAPAN – NOV. 1, 1945

HEADLINES:
1. S.A. DESPOT DITCHED – BLOODLESS COUP IN BRAZIL DEPOSES VARGAS' CABINET (Deposed 15-year dictator Vargas now in protective custody, following threat of civil war by Gen. Montriarie. Supreme Court head Jose Linares now in charge. Elections coming soon.)
2. YENAN TROOPS BEGIN ATTACK (Chinese Communists have secured part of the Peiping-Siuyuan R.R. Nationalists have suffered over 20,000 casualties.)
3. TRUMAN FAVORS WAGE BOOST (Pres. Truman tries to ease a tense labor situation by proposing 48 hours pay for 40 hours work, instead of the 52 requested by labor.)

FROM A 6-HOLER – A DeLong Thomas:

PROPHETIC GLIMPSE

One icy day in February, when snow and sleet were blowing lustily up and down the streets of Laramie, Wyoming, a doddering soak, aged well beyond his years, stumbled into a nondescript barroom.

In a hoarse, cracked voice the bum ordered up a draft and surveyed the three khaki-clad AST-ers next to him.

"Youse fellows sure got a soft touch here."

The three callow college youths nodded yes, embarrassedly, while he continued, "I might've been something if I'd had any breaks, but I stayed in Germany after the last one, just doin' nothin', but... well, nothin' but occupyin'."

TOKYO GLANCE

Tokyo, which as a pass town, is worse than Rolla, Missouri, finally has an attraction worth seeing. For those who've had the experience of visiting nothing more than the hedges around the Imperial Palace and the facade of the Tokyo Radio Bldg., there's now a must on your Tokyo visit, Mademoiselle X.

Miss X, associated with the American Red Cross, is a petite young French lady with an engaging dark look and most wonderful of all – she's neither brown nor atabrined.

CLUB NOTES

Smart brightly colored convertibles, long crunchy gravel drives, a swank, luxurious club house mark the scene provided for our sophisticated pass goers. For three days, lucky men will be plied with tall cooling drinks and feted to rounds of golf on the playground of emperors, provided Moosehead Country Club lives up to the advance notices.

EDITORIAL:

ADIOS, GETULIO:

As Japan is famed for her cherry blossoms, so shall ye know the republics of Latin America by their revolutions.

In fact, it has become practically an SOP for a daily to hold space open on its front page for such capers.

However, the latest manifestation of Latin virility which took place in Rio de Janeiro did not occur because of the whim of some pistol-waving militarist.

Tom Paine once said, "Tyranny, like Hell, is not easily conquered.", and it has taken 15 years for the people of Brazil to depose the slickest dictator south of Nome, Alaska.

Getulio Vargas devoted a great deal of his time to the buttering-up of the U.S. State Department.

We, in return, were buddy-buddy with him, and Brazil was well supplied with Lend-Lease equipment.

The whole business backfired yesterday, when U.S.-built tanks and guns formed the backbone of the army which dumped Getulio.

(EDITOR'S NOTE: Again, there are no bylines on the editorials, but I think I hear my father's voice in this one, just from the way he uses language. The Tom Paine quote is another strong clue.)

HONSHU PIONEER – VOL I, NO. 35 – URAWA, JAPAN – NOV. 2, 1945

HEADLINES:
1. "CHIANG BAITS RUSSIA" - REDS – YENAN CLAIMS NATIONALISTS (Reds: Chiang is accusing us of using Outer Mongolians to drive tanks – not true.)
2. ALLIES TO OCCUPY SOON (British, Russian and Chinese troops to arrive "soon".)
3. IKE REPORTS GERMAN UNREST (Several Americans injured – civil government will rule Germany after June 1.)
4. SULLIVAN SAYS 44 PTS BY FEB. (Army critical point score to be lowered to 55 on 12/1/45, 50 on 1/1/46, and 45 on 2/1/46.) *(EDITOR'S NOTE: Is 44 a typo or a wish?)*
5. MOURNING REPORT - "At the Daizingu Shrine, where the Goddess of the Sun is worshiped, Emperor Hirohito is going to bow low and report that Nippon failed to conquer the world."

FROM A 6-HOLER – BY A. DELONG THOMAS – ESQ.:

LOST: One columnist... medium height and weight. Can be identified by the predatory gleam in his eye. He was last seen heading toward Tokyo, after he had described, in his column, a soulful young Frenchwoman at the Red Cross Club. We lose more columnists that way.

★ ★ ★

Tips to you nicotine fiends, who have been hard hit by the prevailing cigarette shortage: We understand several members of this command are smoking coffee grounds lately. In our day, it was corn-silk, but "chac un a son gout", as we said in Paris. We understand cigarettes are worth two bucks a pack there, too.

Trick in rolling your own, it seems, is to grasp the paper firmly with the thumb and two fingers of each hand. Dump in the tobacco, and then roll, using both hands, one foot, and as many members of your squad as are around. Tie firmly with tent-rope, and then toss the whole thing away, if it's anything like the ones we make, and bum one from the nearest Jap laborer.

EDITORIAL:
"PAL CHIANG"

China is in the throes of civil war. This is not a new conflict. It goes back to the birth of the present Chinese republic.

Sun Yat Sen, father and founder of the new China died of cancer in 1925. His mantle fell to Chiang Kai-shek.

It is not news that Chiang betrayed the democratic revolution for which Sun Yat Sen fought.

He dealt out torture and death to hundreds of Communists, Russians and Chinese, and to thousands of farmers and coolies who had looked to Kuomintang for support against their exploiters.

Through all these early years of struggle his course towards Tokyo was appeasement. He concentrated all his power and venom on the Communists.

The Reds banded together and waged war on the well-to-do. Every year Chiang sent an army against them.

Finally they marched 6000 miles to safety, defied Chiang, and were the first to declare war on Japan.

(EDITOR'S NOTE: You must remember that American Marines were stationed in China at this time, clearly aligned with Chiang. The author of this piece does not point that out because his readers would have been well aware of it. He was not the only person to wonder if we were helping the right side in this conflict, or if we should have been involved at all.)

HONSHU PIONEER – VOL I, NO. 36 – URAWA, JAPAN – NOV. 3, 1945

HEADLINES:
1. U.S. - U.S.S.R. COMPROMISE – TRUMAN, STALIN AGREE ON MAJOR ISSUES (Pacific areas to be the joint interest of the Big 4, with U.S. Playing dominant role – U.S. Reparations committee sent to Japan.)
2. MAC ANSWERS U.S. PRESS (MacArthur: Prince Konoye was chosen to draft a new constitution for Japan by Premier Shidehara, not by GHQ.)
3. YENAN FORCES MOVE TO BLOCKADE MANCHURIA (Communist forces drive to stop flow of National Government forces to Manchuria.)
4. BRITAIN BEGINS SOCIAL PROGRAM (Atlee: government taking over 3 airlines and communication systems – general housing improvements in all England next.)

FROM A 6-HOLER – BY A. DELONG THOMAS JR.:

MOVE OVER BUDDY

All the reassuring talk coming out from 8th Army I and E about mild Tokyo winters means boo to K Company. To heck with 'em; K will make preparations for keeping warm, come what may. First move to safeguard warm temperatures in billets is to see how many men can be crowded into a single room. Biggest difficulty now would seem to be no room for stoves.

★★★

Part of moving day was marked by the non-coms getting clubby again. They've had to associate with their squads for some time now and getting back within their fold will make things look quieter, more garrison-like – and more permanent BUTT BONANZA NIGHT.

Just about the time the most fanatic nicotine addicts were about to renounce the smoke habit out of utter despair, Regimental Breakdown broke down with four packs per man.

✯ ✯ ✯

As if cigarettes weren't enough, somebody came up with a movie. All the theater goers of the neighborhood turned out, trustingly. Cigs and movies were too much, however. You've got to stagger your good things.

Most of the audience didn't take the trouble to change into their best kimonos, and most didn't know what movie it was they weren't going to get a chance to see.

EDITORIAL:
EMPEROR MEIJI:

Today is a national holiday in what remains of the Japanese Empire. November 3rd is the birthday of the Emperor Meiji, 122nd descendant of the Sun Goddess and father of modern Japan.

Meiji ascended the throne in 1867, at the age of 16. A year later, supreme authority was wrested from the feudal lords known as the Shoguns and once again placed in Imperial hands.

At that time Japan was an isolated group of islands. Foreigners were visiting the country after over two centuries of exclusion.

The early years of the Meiji era saw the granting of a Constitution and the first sessions of the Diet.

Western ideas and methods were injected into every phase of Japanese life.

Under his leadership, Japan went to war with China in 1894 and defeated Russia in 1905. Korea was annexed in 1910.

By the time of his death in 1912, Japan was recognized as the leading Asiatic power.

(EDITOR'S NOTE: This history lesson would normally make me suspect that my father was the author, but not this time. Informative and interesting as it may be, the language is flat, dry and textbook-like – not the way Dad usually wrote. Still, it's a nice attempt at increasing the level of understanding of the country they were occupying among the American troops.)

HONSHU PIONEER – VOL I, NO. 38 – URAWA, JAPAN – NOV. 5, 1945

HEADLINES:
1. BYRNES STATES U.S. POSITION – BYRNES IN DILEMMA (The U.S. Has 2 courses of action in China: 1) consider the Reds to be bandits and aid Chiang; 2) regard the war as an internal affair and take no action. No decision has been reached.)
2. CHUNKING OFFERS TERMS – COMMUNISTS STUDYING FOUR POINT PROPOSAL (The government has offered 1) All troops hold present positions; 2) Reds withdraw from railroads; 3) Government will consult with Yenan before moving troops by rail; 4) People's Council to investigate the causes of hostilities and solutions.)
3. NICHTS NAZI (Nuremberg Trials have been postponed 6 weeks per defense requests for more preparation time.)

FROM A 6-HOLER:

FIGHTING WORDS

News Item: Major Alex Seversky stated that 2,000 B29s each loaded with incendiary bombs could have wrought as much havoc as the atom bomb did in Hiroshima and Nagasaki.

And then there's my old friend, the axe manufacturer that predicted a regiment of men armed with axes is as effective on the fields of battle as an infantryman with an M1. Mr. Seversky's trouble and the trouble with the axe manufacturer is that the times are moving too swiftly.

MONKEYSTUFF

Attention Capt. Arthur and other stateside bound K Co. men: You're permitted to take any pets, which might have captured your fancy in the Pacific, so long as it isn't a lemur, a koda bear or a monkey. On the approved list were kangaroos, ostriches, antelopes, and the Giant Eurasian Manalvarix.

AIR FORCE POINTMAN

The word has gotten around Tokyo that Urawa is a better pass town than their own city.

On a Urawa-bound interurban, a pleasure-bent Air Force man was garrulously, alcoholically attacking the point system.

"I been at New Guinea, Marianas and Solomons. What I wanna know is how come those guys in the States are getting out and they keep me here pushin' me around from one Hotel to another?"

(EDITOR'S NOTE: No, Virginia, there is no such thing as a Manalvarix, giant or otherwise.)

EDITORIAL:

WE'RE WAITING:

Not long ago we made mention of the fact that 55 C-47 transport planes had been sold to the Chinese government by the Surplus Property Board.

We didn't like it because it meant that the planes would not be used to take high-pointers home.

Once again the news from China is unpleasant. It has been announced that American ships are being used to move Chinese troops into Manchuria.

Although the Nationalists would rather send their troops overland, it seems that several hundred thousand men of the Communist 8th Route Army are in their way.

There isn't much to be done about this deal now, as the troops have already been moved. However, let us hope that the government delays any further actions until we take one more ride on the ships that were built at the expense of the American people.

We don't want to appear to be impatient, but <u>WE WANT TO GO HOME</u>.

HONSHU PIONEER – VOL I, NO. 39 – URAWA, JAPAN – NOV. 6, 1945

HEADLINES:
1. CHINESE BATTLE CONTINUES; U.S. ALERTS PIEPING TROOPS – MARINES STAND BY – RUSSIA COOPERATES IN MANCHURIA OCCUPATION (Rumor: Yenan may attack airfield occupied by U.S. Troops. Marines there are confined to barracks. Russian occupation forces prepare to turn over posts to Chiang. Battles are spreading, but negotiations to avert all-out war are planned.)
2. NEAR AUTONOMY FOR CAMBODIA (France has offered autonomy to Cambodia, the most loyal of its colonies, as an example of what may be in store for others.)

FROM A 6-HOLER:
KALEIDOSCOPE TOKYO

What with Radio Tokyo, PX Tokyo and GHQ Tokyo and similar institutions all Tokyo, our life seems to be entirely woven about City Tokyo.

Tokyo prevails over provincial Japan as completely as Paris does over France. And is as much the Mecca to gaping tourists of the Orient as New York, London and Paris are to the west.

US forces have grabbed on to pseudo-cosmopolitan Tokyo with the zeal of a provincial first seeing the bright lights. Drunken sailors are spending money like drunken sailors. GHQ officers and enlisted personnel are seizing the most luxurious accommodations possible and are making up for the times they've had to live in tents and wash in helmets. The Air Force, always the best outfit when it comes to looking out for themselves, have made the best of every opportunity (and they sure have a way of popping up.) FEAF have commandeered Tokyo's most pretentious hotel, the Hotel Imperial where AAF men are led to their tables by a grinning head waiter and presented with individual coffee pots by obsequious, toothy little Japaneseys. For all this US Airmen remain blasé and wonder as much as we why we're here.

★ ★ ★

Incidentally, the business that the engineer and conductor on the interurban give out with is "Eat-your-cheese-and-wash-and-let's-go."

EDITORIAL:

LET'S GET OUT OF CHINA:

Late news from Peiping to the effect that the U.S. Marines have been alerted and confined to their barracks doesn't sound good to us.

The latest scuttlebutt in the Marine area is that the Communists are preparing to attack an airfield which is occupied by the Americans.

It is very difficult to believe that the Yenan government would attempt to take on the U.S. in a full scale war, even if it had any grievance against us.

It is possible, however, for an unfortunate incident to take place, considering the tension in the air.

We have no reason for keeping troops in China except as a method of maintaining world peace. According to the decision of the San Francisco

Conference, such things are the job of the Security Council.

It would be very hard to halt a major war with a lone Marine detachment anyway.

(EDITOR'S NOTE: The general dissatisfaction with the China situation and the fear of deeper U.S. involvement are persistent themes with the <u>Honshu Pioneer</u> editorial staff.)

HONSHU PIONEER – VOL I, NO. 40 – URAWA, JAPAN – NOV. 7, 1945

HEADLINES:
1. CHIANG SENDS REINFORCEMENTS (Fighting in China grows fiercer – Reds take 2 cities in Shansi and hold ports in Manchuria, blocking troop landings.)
2. GOV'T DISBANDS LARGE FIRMS (The 4 richest families in Japan, who own 70% of industry and control 100% by intermarriage, will have their holdings dissolved.)
3. BARS, CAFES TO OPEN FOR G.I.S (The Office of Sanitation and Soldier Welfare will inspect all restaurants and cafes in Tokyo, to offer more choices to G.I.s, and films from all major studios are being released for immediate delivery to Tokyo theaters.)

FROM A 6-HOLER – BY A. DELONG THOMAS JR.:

THE STORY OF THE BIG WHITE HORSE

Attention in Japan, at present, seems to be focused on nothing more important than a horse; not a purple horse, or a green horse, but the same sort of horse you might expect Hiram to use in pulling his tomatoes to market. White horses, chocolate bars, and pretty girls are at a real premium around here.

The whole business started when Admiral Halsey inadvertently boasted that he would ride Hirohito's horse through the streets of Tokyo. Since the old sea dog's swaggering announcement, everyone seems to have conspired to give him a hard time. Admiral Halsey's first embarrassment came at the hand of erstwhile well-wishers, who took the Admiral's statement seriously. When saddles, spurs and general equestrian accoutrements started pouring in "Bull" probably wished he weren't so talkative when imbibing. Imagine his chagrin when he learns that some first lieutenant from a cavalry outfit will ride the fool horse.

With all this to-do about who's going to ride whom and whether it's to be in Meiji Stadium or the Ginza, Hirohito's horse remains perfectly calm. His reaction to everything has been a repeated horse laff.

An answer to the whole horsey affair, one with which we're sure Admiral Halsey would be in agreement, is to enter the horse on the industrial survey and boil him down to glue.

HONSHU PIONEER – VOL I, NO. 41 – URAWA, JAPAN – NOV. 8, 1945

HEADLINES:
1. MARINES TO LEAVE CHINA DEC 1ST (First Marine Division to leave for home on 12/1/45 – Fighting expected to develop into full scale civil war by January.)
2. SAILORS PROTEST AID TO DUTCH (39 officers plus crew of USS Hammon petition Pres. Truman that ships be used to transport U.S. Troops home, before any further aids to the Dutch in their fight against the Indonesian Peoples Army.)
3. RUSS ACCUSE U.S., BRITAIN (USSR Commissar Molotov accuses the U.S. and Britain of "keeping the atomic secret for military purposes".)
4. G.I. BILL UNDER REVISION (Senate Finance Committee: Every returning veteran to be eligible for a loan at reduced rates with long term payments.)

FROM A 6-HOLER – BY A. DELONG THOMAS JR.:

PATHWAYS OF PEACE

Getting back to the ways of peace isn't the impulsive, throbbingly patriotic march the road to war is. War makes a person's blood race around; makes a nation draw up to their full patriotic height and buy bonds, enlist and generally get into the scrap.

After six months of conflict, war dept. telegrams, rising prices, gas and food deprivations make it a lot less fun, the sight of a soldier doesn't any longer boost your patriotic fervor; you just want to forget the soldier and make your way to the nearest bar.

Soldiers are intended for one thing – war. They don't look well wandering about town; it embarrasses people. The citizenry can't feel sorry and charitable toward GI's who aren't brandishing bayonets and eating K rations in muddy foxholes.

The Hollywood and New York Canteens are closing shop; USO entertainers are too busy signing contracts to come overseas. Cheesecake photos of budding starlets getting typhus inoculations in their arm or leg aren't going over so well any more. Betcha the people of North Platte aren't even passing out cakes to GI's with imaginary birthdays. Take down your star, mother, the war is over. The nation has won a war and deserves its rest.

HONSHU PIONEER – VOL I, NO. 42 – URAWA, JAPAN – NOV. 9, 1945

HEADLINES:
1. FURLOUGHED 50'S OUT – ELIGIBLE FOR DISCHARGE ON RETURN TO STATION (War Department: All men with 50 points or more who are now in the U.S. are eligible for immediate discharge.)
2. YENAN CLAIMS GAIN IN NORTH (Communists take Hankow RR as far north as Pieping – Red forces relieving guerillas in Fukien – Heavy fighting in the north.)
3. COMMITTEE OK'S SECURITY FORCE (Senate Foreign Relations Committee approves placing U.S. Troops at the disposal of the new World Security Council.)

FROM A 6-HOLER – BY ROADBLOCK DELONG THOMAS JR.:

ON KEEPING OUR NOSES CLEAN

Secretary of State Byrnes saw a way out of unpleasant and embarrassing predicaments in China. The 1st Marines, who are stationed near Tientsin, couldn't have thought of a better move. The answer: Marines are simply to be sent home, before the US is given any opportunity to SNAFU.

Think it over boys! There are revolutions going on all over. There's no reason why one couldn't be arranged for our Jap hosts. The governmental set-up looks as if it could use a nice big revolution to rid it of all its pre-end-of-war hangers-on, such as Konoye and some of his Shidehara cabinet buddies.

We don't know what our compatriots, the Marines, might have had to do with the current hard-feeling in China. There's no job, however, the Marines could have had anything to do with that the Army couldn't improve on.

What's the matter with you Communists here in Japan? - no fight? - no spirit? Come on, let's have a repsnortin' of an old revolution and get the whole occupation force home by Christmas.

HAIL TO THE OLD DHS

Activities going on around here are beginning to look more and more like the activity that goes on around a stateside high school; football games with yell leaders, linesman and bright jerseys, announcements of class schedule changes add up to a civilian-sided sum. Men are even staying after school as punishment for two of their members forgetting to return borrowed bicycles.

(EDITOR'S NOTE: of course, the "DHS" refers to Dearborn High School, where Art attended, met his wife and later taught, not to mention sending all three of his children there.)

EDITORIAL:

A PROMISE REMEMBERED:

The news of the past few days has been very discouraging to all of us.

Officials in charge of shipping at Yokohama have expressed doubt that the quotas for the month of November will be filled, due to the lack of sufficient ships.

Yesterday we learned that our ships were being used to carry supplies to the Dutch, who are fighting an imperialistic war against the natives of Indonesia.

In other words, the ships that should have been used to transport veterans home are instead being used against the cause of the freedom for which we fought.

It is very hard for us to understand why our government insists on taking part in such fiascoes, especially when they are done at our expense.

Maybe Mr. Truman has forgotten the promise which he made to all of us in his V-J Day speech. Or has he changed his mind about wanting us home "as fast as the ships and planes can carry" us.

We haven't forgotten, Mr. President.

(EDITOR'S NOTE: Well, he sounds pretty steamed, and rightfully so. One gets the idea that if these ships were being diverted to support a war against fascism, colonialism, or oppression, the delay in their return to the States would be a lot easier to bear. However, to be using these ships to support an "imperialistic war", that is "against the cause of the freedom for which we fought" is outrageous. Furthermore, the U.S. government keeps getting involved in these messy situations, and why is that? Again, one can see the writing on the wall that would lead us into Vietnam in a few years time – speaking of "fiascoes".)

SPORTS:

UNDERDOG PIONEER TEAM MEETS CO. HQ

Today at 1400 the Greater East-Asia Co-Prosperity Conference will move into second gear when an underdog Honshu Pioneer seven goes up against the favored Company Headquarters team.

The Company Headquarters starting line-up is not known as we go to press, but the Hdqs. Men can be expected to field a bang-up team.

The freshmen "Honshu Pioneer" line-up is as follows: Captain and Quarterback - Bob Ohly; Rt End - Jim Rich; Cen. - Don Anderson; Tkle - A. Hamburger; Left End - Jean Levesque; Left Half - Gary Owen; Rt Half - Art Thomas.

(EDITOR'S NOTE: I was aware that my father had played some football on the JV at Dearborn High, but never heard him discuss his career in military football. He was about 5'10" and 150 pounds, soaking wet, but pretty fast, so Right Half might have suited him. To avoid any undue suspense, we will jump ahead to tomorrow's sports page to see how this momentous struggle resolved itself.)

CRIMSON + GOLD OUTFOUGHT 10 – 6

A valiant Honshu Pioneer team went down to defeat yesterday before powerful Co. Hdqs. By a score of 10 to 6.

Headquarters, momentarily befuddled by the Pioneer attack, permitted the "Crimson and Gold" to score, but from that point on the fracas was completely one-sided.

The Cooks and Supply Roomers drove to a TD late in the second period and after a halftime rest they overpowered the Pioneers in every respect.

In the final moments of the game the stalwart sons of the "Honshu Pioneer" could not fight their way out of the shadow of their goal. Final Score: Co. Hdqs. 10, H. P. 6. Hdqs. collected four points on two safeties.

HONSHU PIONEER – VOL I, NO. 43 – URAWA, JAPAN – NOV. 10, 1945

HEADLINES:
1. MARINES REPORTED IN ACTION – YENAN SPOKESMAN ASKS U.S. GOV'T TO HALT CHIANG AID (Reds accuse U.S. Marines of entering Ching Nan Tao, demand apology, threaten dire consequences. Marine garrison doubled to 2,000 men.)
2. SOE KARNO GETS STERN ULTIMATUM (Dutch and British commanders warn all East Indies natives to lay down arms by 0600 today or be seized and shot.
3. PROFS REPEAT ATOM WARNING (Dr. Compton and Dr. Hutchins favor internationalization of the atom bomb, and warn that "immeasurably more horrible" world conflict will result from trying to keep it secret.)

FROM A 6-HOLER – BY ROADBLOCK DELONG THOMAS JR.:

There's method to our new orange "Japanese Phrase Book". There's no end to what can be accomplished with a little application. The whole answer is you mustn't feel you're restricted to any one department (Emergency Expressions, General Expressions, Personal Needs, Additional Terms). The secret of your success lies in your ability to skip around. Here's an example of only one end to which this little elixir can be put.

You've received the glad eye from a little Nipponese. While you are acknowledging her greeting, you turn to page three.

"Help!" (ta-SKET-ay)

"Please help me." (ta-SKET-ay ko da-SA-ee)

"I am lost." (me-chee-nee ma Yoat-ta)

"Yes!" (HA-ee)

"No?" (EE-ay)

"I don't understand." (wa-KA-ree ma-SEN)

"Please speak slowly." (yook-KOO-ree ha na-shtay koo-da-SA-ee)

"Speak slowly!" (same without koo-da-SA-ee)

Then it would be safe to repeat, "I don't understand."

If at this juncture things are not progressing any better along lines you had hoped they might, turn to page four, quickly.

"You will not be hurt." (hee-DOY koat-o we shee ma-sen) and to cinch the affair you have only to add, "You will be rewarded." (HO-SHOO o AH-gay mahss).

(EDITOR'S NOTE: If you have not read Mark Twain's essay, "The Awful German Language", I strongly recommend that you do so. My father's offering above is not a patch on that hysterical classic, but it is reminiscent of it in some ways.)

EDITORIAL:

We are wondering whether anyone is interested in finding out what is going on in Japan.

The obscurely-worded directives emitting from Supreme Headquarters are becoming more numerous than the many field-grade officers infesting the Imperial Hotel in Tokyo.

Enlisted men from the numerous countermanding authorities can be found on furtive missions in many a rice-paddy, grading soil or measuring the depth of the water. At last reports from one such group, it was still looking for 2000 unaccounted-for hospital beds.

Then, of course, there are the reparations men.

The group headed by Mr. Edwin C. Pauley, California oil-magnate and newcomer to the field of national politics, is very optimistic.

After a 45-day tour of Japan and Nip-conquered countries, (an area of several hundred-thousand square miles), they expect to have a complete report for the President on just about anything he'd care to know about reparations.

Let's hope that everyone has a good time, anyway.

(EDITOR'S NOTE: Clearly the author feels that too many Americans are involved in too much meaningless activity in Japan. This has the ring of truth to it, but is he also implying that all this activity is being used as a pretext to keep so many men in Japan? I would say yes.)

HONSHU PIONEER – VOL I, NO. 44 – URAWA, JAPAN – NOV. 11, 1945

HEADLINES:
1. BIG THREE MEETING IMMINENT (Atlee and Stalin en route to Washington to meet with Truman to "iron out differences" arising out of foreign ministers meeting 3 weeks ago.)
2. REDS AGAIN MAKE "HANDS OFF" PLEA TO WHITE HOUSE (For the fourth time, Chinese Communists request that US Marines be withdrawn from China, and all aid to Chiang be halted. Fierce fighting continues on all fronts. Yenan estimates troop strengths as Chiang: 1.6 million; Reds: 1 million.)
3. JAP LABOR UNIONS GET GREEN LIGHT (All wartime labor laws abrogated – unions free to organize and force the Diet to consider new laws to their benefit.)
4. HST SIGNS TAX REDUCTION BILL (Taxes reduced by $5.9 billion – should aid reconversion and prosperity.)

(EDITOR'S NOTE: Unfortunately, my copy of this particular issue only made one trip through the mimeograph machine, so Pages 2 and 3 are blank. We can only try to imagine what the editorial page and my father's column might have said.)

HONSHU PIONEER – VOL I, NO. 45 – URAWA, JAPAN – NOV. 12, 1945

HEADLINES:
1. US ADMITS CHINA ACTION – GEN. WEDEMEYER ANSWERS QUERIES (There have been clashes, but the U.S. Did not initiate them – U.S. only there to disarm Japanese troops – U.S. Ships will continue taking Chinese troops to Manchuria.)
2. MERCHANT MARINE CUT (Over Army protests, War Shipping Administration releases all seamen with 32 months of service, and makes them exempt from the draft. Will this cause a reduction in the number of ships in service?)
3. PEARL HARBOR PROBERS REQUEST PRIVATE PAPERS (Politicians request diaries and letters of Stimson, Churchill, FDR, to see who knew what and when.)

FROM A 6-HOLER – BY ROADBLOCK DELONG THOMAS JR.:
```
GOAL: 100% GOOD CONDUCT
```
The Germans have been telling General Ike that his boys are ill-behaved, dress sloppily, drive crazily and behave abominably toward the civilian population. Tsk Tch! Eisenhower has come to their defense, but the criticism from the Germans must have caused him a little embarrassment.

Nobody is going to say anything to Col. Lansing about his occupationers carrying on in anything but the most approved Army fashion.

Col. Lansing has anticipated Ike's trouble and taken every kind of precaution.

The colonel's system, devised to thwart local criticism: a chart bearing the name of each member of the regiment (and the 3rd Bn. 303). There's more to it than that. The chart's devised to keep a close check on each man's personal appearance, attitude toward natives, attitude toward the Army, etc., etc.... The minute a slip-up is evident in any man's record, he's called on the carpet.

MARINE ANNIVERSARY

While General Vandergrift and Admiral Nimitz are making speeches on the occasion of the Marines' 173rd anniversary, Marines are writing another glorious chapter in Marine history – this time in China. The United States throughout history had always looked after its corps, and provided them with all kinds of exciting campaigns.

EDITORIAL:

One of the most popular diversions on Capitol Hill since V-J Day has been the investigation of the Pearl Harbor disaster.

The way certain rabble-rousing members of Congress have used the probe as a means of getting themselves in the public eye is very disgusting.

It is to the best interests of the nation that a study of the facts be made in an attempt to prevent a recurrence of such an attack in the future.

However, it is unfair for these men to use it as an opportunity to blacken the names of all those concerned.

Even if it were possible to pin the blame on a few men, the fact that the entire country was asleep at the switch cannot be erased.

It should be remembered that only a few years ago some of these same Congressmen were telling the Way and Navy Departments that it wasn't necessary to "waste" the taxpayers' money on the construction of bases in the Pacific.

Maybe this could bear a little investigation.

(EDITOR'S NOTE: It appears that Congress has changed very little in six or seven decades, and it is pretty clear that this investigation was a witch hunt, seeking publicity. I didn't bother to research the findings of this particular investigation, but I have learned from other sources that there were plenty of secret negotiations between the Japanese and the highest levels of U.S. government, including Roosevelt himself, right up to the time of the attack. It was the failure of those negotiations to provide an acceptable solution [to the Japanese] that triggered the attack. A number of highly placed people had good reason to expect the attack, right down to the date. However, it would not have been healthy to anyone's career to point this out. My guess is that all this was known to these "investigators", at some level, and that they were not interested in digging into that aspect of the situation. I think they were looking more at the lack of military preparedness for the attack. By the way, John Toland's historical novel "Occupation" contains all the details anyone could want, regarding what actually happened in the last days before the attack – who knew what and when.)

HONSHU PIONEER – VOL I, NO. 46 – URAWA, JAPAN – NOV. 13, 1945

HEADLINES:
1. PEACE BID MADE IN CHINA – THIRD PARTY TO MEDIATE (Chinese Democratic League offers to act as arbiter between Communists and Central Government.)
2. GOV'T ACCUSES REDS OF USING JAP TROOPS (94th Nat'l. Army makes claim – No denial from Communists.)
3. SOERABAJA RAZED BY BRITISH GUNS (Karno: Modern weapons being used against defenseless Indonesian native villages – vast massacre in progress.)
4. VET JOBS INSURED BY COURT ACTION (US Attorney General: Federal courts will prosecute any employers who fail to take back men who were drafted.)

FROM A 6-HOLER – BY ROADBLOCK ¥ CRAZY DELONG THOMAS:

BUSINESS FORTITUDE

While reparations commissions and newly-appointed presidential appointees made ambitious plans to gauge Japan's industrial wealth, a rifle co. of the 97th made a practical move toward getting part of what they considered the Jap debt to the U.S.

The enterprising soldiers of a more northerly station sold a plant in their area to some members of that disappearing caste, the Zaibetsu; and pocketed over ¥1,000 per man. That beats selling candy bars and cigarettes.

Wonder what sort of a price the Kagoyama Machine Tool Works would draw on the market?

EDITORIAL:

Yesterday, President Truman said in a speech... that the U.S. needs a foreign policy "not dictated by any political party, but one of the people."

By reason of that statement, one might be led to believe that the U.S. has a foreign policy. This will come as a surprise to those who have been following the recent events in Asia.

What people does the administration have in mind when surplus war material is sold to the Dutch Government for use in Indonesia?

Certainly not the native peoples fighting to free themselves from the yoke of Dutch exploitation.

Maybe it is a policy for the support of the Dutch people. They stand to lose a rich colonial empire which was won in the days of militant and grasping mercantilism.

What people is Mr. Truman referring to when he permits the U.S. Navy and Marine Corps to intervene in China on behalf of a one-man government?

Certainly not the Chinese people, who have just completed an 8½ year struggle against foreign tyranny and are now striving for a democratic way of life.

Maybe he meant the people in U.S. financial circles, who have so much invested in Chiang-ruled China.

When he so artfully conceived this phrase, was our President thinking of the way the State Department has constantly arrested the formation of Korean self-government?

Was he thinking of the people of Korea, whose fifty-year battle for freedom has won the admiration of the world?

Is it possible that he was thinking of the people of the United States?

If such were the case, he should make more of an effort to find out what the people want.

Instead of relying on career diplomats and men in high places who have financial axes to grind, he might get in touch with Mr. Average Citizen and find out his views.

Before committing the nation further, he should be sure that the people want the isolationism of prewar days replaced with interventionism.

(EDITOR'S NOTE: Wow! This piece just about took my breath away. I hope, for his sake, that the author has not lived long enough to learn that his worst fears did not even come close to our current reality. This is pretty strong stuff for a small-time Army paper, and amazingly predictive of future "foreign policy" decisions, as well.)

HONSHU PIONEER – VOL I, NO. 47 – URAWA, JAPAN – NOV. 14, 1945

HEADLINES:
1. U.S. EVACUATES TROOPS OVER HUMP ROUTE (American troops being flown out of China to India as fast as planes can take them.)
2. CHIANG, REDS AGREE ON COUNCIL AS MEDIATOR (Communists deny report that both sides have agreed to mediation, saying it's up to Chiang. Meanwhile, Gov't is preparing to drive into Manchuria, despite heavy Communist presence.)
3. INDONESIANS ASK RUSS TO INTERVENE (Indonesian People's Republic asks Commissar Molotov to help them.
4. GOVERNMENT RAPS GE-WESTINGHOUSE (Civilian Production Administration accuses makers of withholding appliances from the market to avoid price controls.)

FROM A 6-HOLER – BY ROADBLOCK DELONG THOMAS:
WINTER QUARTERS

This column's editorial office has been moved ten feet eastward. Since circumstances absolutely require the change of site, one might think it could have been moved inside a building and provided with a stove. Now it's so cold that the only thing humanly possible is to find a warmed-over hole, sit down and make as speedy an exit as possible. There will come a time when it's so cold that about the time the pencil comes out from behind our ear, we'll have to leave.

NO SOAP

Estrangement with bars of soap is no novelty to infantrymen, being forced into a compromising position with dirt in comparatively civilized surroundings doesn't sound like the wishes of a spic-and-span, spit-and-polish higher echelon.

Col. Lansing can't very well put black marks on personal appearance charts if the men of his command are forced to go soapless.

GRIDIRONY

That field in which K Company stands retreat wasn't made with the idea of retreat in mind. The wooden crosspieces at either end facilitate the playing of football. If the men who made the field could have known to what end their labors would be put, they wouldn't have worked on it so enthusiastically.

(EDITOR'S NOTE: You did realize that the "editorial office" referred to is the Company latrine, didn't you? "From a 6-Holer" and all that? Apparently it was getting pretty cold out there, and Fred Stark did a number of cartoons on this subject, as you will discover, if you read to the end.)

LETTER TO THE EDITOR:

Editor:

In your editorial yesterday, you made several references to the foreign policy of the U.S. at the present time.

Is it your opinion that we should support a Jap instigated rebellion in the Indies against one of the United Nations?

The Dutch fought against the Germans and Japanese during this war, and the Dutch Government has always been friendly to the U.S.

The natives of Java not only accepted Jap rule, but went out of their way to co-operate with the Jap Governor in the Indies.

Also the case of Korea, where the people have accepted Jap rule for many years.

The Korean troops treated American prisoners worse than the Jap troops in Jap prison camps.

The Koreans volunteered to work in Jap industries during the war.

Are these the actions of a country striving for its independence?

In China today we support the man who led China through her war years.

The Communists during the war were concerned with furthering their own power, not with fighting Japs.

ANON

(EDITOR'S NOTE: I include this letter more to show that the <u>Honshu Pioneer</u> was willing to print it than to support or applaud its point of view. Mr. ANON sees the world as pretty black and white. Everything Japanese is pure evil, and anyone who did not fight them to the death is equally evil. Anyone who <u>did</u> fight them can do no wrong. Every accusation he makes ignores the question, "What were their alternatives at the time?" The Koreans volunteered to work in Japanese factories? Horrors! Did they have any other way to feed their families? The Javanese accepted Japanese rule? Awful! But they were accustomed to being ruled by the Dutch. Were the Japanese any worse? This type of thinking – support our allies no matter what – also infected the U.S. State Department and helped get us into Vietnam.)

HONSHU PIONEER – VOL I, NO. 48 – URAWA, JAPAN – NOV. 15, 1945

HEADLINES:
1. MAGIC CARPET TAKES BEATING – SENATE GROUP HEARS FACTS ON SHIPPING (High-point Navy men must be discharged, not take extra trips to bring Army men home.)
2. CHINESE REPORT NEW BATTLES IN NORTH (200,000 civilians injured or killed and 1,000,000 homeless in Shantung Province. Communists seem to have the advantage in the north, killing over 30,000 Gov't troops.)
3. ASAHI CRITICIZES MACARTHUR (Japanese newspaper says measures taken by Americans against Mitsubishi and other large firms are not thorough enough. The rich are still in control, even though stock has been parceled.)

FROM A 6-HOLER – BY ROADBLOCK DELONG THOMAS:

LOTZA SPIRIT

Watch it men! All these alleged firsts, all this braggadocio and bravado about who's the most traveled unit in the occupation farce; all this hullabaloo about who was first in Tokyo and who was first in Nickinacky is very apt to give the Brass the wrong impression.

Somebody may have the idea that we're enjoying ourselves here, since we're showing so much pride in the various meaningless accomplishments of our particular outfit.

If any of you do have any pride in your unit – please; won't you keep it to yourself; repress it. If you write home, or if you must write the <u>Stars and Stripes</u>, won't you wait for a particularly glum period (and they shouldn't be infrequent).

It won't do to have any more of this kind of thing get around:

(Letter reprinted from <u>Stars and Stripes</u> of November 14.)

A 72 HOLER

In regard to Pfc Wm. Stevenson's letter concerning a 30 hole latrine we wish to advise that the Seventh Major Port, also on Honshu, has a 72 holer. Can anyone top this?

T/5 B. L. Wellman and 3 others

Now T/5 Wellman and three others, nobody wants to top this; we get along famously, although we have only six. I couldn't work up any more enthusiasm seated in a 72-holer than I can in six, nor would I take any more pride in the 97th if instead of a QM box and a tent, we were provided with a fur-covered porcelain bowl in the grand salon of the Imperial Palace.

What most of us are interested in is getting back to the room upstairs (first door on your right) and 30- and 72-holers be damned.

We're not going to get back by taking an interest in being first anywhere, or being biggest, best or greatest, nor by becoming excited about who's got the most holes.

(EDITOR'S NOTE: for some reason, I just love this piece. I laughed out loud the first time I read it, and it still makes me smile. "Now T/5 Wellman and three others, ...")

EDITORIAL:

Yesterday's news carried a story which concerned the ardent cooperation the Japanese are giving us in finding and punishing war criminals.

It seems that two Japanese officers were sentenced by a Nip Army Court to 10 months in prison for attempting to extract military information from two American Naval officers by torture.

If these Japs were given the same treatment for ten months that many Americans in Japan received for over three years, it would be a difficult story; but as it stands the whole business looks fishy to us.

Is it possible that our bandy-legged friends are trying to pull a fast one on our War Crimes Commission?

No doubt they are familiar with the law of western jurisprudence which states that a man cannot be twice put in jeopardy of life or limb for the same crime.

If we give the Japs enough time, they'll have all the war criminals in jail.

That's better than we seem to be able to do with Lt. Gen. Yamashita in the Philippines.

(EDITOR'S NOTE: Yamashita's trial had started a couple of weeks earlier on October 29. He was found guilty on December 7, and hanged on February 23, 1946. Apparently all this was much too slow for the author of this piece, but the War Crimes Commission in Tokyo did not even start trying anyone for five and a half more months, so I'm not sure what he was complaining about. [Of course, he wouldn't have known that at the time.] I do think he had

a good point about this case being a Japanese trick, however, because 10 months was a far more lenient sentence than most that were handed down by the Commission.)

HONSHU PIONEER – VOL I, NO. 49 – URAWA, JAPAN – NOV. 16, 1945

HEADLINES:
1. W.D. W.S.A. PASS BUCK ON DEMOBILIZATION SHIPPING – NEW DEMOB PLAN IN OFFING - "ENOUGH CREWS" SAYS N.M.U. (NO shortage of sailors - Men are awaiting assignments. New plan being made – lower points & 18 months of service.)
2. CHIANG INVASION SUPPORTED BY U.S. NAVY GUNS (Under U.S. Protection, Chinese Gov't. Troops wading ashore on Shantung peninsula – major battle expected.)
3. JAPAN CAN'T PAY – PAULEY (Reparations chief Pauley is not optimistic that Japan can even pay the cost of the occupation, let alone any fines.)

FROM A 6-HOLER – BY ROADBLOCK DELONG THOMAS:

```
NO VACANCY
   For those of you who've been moved from one
barracks to another to try and thwart the local
housing problem - listen and mark well what's
happening to the poor unfortunate discharges in
the States:
```

In the Bronx, which has nothing to recommend itself to the prospective homemaker except its proximity to Brooklyn, 800 ex-servicemen lined up to get into an apartment hotel recently vacated by the WAVES.

In Boston, show girls pitched tents on the lawn of the Common and some servicemen pitched tents in New York's Central Park.

It all adds up to another reason for our being kept here; they simply don't have any room for us back in the States.

★ ★ ★

Accommodations around here aren't what are ordinarily considered suitable for a middle class family, and it might be that the privacy afforded here isn't any more than you'd expect in Central Park, but still the fact remains that the housing situation has been somewhat alleviated by our presence here, and that, of course, is the important thing.

★ ★ ★

The Federal Housing Administration is interesting itself in the house shortage. A few suggestions that might help: outside latrines and double-deck bunks.

EDITORIAL:

There is a marked difference between the reactions of the two former Axis powers to the Allied occupations.

From Germany come tales of unrest and bitterness on the part of the Germans. Every misstep on the part of our overworked AMG is reflected in gripes from our GI's and the German civilians.

In Japan everything is rosy. We have had no trouble with Nip authorities; no trouble in handling War Criminals. To look at the people, one would think they actually enjoyed this phase of their World Conquest dream. We have made a point of being just and mild. We have made a tour de force of being fair.

Why no hitches in our so newly formed Occupational Therapy? Why the abject eagerness with which War Criminals are discovered and turned over to be punished? Why are Kido and Konoye, former flagrant military fascists, yet in the saddle? There is something cooking below the surface of tranquil Japan. The Japs are no fools. More may lie below their bowing inscrutability than we think. Is our halo worth more than our face?

(EDITOR'S NOTE: This sounds like the same guy who wrote yesterday's editorial – suspicious of the Japanese and impatient for vengeance, er, justice. Marquis Kōichi Kido was Lord Keeper of the Privy Seal and one of Hirohito's closest advisers during the war. He kept a private diary that was subsequently used by the War Crimes Commission as one of the definitive sources for the prosecution against Japanese defendants. He was convicted himself and sentenced to life imprisonment, but paroled in 1955.

Both Konoye and Kido were extremely close to the Emperor, and any "slowness" in arresting and prosecuting them was probably due to the monumental power struggle going on within the highest levels of the U.S. government and military at that time. There was a considerable faction that wanted to see Hirohito tried, convicted and executed. Others [including MacArthur] thought that his cooperation might be very helpful in bringing about the sort of changes they were hoping to see in Japan's culture and government. The latter group eventually carried the day, but it was not much help to Konoye or Kido.

Again, for a lot more detail on all this, I recommend John Toland's historical novel "Occupation", which is hard to find, being out of print, but is meticulously researched, and contains intimate details that you would not imagine.)

HONSHU PIONEER – VOL I, NO. 50 – URAWA, JAPAN – NOV. 17 1945

HEADLINES:
1. WORLD OFFERED A-BOMB – NATIONS TO SHARE SECRET (Only for humanitarian and industrial purposes, after Russia and others offer reciprocal agreements.)
2. JAPS GUARD CHIANG BRIDGES (Armed Japanese troops guarding Chinese bridges and railroads for the Government.)
3. US GENERAL FIRED ON (A train carrying Maj. Gen. Dewitt Peck of the 6th Marines was fired on – the General is planning retribution.)
4. NAVY CONVERTS SHIPS (11 more war ships are being converted to troop carriers, just after a Navy spokesman said this was "impractical" - by 1/1/46 over 400 Navy ships will be involved in the "Magic Carpet" bringing Pacific troops home.)

FROM A 6-HOLER – BY ROADBLOCK SAD SAKE THOMAS, JR.:
REMODELING

There were times when the Day Room was nothing more than a place to get a Coke (they were usually all gone by the time they got cold). The only time anyone got close to the Day Room was when he was forced to attend a class on interior guard or sighting and aiming.

Not so the Day Room of our present station. In fact, it has been suggested that the name "Day Room" not be used to apply to our new recreation hall. Day Room has an unpleasant sound to it. It brings up old memories of weekends spent in camp when a pass was refused. Only then did the Day Room have any function. It was a wonderful place to go and brood. It was possible to sit on the floor (I don't remember there ever being any chairs) and think of all the fun you might have had, could you have gone out on pass – a brood chamber for the crocodile tears of men refused passes.

HONSHU PIONEER – VOL I, NO. 51 – URAWA, JAPAN – NOV. 18, 1945

HEADLINES:
1. NATIONALISTS KNIFE INTO MANCHURIA (Gov't. Troops cross Great Wall and break through Communist lines. Peace talks scheduled for Nov. 20 have been postponed.)
2. END IN SIGHT FOR SHIDEHARA CABINET (Reeling from US reparation demands and general disapproval, the Japanese cabinet is preparing to resign.)
3. DEGAULLE RESIGNS AFTER FAILURE TO CONCILIATE PARTIES – CAUSES POLITICAL CRISIS (Violent disagreements over cabinet appointees have caused Charles DeGaulle to resign as provisional President of France.)
4. SHORT ACCUSED AT PEARL HARBOR INQUIRY (General Short's order to turn off the radar equipment at 7:00 AM on 12/7/41 questioned by Congress.)

FROM A 6-HOLER – BY ROADBLOCK DELONG THOMAS, JR:
KEEP MOVING BUMS

K Company's stakes are nothing more than slivers of their former selves from having been pulled up so often.

The time K Company has spent on the move must even exceed the time consumed on Interior Guard classes. Quite a debate might be had as to which is a greater waste of time, moving or Int. Gd. classes.

The proposed move comes as a bit of a surprise, coming as it does 30 days after arrival. If the orders had come down the first time the cots were being moved from one building to another (or back), K Co. would have thought nothing of it.

The men were fooled, however, by permitting K to become so firmly entrenched in the present area.

Things must have been moving pretty fast in the G17 office this past month for them not to have found another factory site before this time. G17, which has nothing to do but ride around in Jeeps looking over proposed sites recommended by the Japanese, must have strayed far afield to have taken so long before announcing our next movement.

That seems to substantiate the rumor picked up at the Urawa RR Station yesterday. A big hairy Ainu of a northern tribe was heard saying that an unidentified rifle co (ostensibly us) from the 303rd Regt. was making a safari into the hills, 135 miles north of here.

SUNDAY SUPPLEMENT
BLAIR FINDIE'S DAUGHTERS — A. D. THOMAS

Sunday breakfast at the rectory was a snappy affair of wheat flakes. For the Rev. Mr. Blairfindie, his wife and three daughters, this was not the day to dawdle over coffee; there were sermon notes to be gone over, the lesson to be read aloud and flower arrangements for hard-working Mrs. Blairfindie's attention. Mr. Blairfindie's daughters (now that Shirley had grown up) spent most of the morning thinking over what they were going to wear, and the rest of the morning changing their minds on whatever they had decided upon.

This morning's breakfast was a particularly glum affair. The Blairfindies, husband and wife, looked at each other, their daughters' empty places, and went back to crunching their breakfast.

In the next moment there was a rhythmic patter of feet, and the third member of the Blairfindie breakfasters seated herself in front of her flakes.

"Good morning, Mother; Morning, Father."

"Morning, Shirley," he said to the youngest daughter of the household, a pert high school senior. "Did you hear Gertrude and Pamela come in last night?"

"Why, no, Mums. Don't tell me you're worried about Gert, now that she's so taken with a nice, crusading Bill Giles."

"Don't be impertinent, Shirley. I didn't say I was the least bit worried about Gertrude. It was just that I didn't hear them come in." And then she added, as if she were reassuring herself "I'm so happy... Gertrude met him and has given up that worthless crowd she was running around with."

Prelate Blairfindie looked up from his fodder, "Don't forget, Mildred, Mr. Giles is a Congregational minister."

Mrs. Blairfindie never permitted herself to be interrupted by her husband, and now she turned her attention to him. "I notice that since Mr. Giles' arrival there are an increasing number of cars in front of the Congregational Church Sunday mornings, and I rather imagine that their church isn't having the difficulty ours is in raising this year's pledge for last year's debts."

The old boy, feeling more frisky than usual, wasn't to give in so easily, "Mildred, my dear, you must remember that Bill Giles is a good deal younger than I."

Mildred wished to bring the unfavorable conversation around in her favor, turned to Shirley. "Shirley, tell your father what Mr. Giles is doing for the young people of the whole town."

"Mother, really, you can't mean the Young People's Community Center? It's impossible, Moms. It's absolutely droopy, and ever since Gert has been seeing so much of Bill Giles, I've had to go around there once in a while."

"Why, what on earth do you mean, Shirley?" which was Mother's favorite answer to things she didn't wish to understand and had no intention of trying to understand.

"Pu-lease, Moms, everybody at school feels it's not real. Why the juke box is six months behind the time. When Gert was a senior in high school she wouldn't have swallowed this good fellowship, holier-than-thou guff."

Mother wasn't going to budge an inch, "Well, you must remember what a difficult time your father and I had with Gertrude before she met Mr. Giles, and now, Shirley, you can't help seeing what a change there's been in Gertrude lately."

"It isn't as though I were worried about only Gertrude, but you and Pamela were always so influenced by what your sister did. It was enough worrying about what our congregation thought of Gertrude without having to worry about you and Pamela. Now that Gertrude has given up going to those awful places outside the city limits and isn't smoking nearly as much as she was, I can take more of an interest in my other two ladies."

"Wasn't it you, Father, who noticed how little Gertrude's been smoking lately?" This last bit was directed at her husband, who was busily engaged in reading the Sunday funnies.

"Why-uh, yes dear, I do remember saying something of the kind."

This interruption prompted Papa to begin stirring his coffee again. He never permitted himself three cups, but by stirring continually his two, he was able to make them last the desired amount of time.

Now that Mother, in so roundabout a way, had scored her point, she went back to Shirley. "Now you see, Shirley, Mother and Dad don't try to make things unpleasant for you. Our only concern is that you children grow up into fine upstanding ladies of which your father and I can be proud. I'm sure you will, child."

Shirley wasn't sure, and she did wish Mother wouldn't persist in calling her child.

Mother, of course, might disagree, but Shirley thought Gert used a lot of discretion in making the life of a minister's daughter exciting. There were times when she might have exercised more decorum at church Boy Scout rallies and Ladies' Guild meetings.

Shirley remembered the morning, just before the appearance of sobering Mr. Giles, when Gert had returned from the Green Gables to deliver one of her father's sermons, dressed only in a flimsy chemise. Pam and Shirley thought very highly of the performance, but not so Aunt Martha, Mother's visiting sister, who had been awakened by loud sermonial expletives.

Poppa Blairfindie adjusted his spectacles, put away the funnies, and picked up three formidable looking sheets of typed paper. He shuffled them several times with a resigned air.

Shirley could see something was disturbing her father. "What is it, Dad? Can I help?"

"No, Shirl, it's just that every once in a great while the congregation needs to be brought down to earth with an old-fashioned fire and brimstone sermon. And I'm not satisfied that this is enough down to earth. I really had intended to go all out and say the wages of sin are paid for by everlasting damnation, and... Oh, good morning, Pam. I think the place for you is back in your bed. You look like the wrath of God."

"Thanks, Dad. You always say the nicest things on Sunday mornings. I do think I go a long way toward putting you in a proper frame of mind to harangue your flock."

Mother looked up annoyedly from pushing gladiolas and ferns around. "Pam, what time did you children come in last night?"

"If you mean what time did I get in, Jerry brought me home at approximately four o'clock."

"Why, I thought you were with Mr. Giles and Gertrude?"

"Um-hmm, I was, but about three, Bill and Gert decided that we had laid in such a supply of bourbon, they'd run up north to our cottage and rummage through the icebox, to look for mixer. Jerry and I thought the whole setup sounded too much like a private party for us to insist on going along."

-Arthur Thomas-

(EDITOR'S NOTE: I hardly know what to say about this story, except that I was stunned to find it here. Not that I thought my father incapable of writing fiction and dialogue, for he was an excellent inventor of bedtime stories, but that he should produce such a story under these circumstances was totally unexpected. That he should write about a minister's family, however, would not surprise anyone who knew him well. He wrestled with the idea of becoming an Episcopalian minister himself, and both he and Sarge were heavily involved with Christ Church Dearborn [where their ashes are now interred]. Art was active as a lay reader [see photo above], sometimes preached sermons [his were sort of religious history lessons – not the fire and brimstone kind], and when the Church decided to open a mission in Garden City, Michigan, Art was put completely in charge of the project, to the point of conducting the Morning Prayer services himself, until an ordained minister could be found.)

HONSHU PIONEER – VOL I, NO. 52 – URAWA, JAPAN – NOV. 19, 1945

HEADLINES:
1. BATAVIA PEACE TALKS FAIL (Fighting continues to spread – British troops extending bridgehead into Soerabaja – US-trained Dutch marines to arrive next week.)
2. 117 HOMEBOUND CIVVIES TAKE GI'S BUNKS AT SHANGHAI (Widespread protests against the "redeployment farce" and civilians bumping high-point soldiers from ships.)
3. SHARP DISPUTE ON A-POWER DECISION (Congressmen denounce Truman's stand on releasing atomic power secrets to the world – Senator: He exceeded his authority.)
4. THIS ARMY BEST – SEC'Y PATTERSON (Best-behaved army in the world – only 1 in 400 has been court-martialed – better record than 1917-19.)

FROM A 6-HOLER – BY ROADBLOCK VOLTAIRE THOMAS:

WASHINGTON CARNIVAL

Washington, which always provides its local population and numerous visitors with diverse forms of entertainment (everything from sophisticated satire at the Terrace of the Statler to much less sophisticated stuff in the chambers of the House and Senate) is currently host to a new kind of dramatic show – the investigation of the Pearl Harbor attack.

The Senate is always pretty good for a laugh. Reading the Congressional Record, however, isn't any more satisfactory than reading the script of a 22 night run comedy. It's entertaining all right, if you are fortunate to be up in the gallery watching them perform. It must be even more fun to be in on the ground floor, but you have to be elected to do that.

★ ★ ★

It might have been George Nathan who said rightly that the audience was almost as important as the cast in making a play realize all its potentialities. Mr. Nathan's observation never applied more accurately than it does to the present Senate Pearl Harbor Investigations. As is so often the case, there were too many advance publicity notices on the Pearl Harbor play to expect a very good performance. The present gallery in Washington spoils the whole performance. They've gone to Washington with entirely the wrong attitude. The present audience is in Washington for much the same reason that prompted French revolutionaries to visit the guillotine – they want to see heads fall. The playgoers have a sadistic urge that is responsible for their attendance. They're in their seats to see men of responsibility, trusted servants, be sentenced as scapegoats for the Pearl Harbor disaster. The all-star cast has ensured them of pretty good pickings. The sentence mongers have turned the Comédie Américain into chambers for a travesty of justice.

The cast doesn't lend itself to discussions on anything so tragic as the Hawaiian disaster. They would do much better to occupy themselves with the trivia ordinarily before the Senate. Let's not print another black chapter in American history by making such a monstrosity of unpreparedness.

(EDITOR'S NOTE: Although he makes his points with sarcasm and ridicule, this is much more political than the usual fare in Dad's column. Clearly, he saw the whole Pearl Harbor investigation for what it was – a political sideshow to amuse the public and hopefully find a scapegoat or two. He does make fun of the perpetrators, but there is nothing humorous about his condemnation of this witch hunt.)

EDITORIAL:

There is no bogus answer to the world's ills quite so dear to the hearts of diplomats as the idea of occupation.

No one can seem to agree on what the underlying principle of occupation is.

There are those who feel that a large occupation force is warranted for the psychological effect it might have on the enemy. The U.S. occupation of Germany after World War 1 did not have a very lasting effect on the German peoples.

If the object of occupation is one of humiliation, our casual acceptance of the various Jap ministries and our all too willing administration of their public welfare hardly caused the Japs to lose face.

The time to occupy a defeated nation is not after they have recently been defeated, but 25, 10 or 40 years from now, when there is a little more likelihood that the enemy is ready for another war.

The United States cannot make up for previous blunders by guarding Japan and Germany so zealously now. What the U.S. needs is a more discerning eye for future threats.

(EDITOR'S NOTE: At first glance, I thought this was a joke, and that it might be my father's handiwork, but on closer examination I changed my mind. I now believe it was written by one of the other members of the editorial staff, and that it reflects nothing deeper than the widely shared sentiment of, "Why the hell are we here, and when do we get to go home?")

LETTER TO THE EDITOR:

Editor:

In a recent edition of the Pioneer there appeared a letter criticizing your editorial opinion of the Asiatic situation.

The writer speaks of a Jap instigated rebellion in the Indies. There is no doubt that during the Japanese occupation of these conquered countries they did not hesitate to fan the flames of an age-old hatred for the western democracies, especially Great Britain.

But to say that the present rebellion is Jap instigated is to forget that the masses of the Indies, of Burma, and of Indochina have for many long years been under a despotism only surpassed by Hitler in Europe. And that they looked with great hope towards the war's end and the application of the principles of the Atlantic and World Charters.

The Koreans, almost 100 years ago, were the first to halt the advance of Jap imperialism. Then it was with the help of material received from the United States that Japan managed to create a military machine which made it impossible to resist her rule.

The British would not enlist the support of the Burmese against the Jap advance, instead leaving them to the bombardments, while the British industrialists fled by plane.

Chiang, condemned by the irrefutable facts of history, has betrayed his nation innumerable times. And it was the Communists who fought first and longest against the Japs, and who have proved that it is with the interests of the great masses of Chinese in mind that they are now fighting.

(EDITOR'S NOTE: It's nice to see that I was not the only reader who disliked that letter from Mr. ANON a few days ago. As Daniel Patrick Moynihan supposedly said, "Everyone is entitled to his own opinion, but not his own facts." This writer seems much more in touch with reality, and is able to distinguish some shades of gray in the world.)

HONSHU PIONEER – VOL I, NO. 53 – URAWA, JAPAN – NOV. 20, 1945

HEADLINES:
1. CENTRAL TROOPS CONTINUE STRONG MANCHURIAN ADVANCE (Nationalist troops advancing across a 200-mile front – reach Chengtehfu, 50 miles past Great Wall.)
2. BOWLES DISCLOSES '46 AUTO PRICES (OPA: With '42 as a base, Fords up 2%, Studebakers up 9%, Chryslers up 1%, GMC down 2%.)
3. 11 JAP WAR CRIMINALS JAILED (Among these "ardent militarists": Matsuoka of Tri-Partite Pact fame, Gen. Kusue of the Black Dragon Society, Gen. Matsui – responsible for the Rape of Nanking, Baron Araka of Konoye's cabinet.)
4. FRENCH DISAGREE ON DEGAULLE SUCCESSOR (All hope for a resolution depends on acceptance of Felix Coign by tee 3 largest parties: Communists [now the 2nd largest], Socialists and Popular Republicans.)
5. S.W.A.K. (GI's in Tokyo now closing letters home with this slogan: "NO BOATS – NO VOTES – GET THE TROOPS HOME")

FROM A 6-HOLER – BY ROADBLOCK GOBBLE GOBBLE THOMAS:

TURKEY LOGISTICS

It's not the regal qualities of the turkey that make him so important on the American scene. The big brown bird is the symbol of the holiday season. To people all over the land, the turkey means feasting and holiday-making. No imposter can ever take his place as the kingbird of the table.

It might appear that all this attention given to a poor dumb feathered bird is ridiculous, and nothing but sentimental drool. But Thanksgiving and Christmas wouldn't be much if it weren't for their sentimentality, their hymns and prayers – and their turkeys.

It won't mean much to the Japs if the men of K Company don't have turkey. (They'd probably prefer we had Vienna sausages, so that there would be more left over.) In the long run it shouldn't mean very much to the men if they go without festive drumsticks, wings and necks. There may be some chicken some Sunday in the future. It's just that some effort should have been made to differentiate Thanksgiving from any day in our monotonous sequence of days.

It should be said that somebody did have turkey in mind for the soldiers. It is unfortunate that those in higher places gave a greater shipping priority to arms for the Dutch than gobblers for Japan-occupying Yanks.

EDITORIAL:

One of the most ruthless dictators found on the international scene in the last ten years is still in power. Francisco Franco has managed to remain unobtrusive and stay off of the war criminal lists while over a million Spanish citizens, whose only crime was opposition to his tyranny, languish in medieval prisons.

The Generalissimo rose to prominence on the tidal wave of Fascism. His old cronies, Hitler, Mussolini, Laval and the rest, are nearly all dead or in custody; while he continues to strut and shout and hold sway over starving millions.

The democratic nations seem to forget that the Spanish Government supported the Axis powers throughout the war. Not only did it give all-out aid in supplies and war material, but even sent troops to fight in Russia.

The Spanish Consulate in Manila in 1942 acted as a fifth column for the Japanese Army, thus helping to betray that city and hinder the American cause.

How long are the enemies of our way of life going to be permitted to make fools out of us?

(EDITOR'S NOTE: It's difficult not to sympathize with the writer here, but I am not enough of a student of history to know what countervailing forces were at work to prevent the Allies from objecting to Franco's regime. I assume that his anti-Communist stance, with the Cold War looming, had something to do with it, as it did in so many similar cases.)

HONSHU PIONEER – VOL I, NO. 54 – URAWA, JAPAN – NOV. 21, 1945

HEADLINES:
1. U.S. PUBLIC DOESN'T KNOW TRUTH ABOUT CHINA WAR (News agencies chafing under 4 weeks of secrecy & surveillance by government officials – only Navy & Marine press releases are allowed – no press coverage of Marine involvement in China.)
2. RER RESOLVES RETURN OF SHIPS (Congress calls for the return of 600 ships chartered to other nations, to speed the return of U.S. Troops.)
3. MAC'S OCCUPATION POLICY CRITICIZED (Zhukov: Demilitarization is too slow and haphazard – Japan may be in a position to wage war.)
4. SCRAPHEAP MAY BE LABOR BILL'S FATE (Clare Hoffman [R, Mich], a "strong reactionary leader against labor", and pals plan to kill the Full Employment Bill, which was to ensure jobs for 60 million.)
5. CIVIL WAR DEVELOPING IN IRAN ("Newly arrived strangers wearing leather boots" instigating open revolt in northeast Iran - "Mother Kremlin" adding another step-child?"
6. H.S.T. ASKS GOVERNMENT HEALTH PROGRAM (Compulsory health insurance for all proposed by Pres. Truman – health fund to be established from an insurance tax and normal revenues - "not socialized medicine", but an aid for the poor.)

(EDITOR'S NOTE: I can't believe I never heard of this last one before. During all the wild debate about "Obamacare", did this plan never get mentioned? It sounds nearly identical.)

FROM A 6-HOLER – BY ROADBLOCK CONTENTED COW THOMAS:

THERE'S NO PLACE LIKE HOME

To those who canceled K Company's move, Kingmen send a rousing vote of thanks.

For the past few days all talk has centered about our projected move. And pretty discouraging sort of talk it was, too.

With chronic pessimism (so much a part of men who've been in this outfit long) the place where K was supposed to go sounded like: (1) an ITRC camp, (2) a frontier outpost, and (3) hell.

Rumorists were in agreement on only one count: that whatever the deal was, it was bad.

At first report, K Company was going to an area infested with scrub typhus, and the entire unit might expect to be in the hospital in a month's time.

Next most circulated rumor: that King was going to an area infested with so much brass that the entire unit might expect to be in the bug house in a month's time. The second setup sounded like a rookie's nightmare. Inspection, guard and parades were to be ordered up on the whims of a general.

The most fiendish rumor had Kingites in the role of exemplary soldats to prove to an artillery general just how well the infantry performed. Perish the thought.

The more rumors heard, the more tears were shed and the more sentimental everybody got toward their Urawa home.

EDITORIAL:

Regardless of the side which we believe to be in the right, our all-out aid to the Chinese Central Government is not only against the agreement in the World Charter, but it shows a lack of long-range thinking in high places.

Our ill-advised acts of today are liable to have drastic results several years from now.

One indication of this was the demonstration held yesterday in the city of Chunking by some of the best known Chinese scholars, artists and educational leaders.

These men are members of the Democratic League – the third largest party in China. At the present time the League is attempting to bring about peace between the two warring factions.

It is their opinion that there can be no peace in China until our country stops sending Lend-Lease supplies to Chiang, training and transporting his armies and spearheading the advance of those armies in the field.

This group said that the United States' hope for peace, as compared to her actions, was like "hoping for eggs while killing the hen."

(EDITOR'S NOTE: My jaw keeps hitting my keyboard as I read these attacks on U.S. policy emanating from a unit of the U.S. Army. Can you picture an Army newspaper published in today's world that would openly question our role in Afghanistan, or drone strikes in Pakistan? My guess is that the author would find himself sharing a cell with Bradley Manning. Clearly, it was a different time.)

HONSHU PIONEER – VOL I, NO. 55 – URAWA, JAPAN – NOV. 22, 1945

HEADLINES:
1. MARSHALL TO RETIRE SOON (George C. Marshall to retire as Army Chief of Staff – Dwight D. Eisenhower, former Supreme Allied Commander, to assume command.)
2. NATIONALIST LEADERS CONFER AS YENAN FORCES ATTACK (Chiang calls meeting of all generals – Communists begin counterattack – Gen. Wedemeyer goes to Chunking to consult with Kuomintang leaders.)
3. RUSS TROOPS HALT IRAN ARMY MOVE (Iranian troops stopped by Russian occupation forces, as they try to halt an uprising – Izvestia denounces British reports that Russia is interfering in Iran's internal affairs.)
4. 56% OF VE-DAY ARMY OUT BY JAN 1ST (War Dept.: More than half of 8,500,000 have been discharged – by 1/1/46, 2,000,000 will be home from Europe, but only 350,000 from the Pacific.)

FROM A 6-HOLER – BY ROADBLOCK POLLYANNA THOMAS, JR.:
BOUQUETS

It doesn't do to be bitter, continually. The passing of the turkey as the Thanksgiving bird was lamented in this column with some irony not so long ago, and what happens; – the bird came from out his bush and our head is low with embarrassment. All of which goes to prove that a Vienna sausage in hand means you haven't reckoned with what our RSO could scare up at the last minute.

It's not the 6-Holer's habit to be free in its orchid bestowals, but somebody has again come through with a praiseworthy action.

★ ★ ★

If there aren't as many cheery, bright-faced lads around you at K Company's Thanksgiving feast and festivities as you think there should be, it's because some men have been elected to stand guard for 3rd Bn. Hdq. Co.

That's a pretty commendable idea, initiating a reciprocal holiday guard system. It wouldn't seem presumptuous of K Company to look forward to a guard-free Christmas.

Curiously enough it would seem Kingites might come out ahead in the long run; it'll be colder 33 days from now.

To those of you who are on guard, it may seem there isn't such an awful lot for which to be thankful, but the rest of K men can be glad Battalion has so few guard posts.

(EDITOR'S NOTE: *To those of you reading this without paying close attention, I will point out that today's alias - "Pollyanna" - clearly refers to the assertion that the holiday guard duty responsibility will be a reciprocal arrangement between K Company and Headquarters. He knows perfectly well that this is a fantasy.)*

EDITORIAL:

THANKSGIVING 1945

A few short years ago, the men of this company could be found in their homes in every corner of the land, celebrating the Thanksgiving Holiday in the custom of their fathers.

We had so much to be thankful for then, even though we may not have thought so at the time.

This year, there are even more things for which we can give thanks. ---

We are thankful that:

The war is over;

This is our last GI Thanksgiving;

We are sweating out a discharge, and not an attack;

We are having turkey today, instead of Vienna sausage or corned beef hash;

We are alive;

All of us arrived in Japan via gangplank and not from the heaving bow of a landing craft. ---

We are thankful for these and many more blessings, though we hope that in future years this day is observed a few thousand miles nearer the scene of the first Thanksgiving.

HONSHU PIONEER – VOL I, NO. 56 – URAWA, JAPAN – NOV. 23, 1945

HEADLINES:
1. MARINE-GUARDED RAILWAY CUT BY YENAN GUERILLAS (Railroad cut in 6 places – Centralist troops driving 16 to 20 miles a day toward the sea – Communists say they've been strafed by American planes.)
2. ANGLO-DUTCH NATIVE TROOPS WITHDRAWN FROM INDIES FIGHT (Native troops taken out of Java fighting for participation in pro-Indonesian demonstrations.)
3. CALIF. LOAN COMPANIES RAP GI BILL RED TAPE (Protest filed against VA – 30 vets dispossessed – loans "impossible at this time" due to red tape.)
4. UAW CALLS GMC STRIKE (325,000 GMC workers to walk out today – demand 30% wage hike – National Maritime Union to walk out 12/1, except on troop ships.)
5. PICKETS PROTEST BRITISH IMPERIALISM (British and Dutch embassies in San Francisco were surrounded by pickets, protesting the wars in Indonesia.)

FROM A 6-HOLER – BY ROADBLOCK GLOBETROTTER THOM.:

Before the three Baltic Republics are completely assimilated by the Soviet, something should be said about the efficient and original contributions made by Lithuania in the field of sewage and garbage disposal. The little Baltic country should make a great contribution to Russia's sewage difficulties.

Mde. Bielogusrsksas, daughter of the Lithuanian State Architect, has been most helpful in making public inside dirt on the Lithuanian's ingenious refuse repositing.

※ ※ ※

In the city of Riga, garbage is emptied by the housewife from stainless steel, chrome-plated receptacles (resembling the outdated coffee table popularized by furniture manufacturers of the 20's) into hoppers operating on conveyor belts that are suspended from the city's electric light poles.

From the hoppers the garbage is dropped into boiling cauldrons of sulfuric acid. The silt at the bottom of the cauldrons is tapped bi-daily by Health Dept.-inspected workers wearing surgical masks, and the contents sealed in cans. The cans are then loaded onto a fleet of plastic and tubular steel barges and taken out into the Baltic Sea, where they are dropped at a depth of 8½ fathoms.

(This is the first in a series of articles by Mr. Thomas dealing with the peoples of Eurasia. - Editor's note)

(EDITOR'S NOTE: In the first place, Riga is not in Lithuania, but Latvia. Whether or not they were aware of that fact, I hope that Dad's readers realized that this entire tale is complete hogwash, and the garbage system would be completely impractical, anyway. Still, I wouldn't doubt that a few were taken in.)

HONSHU PIONEER – VOL I, NO. 57 – URAWA, JAPAN – NOV. 24, 1945

HEADLINES:
1. "JAPS GOOD TROOPS" - BRITISH (British General: Sure we are using Japanese troops against the Indonesians, and they are very good.)
2. EDEN URGES COOPERATION (Eden: "We know Russia's aims are not directed against us; can we be sure of our aims regarding them.")
3. IRAN REVOLT ALARMS TURKS (Turkish government makes formal statement censuring Russia, believing them responsible for instigating rebellion in Iran.)

FROM A 6-HOLER – DR. ROADBLOCK CAVIAR THOMAS, JR.:
STURGEON FISHING ON THE GULF OF BOTHNIA

The little coastal port of Wlav is only a two hour ride from the Russian city of Leningrad for the commercial tourist who wishes to take advantage of the crack Russian train, "The Red Star Empress". The discriminating traveler, however, Can't fail to go by anything but Yak cart.

The road between Leningrad and Wlav is a picturesque series of windings and unwindings. Your first view of Wlav is from one of the several heights surrounding the town.

The most striking thing about Wlav to the stranger is the activity around the waterfront. The wharves of Wlav are a hive of activity with bearded fishermen preparing for the day's catch of sturgeon.

For centuries the people of Wlav have earned their livelihood by catching the elusive sturgeon for the fish's valuable egg yield. (If you haven't tasted Wlav caviar, you have something to look forward to.) The wily sturgeon has pressed these simple Wlavian people to their utmost in ingenuity.

Long combat with the sturgeon has taught the people that the net and hook were of no avail against the sturgeon's unsportsmanlike habit of holing out in shoreline caves. The Wlavians answer throughout the years has been to throw cordons of fishermen-filled dories around the caves and catch the little rascals when they came out.

(This is the second in a series of articles by Professor Thomas on his extensive Baltic travels. The third and final story appears in tomorrow's HONSHU PIONEER.)

(EDITOR'S NOTE: There is no Wlav, unless you are talking about a radio station in Grand Rapids, Michigan. To the best of my knowledge, my father was never anywhere near the Baltic, unless he was playing Monopoly. Also, sturgeons are not "little rascals", but are commonly 7 to 12 feet long. Another flight of fancy and total malarkey that makes you wonder if someone left the cap off the glue jar in the Honshu Pioneer office.)

HONSHU PIONEER – VOL I, NO. 58 – URAWA, JAPAN – NOV. 25, 1945

HEADLINES:
1. CHINCHOW BATTLE BEGINS (Armored spearhead of Nationalist 13th Army in sight of Chinchow – 2 brigades of Communist armor preparing to defend – Russia summons Chiang to confer on future occupation policies.)
2. MAC WANTS WAR-CRIME TRIALS SPEEDED UP (300 Japanese have been indicted for war crimes – MacArthur calls on War Dept. to get trials going, especially Tojo.)
3. JAP ATOM RESEARCH EQUIPMENT WRECKED (3 cyclotrons blown up.)
4. WORLD WATCHES IRANIAN CRISIS (Iran: Azerbaijan insurgents being supplied by Russia in attempt to retain strategic region they have occupied since 1942.)

FROM A 6-HOLER – BY A. DELONG KRIS KRINGLE THOMAS:
MELLIE CLISMAS

Ten yen wasn't much to put out for hand-painted Christmas cards, but there should have been some way of knowing what the well-meaning, but misguided little Orientals intended to do with the sacred American institution of Christmas.

Garish, billboardish posters emblazoned with regimental insignia and the bold lettering INFANTRY, 97th Division are about as reminiscent of Christmas as if the little Nip darlings had drawn a cross-section of the atomic bomb. One thing teacher might have told her artistic hopefuls was that Christmas was the season of brotherly love and the whole idea of the army, although always repugnant, is particularly repugnant to doughs the last few weeks of December.

It must be said, however, that the Japs are completely unaware of their desecration of Christmas; witness an article appearing in the Urawa newspaper, Urawa Shimbun: "Joyful US soldiers with Xmas cards presented by Japanese students of Urawa Middle School... These beautiful cards, full of local color, have been mailed to their families, as a Christmas remembrance."

Local color is right, but I don't think my little sister is going to work up much enthusiasm over a slant-eyed Santa CLAUS.

(EDITOR'S NOTE: I know he is just trying to be funny, but this sounds a bit harsh to me, it being about Christmas and all. Making fun of their ignorance when they were trying to be nice [in a way] seems uncalled for.)

HONSHU PIONEER – VOL I, NO. 59 – URAWA, JAPAN – NOV. 26, 1945

HEADLINES:
1. CONGRESS AFRAID TO FORCE DEMOBILIZATION SPEED-UP (6 different petitions have failed to get backing – Sen. McMahon asks Sec. Patterson and Forrestal to show that demobilization "has not been unduly delayed.")
2. MARINES TO STAY IN CHINA 6-8 MORE MONTHS (Despite their being embroiled in fighting and previous State Dept. statements that they would be withdrawn ASAP, Gen. Wedemeyer says they might expect another 6-8 months in China.)
3. NIP PEOPLE WON'T STARVE – McLOY (Japan has enough food for the winter – 5,000,000 unemployed - Pacific troops returning – food to be imported if needed.)

FROM A 6-HOLER – BY ROADBLOCK DEFILADE THOMAS:

```
ROD AND GUN
   The Jap hunting season officially got under-
way with the announcement by Supreme American
Headquarters that hunting licenses will be grant-
ed to all sports-loving Japanese.
   December is a little late to be getting under
way, but there's still a lot of game afoot.
   It might be that December is the customary hunt
season. The Japs didn't begin the chase in 1941
until Dec. 7.
   Accompanying Japanese sportsmen must be quite
an experience. They must have a whole lot of
tricks up their sleeves on how to surprise crea-
tures of the bush and field.
```

Japanese quail might be on to the huntsmen from long experience with the Japs' crafty woodsmanship. Reports from interested observers say that each covey has a recon patrol in the air all the time.

The American sponsors of the Jap hunting season have not announced any game limits. Evidently it's open season on everything.

Everybody watch your step!

> The pheasant and partridge
> are on the wing.
> They've heard reports
> of the awful thing
> Done by the Yankees in
> behalf of the Jap;
> And are scurrying to cover
> to avoid the attack.

(EDITOR'S NOTE: I learned a new word today, thanks to my father's obsession with bizarre aliases. DEFILADE: to arrange [fortifications] so as to protect the lines from frontal or enfilading fire and the interior from fire from above or behind. Thanks, Dad, but "Jap" apparently rhymes with "attack"? Good grief!)

HONSHU PIONEER – VOL I, NO. 60 – URAWA, JAPAN – NOV. 27, 1945

HEADLINES:
1. U.S. ADMONISHES RUSSIA ON INTERVENTION IN IRAN (Sec'y. Byrnes sends stern note of protest – U.S. will consider any Iran intervention as a direct affront to the San Francisco charter – did not reveal whether U.S. actions in China were discussed.)
2. UNION PROTESTS SHIP MISUSE (Harry Bridges warns they will keep their pledge to strike on all ships not carrying troops or supplies.)
3. BRITISH DENY USE OF JAPS IN FIGHTING (Mountbatten contradicts previous reports - Japanese troops not being used against Indonesians – 5,000 natives killed.)

FROM A 6-HOLER – BY ROADBLOCK SUPERSUDS THOMAS:
SALESMANSHIP VIA THE MIKE

Since no civilian corporation is permitted to advertise on any radio program for GI consumption, Tokyo radio salesmanship is lacking the spark, the zest, the zip of stateside broadcasts.

The occupational audience is tired of hearing staid, humdrum run-of-the-mill announcements which pass for advertising. The announcements are usually tagged on to the end of a nostalgic musical program as if they were an afterthought and not an integral part of the show, which they might easily be, with a little more pep and originality.

Suggested plan for livening up WVTR's programs is something that worked in the States until some of the stations rebelled at having to repeat so often rhyming, jingling ads.

Here are a couple suggested to liven up the most dreary broadcasts. (on VD, sung to the tune of "Hail, Hail the Gang's All Here")

    VD, VD the scourge of Tokyo
      It'll make you batty
      It'll make you bli-ind
    VD, VD the scourge of Tokyo
  It's better to let the Geisha stuff go.

★ ★ ★

(on reenlisting, sung to the tune of "I'm a Yankee Doodle Dandy")

    I'm a reenlisting soldier,
  An eager beaver through and through;
  The Army's got the only place for me,
    A place with happiness for you;
   So why don't you take advantage
    Get furlough, bonuses 'n mo'
    And join the Army right away
    For security with extra pay

If rhymes won't do the trick, take a whirl at soap operas.

HONSHU PIONEER – VOL I, NO. 61 – URAWA, JAPAN – NOV. 28, 1945

HEADLINES:
1. 700 MORE PLANES TO CHINA (10th & 14th Air Forces flying 700 planes "over the hump" from India and Burma – several American lives lost when 22 P-51s hit a cold front – fliers angry to be risking their lives 3 months after Japan's surrender.)
2. SOLONS DENOUNCE CHINA AID (6 Congressmen call on Pres. Truman to stop all aid to China – our troops and planes are "arresting the evolution" of democracy.)
3. INDONESIANS FLEE BRITISH GUNS (Natives in retreat from Soerabaja to Melang – superior British equipment means British victory.)
4. COURT MARTIALS "TOO SEVERE" (Sen. Elbert Thomas [D, Utah] tours ETO – says severe wartime penalties should not apply in peacetime.)
5. WHAT'S THE TARIFF? (State Dept. estimates 100,000 GI's have taken foreign brides since '41 – 22,000 have already applied for permission to come to the U.S.)
6. CYCLOTRON DESTRUCTION DENOUNCED (Oak Ridge scientists compare Major O'Hearn's attack on instruments of science to burning libraries – Allied Command "just didn't want to take chances".)

FROM A 6-HOLER:

WHERE DO WE GO FROM HERE

Occupation for the redeployed 97th dragged on into its third month with no fanfare or renewed resolutions on the part of the government to pursue any kind of a new policy as regards long range occupation strategy, or any kind of strategy, for that matter. Not that the GI's care.

It wouldn't do, of course, to set aside a day for commemoration or re-dedication, since no policy has ever been announced by a higher headquarters, beyond the fact that "it was to be a tough peace for Japan."

Our tough peace seems to be nothing more than an attitude of complete detachment. Maybe the Japs will feel that our unconcern in their general welfare is a personal affront and will go off in the corner, sulk, and come out to dig at being good little boys.

It's not difficult to be disinterested when the only consideration of men in the occupation is when do the ships come.

From Repl. Depots to obscure hinterland stations, the cry is for ships and more ships. The only responsibility the army has given Japanese occupees is to guard against venereal disease and to give some thought to re-enlisting. With nothing more than these two considerations, it's understandable that a good part of a man's thinking is given over to getting home.

(EDITOR'S NOTE: It is surprising [to me, anyway] that this rather bitter attack on the chain of command for its lack of leadership was allowed to reach print. I feel pretty confident that the editor found himself "on the carpet" after this one. It sounds like Dad was having a bad day.)

HONSHU PIONEER – VOL I, NO. 62 – URAWA, JAPAN – NOV. 29, 1945

HEADLINES:
1. HURLEY QUITS CHINA POST – ROOSEVELT APPOINTEE RAPS US POLICY IN CHINA (Major General Patrick J. Hurley, Special Ambassador to China, resigned with a 1500 word diatribe against the State Dept., accusing them of "undermining democracy and bolstering imperialism in China". Successor to be George C. Marshall.)
2. US SHIPS ROT IN PACIFIC HARBORS (52 ships idle in Manila, many more in the Tokyo-Yokohama area, awaiting Government sailing orders. 72 hours of work would convert these for troop transport.)
3. SOLONS CHARGE WSA MISUSE OF TROOP SHIPS (Congress lashes out at Army, Navy and War Shipping Administration for slowness of demobilization.)

EDITORIAL:

President Truman and the American people received a big jolt when Maj. Gen. Patrick Hurley resigned his post as Ambassador to China.

It was the first time in many years that an American ambassador had resigned in protest of the government's foreign policies.

In a public statement, General Hurley laid most of the blame for the U.S. debacle in China on what he called "professional diplomats".

We were always under the impression that the President and Sec'y of State, with the advice and consent of the Senate, were the guiding light of our external affairs.

We would hate to think that unseen hands are, according to the General, "plunging us into a Third World War".

Has the executive branch of the government come to such a terrible state that a complete reversal of the aims of the Atlantic Charter was accomplished by a little group of willful, lower echelon, career diplomats?

It doesn't sound logical to us.

If such is the case, however, things are getting pretty sad on both sides of Pennsylvania Avenue.

(EDITOR'S NOTE: If I may be allowed a bit of criticism: Gazing at this situation from a great distance of time, I think the author may have missed the point. I doubt that General Hurley's main purpose in resigning was to point an accusatory finger at "unseen hands", so much as to sound an alarm that our policies were headed off a cliff. He may have chosen "professional diplomats" as a safer target than the President and the Secretary of State, but to focus on that is a distraction from the real questions of "What's wrong with our China policy?" and "What should we be doing instead?" As other *Honshu Pioneer* headlines have pointed out, there was loud criticism of our China policy coming from many sources, including some within the military. When your ambassador, who is obviously closer to the situation than anyone, resigns in protest, it is time to sit up and take notice. That's the editorial I would have written, I think.)

HONSHU PIONEER – VOL I, NO. 63 – URAWA, JAPAN – NOV. 30, 1945

HEADLINES:
1. MARITIME WORKERS REPEAT DEC. 1ST STRIKE THREAT (National Maritime Union and 4 others to stage 24-hour protest walkout, except for troop ships.)
2. STATE DEPT. SHAKE UP DUE – CONGRESS TO INVESTIGATE HURLEY STATE DEPT. BLAST (Diplomats referred to were George Acheson, Diplomatic Adviser to Gen. MacArthur in Tokyo, and Charles Service, recently exonerated on charges of selling information to newspapers.)
3. RUSSIANS CLEAN UP MUKDEN – RUSSIANS DRIVE OUT REDS FOR CHIANG TROOPS ENTRY (Abiding by previous guarantees, Russian occupation troops have cleaned out all Yenan forces for the entry of the 94th Nationalist Army.)
4. INDIES SETTLEMENT AWAITS END OF WAR (Netherlands Minister expresses doubts of a peaceful resolution – no new government until fighting ends.)
5. NO '45 VET BONUS IN SIGHT (<u>Army Times</u> finds no sentiment in Congress to do anything about a bonus for World War II veterans.)

FROM A 6-HOLER – BY ROADBLOCK PERMANENT ASSET THOMAS:

This business of getting out of the army is different than it was during my first hitch. It used to be you broke a leg to get out or amputated a trigger finger. But the army of occupation has different requirements. Amputees are just as capable occupiers as the next man, provided they have been left that part of them which performs the function of sitting in one place for a long time.

At one time anyone could be a sluggard and a slacker. Now it's only a question of who you know, who your father knows, or who your father is.

Most fathers goofed off. They occupied their leisure time sailing, hunting, hanging around the lodge or local bars. Not so Pfc. Jack McKnighter's father. Jack's father interested himself in the civilian army and as a result is now a Brigadier General, commander of the 158th Combat Team. Jack let the old man know that he didn't think he was much of an asset to the United States sitting here in Japan. Daddy pulled strings and 38-point Jack is now a civilian. It would appear this isn't a case of father like son. Jack couldn't have given much thought to any future McKnighters, taking so little interest in the military.

Certainly Jack must have known that's no way to become a Brigadier Gen. Where would Jack be today if Pa McKnighter had did *(sic)* any such thing in the last war?

(EDITOR'S NOTE: The story of Pfc. McKnighter's [or McNider's] early exit from Japan with a paltry 38 points was reported briefly in yesterday's Honshu Pioneer*, but I elected not to transcribe it, because I thought my father's version was much more entertaining. "Permanent Asset" - get it? At this point, my father was probably aware that Sarge was over 5 months pregnant [with me] and was getting more anxious about when he could get home himself.)*

EDITORIAL:

A very good indication of the way things stand in China can be derived from the Russian Government's policy toward the present Yenan-Chiang civil war.

In accordance with the Sino-Soviet Pact of August 1945, the Red Army has agreed to withdraw from Manchuria by the middle of January.

It has also been agreed that Marshall Malinovsky's troops will "guarantee the safety" of Chinese Nationalists who are flown into the city of Mukden through the courtesy of the USAAF.

They will also aid Chiang in cleaning out "resistance troops" in the province.

This accord was reached after the Nationalists gave Russia certain mining concessions, as well as special privileges on the Trans-Siberian Railway.

In other words, Stalin's boys are fighting the so-called "Communist" Government of Yenan. This group has been labeled by many pundits as being "Moscow-controlled".

Either the Kremlin doesn't intend to foster Communist factions in Asia – which is Kremlin SOP in Europe, or the Chinese "Reds" are not as red as some people think.

HONSHU PIONEER – VOL I, NO. 64 – URAWA, JAPAN – DEC. 1, 1945

HEADLINES:
1. HURLEY DEFENDS YENAN REDS (Hurley: "The only difference between the Chinese Communists and Oklahoma Republicans was that the Chinese Communists carried arms." - Hurley to appear before Senate Foreign Relations Committee.)
2. HST WANTS POTSDAM CHANGE (Truman dissatisfied with Allied control in Germany, due to conflicting authority – wants complete control of each zone by its commander.)
3. FEAC HEAD SAYS ALLIED CONTROL NOT NEEDED (UN Chairman, after 11 weeks of meetings, says MacArthur should remain in command of occupied Japan.)
4. NO LET-UP IN GMC STRIKE (225,000 on strike for 9 days – want 30% wage hike – Company: GM profits are none of the union's business.)

FROM A 6-HOLER – BY MRS. ROADBLOCK MARESCU:
BOOKING PASSAGE

While the redeployed 97th Div. Sits and waits release of ships before giving themselves to any very extravagant thoughts on going home, other quarters are doing something more positive toward getting to the United States.

Mrs. Joseph Marescu, wife of an ETO vet, stationed in Liverpool (she's English), waited until everything was quiet aboard a troopship in the Liverpool harbor and very unobtrusively slipped by the Marine guards.

Ships leave Yokohama as well as Liverpool. The difference being, of course, that ships leaving

Japland go home with Japanese ordnance and the members of reparations commissions instead of troops. That shouldn't make any difference to desperate homesick 97thers, they've had a lot of experience on a variety of ocean-going craft.

The Bureau of Immigration has decided to waive charges that Mrs. Marescu entered the country illegally. Similar consideration from the War Dept. on the part California-bound stowaways is all that's needed to start a mass exodus to Elysian States.

Australian wives of GI's have already left the Pacific for the United States. If you could count on the wifeships putting into Yokohama before taking off for Frisco, the tables might be turned. P.S. Meetcha in Frisco.

(EDITOR'S NOTE: I have not bothered to comment on my father's penchant for inventing words, but you have probably noticed that nearly every column includes a couple of new ones that Spell Check never heard of. It makes proofreading kind of a pain, but mostly I like them. They are usually very logical in their construction and meaning, and so very easy to understand. I wonder if this was due to his training in German, a language where gluing small words together to make big ones is normal.)

HONSHU PIONEER – VOL I, NO. 65 – URAWA, JAPAN – DEC. 2, 1945

HEADLINES:
1. SENATE GETS UNO BILL MONDAY (Leaders are confident the bill to put teeth into the UN Security Council will pass – A U.S. Delegate to this Council is needed.)
2. JAP WAR CRIMINALS TO BE TRIED IN IMPERIAL COURT (More than 100 are on the list – MacArthur to name judges – Prime Minister Shidehara opposes law on criminal liability for the war, saying it would be an "unfortunate precedent".)
3. RUSSIAN TROOPS STAY AT CHIANG'S REQUEST (Moscow radio: Russian troops to stay in Manchuria until Chiang's forces are "free of internal entanglements".)
4. ENLISTMENTS RISE; DRAFT END ASKED (5 Senators argue that draft should end – monthly enlistments now exceed 125,000.)
5. FREEDOM FROM WANT (Japanese Royal Princes will no longer be required to join the military, but can choose their own occupation.)
6. HESS REGAINS SANITY (Rudolph Hess, Hitler's henchman and recent amnesia victim, has recovered his memory well enough to plead guilty to 37 counts in his war crimes trial in Nuremberg.)

FROM A 6-HOLER – BY ROADBLOCK SLEEKBELLY THOMAS:
JAP FOOD SHORTAGE ALLEVIATED

From the first meal at your induction station, it's evident what a big job it's going to be, preparing your stomach for army chow.

Everything has a production line taste about it. It's all there, each piece is identifiable, but there's a mystery about everything on the tray.

While it might have been a mystery to inductees in the States, it hasn't taken the little waifs and strays of Urawaboro long to get used to US Army chow.

The little urchins have been making less work for the KP's for several weeks now, by cutting down K Company's garbage disposal.

More leniency should be shown the hungry little brats. Soldiers are not going to make the peace any "harder" on Japan by depriving its children of an occasional pea or crust of bread.

Their spirit should be admired. Anyone mastering the art of digesting GI food in the short space of time they have is deserving of every sort of cooperation and every stray pea they get.

The little food gatherers have a wonderful impish, Puckish spirit that puts them across with some members of the Company.

"Hulloo, hull-o" and then there are little frantic gestures of pointing with their fingers toward your mess kit and toward their nose and if they have succeeded in getting anything they are sure to say, "Sank you, sank you."

EDITORIAL:

The President made a statement the other day, saying that in his opinion, Russia's policies are not leading to another war.

Why this was considered to be of news value, we know not.

Maybe the folks back home look at things differently than we do.

For all we know, they may be found huddled together in little groups discussing war with the Soviets. However, the tone of letters from the land of separation centers wouldn't lead a person to believe that to be the case.

If Mr. Truman had had any desire to reassure the world on the possibilities of future world peace, he could have explained, or at least attempted to explain, a few of the whys and wherefores of U.S. Policy toward the Netherlands East Indies and China.

Maybe he could reconcile our intervention in the internal affairs of these countries with the twelve points of his Navy Day speech.

The peoples of Asia will extricate themselves from the bonds of imperialism in spite of our attempts to retard this natural democratic movement.

In the meantime, however, guns and tanks with the "Made in U.S.A." markings hastily removed are killing the vanguard of Asian freedom.

(EDITOR'S NOTE: I suppose by now I should not be surprised any more by the political opinions expressed this paper. Fox News would throw an embolism if views so far to the left of center were expressed by any member of today's military, especially when they flew directly in the face of current U.S. foreign policy and military action. On the other hand, this view of what was going on in Asia at the time was better informed and far more prescient than

anything coming through "official" channels. If only somebody important had been listening. I'll bet Hanratty got is ass chewed again after this one.)

SUNDAY SUPPLEMENT
Lament – A.D.T.

LONG, LONG AGO, MANY YEARS BEFORE Christ, there lived in Persia a man named Azibillik.

In his day Azibillik was not considered much. He spent his time carving his memoirs and commentaries on marble slabs. The things old Azabilly had to say about the world in which he lived were generally pretty rough. He found little in his Persian world that warranted his praise. (He would have found even less in this world worth condoning.)

Azabillik can be said to be the first of a long line of fault finders. For this reason history has carved a little niche to the memory of Azabillik and all the Azabilliks throughout time.

Azabillik's precedent of lamenting the awful goings on in the world around him has been carried on by some admirable successors.

There have always been those appointed or who have elected to stay on the sidelines of the cockeyed world and criticize, one way or another, the dizzy pace of our planet.

Some lamenters chose a path of poignant irony, such as Diogenes, who carried on a futile search for an honest man, with no more assistance than a crude lamp. Some contemporaries of Mr. Diogenes felt he didn't try as hard as he could have.

Down through history, many names might be added to that of Azibillik. Certain epochs have been completely dominated by this school of sour-faced reactionaries. The stout but stony-hearted Puritan that settled our country was completely under the influence of these 18th Century Azibilliks.

In modern times, however, this business of chastising the modern generation for their "hare-brained ideas" has been pretty much left to white-haired crotchety grandparents, who "Tsk tch", but seldom publish anything, and never commemorate their "Tsking" by carving their observations in marble tablets.

Within the last few years the grandparents have been losing ground and have banded together to make themselves heard. Missionary organizations, the DAR, and temperance societies have sprung up to declaim the awful quirks and spasms of a world running away with itself, and even that has not been enough.

The late war has come almost to the point of silencing the last vestige of reactionaryism as typified by these organizations.

The atomic bomb seems to have been too much for them. Everything goes now. Some of the old guffers are even suggesting things which a century ago the wildest and most anti-social person would have rejected as being too diabolical.

A nice old gray-haired grandmother of Washington, D.C. suggests that any woman who feels in the mood to have a baby should have only to avail herself of a central spermatozoa agency, where she can pick up all the necessary ingredients without having to go to the trouble of tying herself down with a husband. As yet there have not been any counter proposals from any nice gray-haired grandfathers.

Mr. Nathan B. Southey, octogenarian assemblyman of Massachusetts' legislature, has a bill before the House to repeal the "Blue Laws", thereby making it possible to play baseball in Boston on Sunday; buy liquor on Sunday; and Mr. Southey wants to go so far as to remove bans on books.

Grandmothers in Kankakee, Ill. are tearing around the country with Greatuncles from Marshalltown, Iowa. The sports are desecrating elm-shaded lanes with sporty convertibles and spiking the punch at socials.

This senile reaction to prissyism, so manifest in the world today, would seem to mark the end of a long line of Azabilliks. There's no one left to cluck his false teeth any more; there's no one left to be shocked by the next generation.

(EDITOR'S NOTE: Dad's "attacks" on the DAR, Puritans and temperance organizations are more entertaining if you know that his own mother was a stalwart member of the DAR, and descended from the Mayflower, while his mother-in-law was a lifelong member of the WCTU. I had no idea that the Red Sox could not play Sunday games at Fenway in 1945. The sperm bank proposal is interesting, as is my father's reaction to it, but the idea had to start somewhere. It would be another 10 years before the first state [Georgia, of all places] legalized sperm donation, and 26 years before the first commercial sperm bank opened. Of course, there was never such a person as Azibillik, but you knew that.)

HONSHU PIONEER – VOL I, NO. 66 – URAWA, JAPAN – DEC. 3, 1945

HEADLINES:
1. GUERILLA ACTIVITY INCREASES (4 Gov't. Officials captured by Reds in Chinhwangtoa – Chiang's forces arrive in Soviet-held Changchun, believed to have been flown in by U.S. Planes.)
2. JAP CRIMINALS TURNED OVER TO GEN. MACARTHUR (56 industrialists, bankers, former premiers, etc. have been ordered turned over for trial on war crime charges.)
3. RUHR INDUSTRIALISTS TAKEN IN MASS RAIDS (British troops arrest 76 war criminal suspects on Montgomery's orders – some of Germany's richest men.)
4. 829,000 BUNKS AVAILABLE (War Dept.: 515 ships in Pacific with capacity of 829,000 passengers – West Coast transportation getting chaotic – may delay redeployment.)
5. HODGE WANTS DISCUSSIONS ON KOREA (Commander of US forces in Korea: Russian-American conference needed to resolve administrative problems and economic ills caused by the 38th parallel "internal barrier".)

FROM A 6-HOLER – BY ROADBLOCK 2 POINTS THOMAS:
ANOTHER DISCHARGE PLAN

Back in May when Germany was folding up her Wehrmacht, Congress had a bunch of knocked out sessions on a plan (a gradual plan) for dismembering the US armed forces.

Congress always manages to make a lot of any plan emanating from their dusty chambers. Right off the bat, certain legislators came out with an orderly efficient system for discharging servicemen. They wanted to discharge men using the date of induction as a basis of discharge. But it was too easy for them. A way had to be found to make it look like more work had gone into the bill. After going before 15 committees and consulting with several big wheel generals, the experts finally hit on a plan worthy of their usual complexity. The bill did provide a fairer method of discharge, but it still didn't put enough premium on men who were in combat, and it still represented the civilian's conception of something peculiarly GI.

After the approval of the point system, a storm arose, and everyone took it upon himself to blast Congress and suggest a system of discharge he considered more fair.

Congress brushed everything off on the War Dept. and have continued to do so for several months now.

Here's something else to go to the War Dept. about. Pfc. Jack MacNider, son of a Brig General, was recently discharged with 38 points. Since nobody seems to be paying much attention to the scores any more, it's time to suggest a new method for discharge.

K Company men are now authorized to wear four ribbons: ETO, Asiatic, American Defense, and Good Conduct. What's more, men will be authorized two more ribbons shortly: the Victory ribbon and the Japanese Occupation ribbon.

The new plan: To discharge all men with six ribbons or more.

HONSHU PIONEER – VOL I, NO. 67 – URAWA, JAPAN – DEC. 4, 1945

HEADLINES:

1. PATTERSON DECLARES DRAFT NECESSARY FOR DEMOBILIZATION (To shed 7 million men by 7/1/46, enlistments must rise, or the draft will be needed indefinitely.)
2. SHIP CREWS STRIKE (24-hour walkout will be "100% effective" except for troop ships – also protesting use of Merchant Marine for trade before all troops are shipped home.)
3. GERMAN UNREST INCREASES (German protest to U.S.: Administration is lax – unable to cope with mounting brigandry, rape and violence.)
4. CHIANG TROOPS GET US AMPHIB TRAINING (Admiral Barbey: Chinese troops being trained to help "effect the disarmament" of remaining Japanese troops.)
5. FRANCE VOTES CREDIT NATIONALIZATION (DeGaulle's new government took over the Bank of France and 4 other large banks – electricity and gas industries are next.)
6. LABOR CONFAB SETTLES NOTHING (2 weeks of labor-management meetings adjourned with no answers – new array of anti-union legislation expected.)

FROM A 6-HOLER – BY ROADBLOCK BLUSHING THOMAS:
RIBBON MIX-UP

Anyone who talks of ribbons and awards with men of the 97th Div. is in for a hard time.

The subject of theater ribbons and battle stars is touchy business with Trident-men. Ever since there was discussion on the subject of a second battle star, extreme caution has had to be exercised for fear of treading on sensitive toes.

Toes were stepped on by this columnist yesterday, when it was reported that K Company men were authorized four ribbons, including the American Defense Ribbon.

This was a glaring error, and to date, no less than eight men have made it quite clear just how much of an error has been made.

The most outspoken of these in their attack on misinforming the public of King Company's ribbon status was Sgt. Robert Farmer, wearer of the aforementioned American Defense Ribbon.

Sgt. Farmer said, "I want to see a written retraction."

Wishing to cause no embarrassment to Sgt. Farmer (or anyone else in K who might be the proud possessor of the American Defense Ribbon) let it be said that the A.D.R. is presented to those who served in the army prior to the bombing of Pearl Harbor, and therefore, everyone is, of course, not eligible. What was obviously meant is not the American Defense Ribbon, but the American Theater Ribbon.

HONSHU PIONEER – VOL I, NO. 68 – URAWA, JAPAN – DEC. 5, 1945

HEADLINES:
1. RED APPLE DEAL ROTTEN SAYS WYOMING SENATOR (Sen. Robertson: Shipping priority for low-point re-enlistees is wrong – high-point men are becoming so discouraged with slow demobilization, they are re-enlisting just to get back to the States.) *(EDITOR'S NOTE: And the Senator thought this was an unintended consequence of a poorly planned policy? Want to buy a bridge?)*
2. TRUMAN INTERVENES IN LABOR CRISIS (Pres. Truman calls for a new labor bill to speed up reconversion without strikes – wants fact-finding committees for arbitration.)
3. REVOLT SPREADS TO SUMATRA (Indonesian snipers and swordsmen attack – British patrols are busy in Java.)
4. RUSSIAN SPY REPORTED HAVING A-BOMB (Spy entered US on a stolen passport in '38 – worked in a music shop for $75 per month, but had hundreds of thousands in the bank – has successfully stolen plans for manufacture of the A-Bomb.)

FROM A 6-HOLER – BY ROADBLOCK GOURMET THOMAS:

```
CUISINE VAGARIES
```

Mention of the new K Company Mess Hall has been withheld by design. It wouldn't look right to offer comment before the new beanery had a chance to establish itself.

And establish itself it has, too. All sorts of new ideas have been incorporated into the new mess arrangement.

Some of the ideas are holdovers from San Luis Obispo and the non-talking in the mess hall regime. One in particular is the idea of appearing for chow dressed in complete uniform, even to headgear.

SIGNS OF THE TIMES

Directly over the sauerkraut is the mess hall's art work, depicting a converted dinghy carrying troops back to the United States with the inscription "Don't Miss the Boat – Avoid VD". It might not be as convincing a job of reproduction as some other VD signs, but good judgment was shown in hanging that particular one in the mess hall, and not one of its brother posters.

BUCKET BRIGADE

The little Nipponesies who hang around the garbage pail with their little buckets are becoming bolder with each meal.

It's not uncommon now to look up from your plate of chili into the doleful eyes of a little Jap panhandler and watch him follow your every mouthful with drooling mouth and running nose.

(EDITOR'S NOTE: the issue of hunger among the Japanese is not often mentioned in these pages, but other sources suggest that it was a significant problem, and one that MacArthur was very concerned about, and that it got even worse in the next couple of years.)

EDITORIAL:

Commander W.C. Peet, spokesman for the War Shipping Administration, told newsmen the other day that it is necessary to use many U.S. ships for commercial purposes instead of using them for troop transport.

According to the Commander, other nations have already begun the shipping race, and if we expect to have a high volume of trade carried in American ships, we must secure our postwar maritime markets now.

He gave this song and dance when queried on the shipping shortage in the Pacific. The reporters wanted to know why certain ships formerly used as troop transports are now plying South American waters.

Considering the fact that over two-thirds of the merchant ships in the world are U.S.-built and U.S.-owned, Commander Peet's argument doesn't amount to much.

Until the other prewar maritime nations have had a chance to replace their sunken fleets, they will have to rely on the United States to do their business for them.

This situation will no doubt exist for several years, so we can't see why WSA is getting excited.

Someone should tell Commander Peet and the WSA that the men overseas waiting to go home (which includes 99.9% of the men overseas) aren't worried very much about world trade at the present time.

A dollar sign arouses no interest, and the only thing that appeals to us is that magic word – Home.

SPORTS:

DOC BLANCHARD WINS HEISMAN TROPHY (The Army fullback was followed by Glenn Davis, Army; Bob Fennimore, Oklahoma A&M; Herman Wedemeyer, St. Mary's; Harry Gilmer, Alabama; Frank Dancewicz, Notre Dame; Pete Pihos, Indiana.)

(EDITOR'S NOTE: This issue was the first to contain the following statement in its masthead:

```
Honshu Pioneer receives Camp News Service material. Republication of credited matter prohibited without permission of CNS-205E 42d St. NYC
```

Every subsequent issue included the same warning, so I assume that this date marks a watershed, where the amount of "wire service" content started to increase. I am pretty sure I have not included any "credited matter" that would violate this – just content that was created locally by the staff.)

HONSHU PIONEER – VOL I, NO. 70 – URAWA, JAPAN – DEC. 7, 1945

HEADLINES:
1. MURRAY-TRUMAN BREAK (Phillip Murray, CIO President and formerly a loyal Truman supporter, condemns new labor laws proposed by the President as endangering the existence of unions and hampering the development of a new era of prosperity.)
2. FATHERS' BILL DEFEATED (A bill to discharge all servicemen with one child was defeated 6-3 in committee.)
3. MACARTHUR ORDERS KONOYE ARREST (Japanese Government ordered to surrender ex-Premier Prince Fumimaro Konoye and several other cabinet figures, including Marquis Kido. Both have been under attack by US press.)
4. HURLEY TESTIFIES AT SENATE HEARING (Gen. Patrick Hurley names Acheson, Ringwald, and Davies as having worked against him when he served as Ambassador to China during the last years of the war.)
5. U.S. FOREIGN POLICY SCORED (Sen. O'Mahaney [D-Wyo.] assails foreign policy in the Far East as sponsored by "totalitarian and imperialistic interests." He also slammed our "abject apathy" in allowing Britain to aid in subjugating Indonesia.)

FROM A 6-HOLER – BY A. BUDDING BAEDECKER THOMAS:

```
THE DAI ICHI BUILDING
   The most imposing building in Tokyo is the
Western-looking, gray stone structure called the
Dai Ichi building.
   The impressive Dai Ichi building is fitting
for the important activities carried on by the
```

administrative department offices of the occupation forces.

The various functions performed by GHQ within Dai Ichi's walls vary from the Welfare and Health Dept. to the group of artists working on the design for the proposed Japanese Occupation Ribbon.

An informant close to Dai Ichi says design circles are talking of rising suns on a field of blue, of little red suns on white, and of blue and white Mt. Fujis on O.D.

Some of the statisticians confined in the Dai Ichi's somber walls have suggested horizontal black and white stripes with a ball and chain cluster.

BED COUNTING DEPARTMENT

Ground floor offices include those of the bed counting department.

Among the enlisted personnel of Dai Ichi's bed counters is a T/5 from the 7th Division. The T/5 asked that his name be withheld, not for fear that he would be called on the carpet for giving away trade secrets, but he wanted to be sure that his family did not discover the kind of work required of him in the important task of Jap occupation.

The ex-7th Division man explained that he compiled long charts of the number of beds in Japan, and checked them against previously prepared lists submitted by the Japanese.

EDITORIAL:

Today is the fourth anniversary of the bombing of Pearl Harbor.

For the past few weeks, a joint Congressional committee has been investigating the series of events which led up to the incident which has become the symbol of Japanese treachery and American unpreparedness.

In its search for a scapegoat for America's unpreparedness, and in order to keep the spotlight on the individual members as long as possible, just about everyone who has sung "Aloha" has been, or soon will be, a witness.

Although the findings of the committee will no doubt prove to be of interest to historians of future generations, and the press reports have been more than adequate, very few important facts not already known have been brought to light.

It would seem that men who speak with such enthusiasm about tax reductions and governmental economy could think of a better way to spend the people's money.

If this investigation proves to be a howling success, our legislators will probably continue to do this type of thing indefinitely.

A great tragedy in American military history which has been long overlooked is the poor housing facilities and lack of adequate clothing, food and fuel at Valley Forge.

Probably the lack of available witnesses will rule this one out.

SAN FRANCISCO CHRONICLE – EDITORIAL:

Secretary Byrnes can hardly be said to have cleared the air with the current explanation of the presence of US Marines in China.

...he says that Japanese soldiers would be returned to Japan as part of the terms of Japanese surrender. ...no such assurance was made known at the time...

...we think the real reason we are in China is....to help the Chinese Government put down the incipient revolution of the Yenan Chinese. Nowhere have we seen a clear admission to this effect from the State Dept., the Army or the White House. This evasion of the true issue making it impossible for the American people to judge it on its merits, and the series of beside-the-point "explanations" constitute an insult to the popular intelligence.

(EDITOR'S NOTE: Although his area of expertise was American history before the Revolution, my father had a lifelong fascination with China. A voracious reader, he was always adding books to his "China Shelf", which eventually occupied several shelves. It never occurred to me to wonder where this interest sprang from, but after reading about the events taking place there during his career in journalism, it's not hard to understand how an abiding interest could have been kindled.)

HONSHU PIONEER – VOL I, NO. 71 – URAWA, JAPAN – DEC. 8, 1945

HEADLINES:
1. EDWIN C. PAULEY SAYS: **STRIP JAPAN** (Ambassador Pauley: Japan should be completely stripped of her war potential – 50% of industrial assets to other nations.)
2. STATE DEPT. PROBE TODAY (Fireworks expected in Hurley questioning – why did Truman not support Hurley when "career diplomats" opposed him?)
3. WAR CRIMES GROUP ARRIVES IN TOKYO (Special Counsel Keenan: Jap war criminals must be punished, humiliated and go down in history as "felons of the lowest type".)
4. A-BOMB PRODUCTION CUT (US production of A-bombs tapering off – Oak Ridge employees being laid off, bringing Nashville unemployment to a new high.)

FROM A 6-HOLER – BY ROADBLOCK LUC. BEEBE THOMAS:
LIFE AFTER DARK

Showplaces in Urawa are restricted in their fields of entertainment. Their programs follow a well-established pattern. For more diverse amusement and a change in the routine, it's been suggested that night clubbers go abroad for their entertainment.

To be opened soon is the Roseland Ballroom in Omiya. According to advance notices from the "Omiya Special Organization of Entertainment Society", the Roseland is going to be a "SENSATION".

Plans for the Roseland Ballroom call for 200 Beautiful Dancing Partners, 200. Music will be provided by a 15? piece dance band, featuring that lovely oriental songbird, Miss Miyashita, "featured vocalist for Allied troops".

No study in aborigine music and dance is the Roseland Ballroom. Everything is strictly jive. The classiest little jitterbugs in all Honshu will be on hand.

No pounding together of sticks or plinking of medieval mandolins for "Merican solja" - everything is jazz. The band will play nothing but "LATEST AMERICAN HITS".

CLUB OASIS

Another spot on the same idea as the Roseland is the Club Oasis in Tokyo. The music is just as hot, and the dancing girls are just as lovely.

Club Oasis might even be said to have more on the ball because of its strategic location – on the Ginza. Either place is sure to give you something new in the Japanese entertainment world.

No cover, no minimum, just plain American-type fun.

(EDITOR'S NOTE: *I am struggling with this column. It would be well within my father's capabilities to invent these nightclubs out of thin air and describe them in great detail. They do not sound like the kind of places MacArthur would approve of, but who knows if they were real?)*

EDITORIAL:

Now that Joseph Keenan, Special Prosecutor for the War Crimes Commission, has arrived in Tokyo, the Emperor Hirohito's status again crops up in the news.

Since the early days of the war, there have been attempts to estimate the amount of influence Hirohito has had on Japan's policy of aggression.

Some observers who were here before the war have stated that he was familiar with the military leaders' plans and was in favor of them.

Another group, probably just as large, doubt that he had much to do or say about it.

However, when the Keenan staff goes to work, it may try to prove that His Majesty was an accessory to the international crime of aggression. It may claim that if he is considered to be a god, and is so respected by his people, he could have halted the war, had he opposed it, by a direct appeal to the people or by use of his influence.

He may even be tried as a war profiteer. Imperial funds were heavily invested in Manchuria, China and other parts of the new Empire.

The question of his prosecution as a war criminal won't depend too much on the degree of guilt, anyway. If the U.S Government decides it can run Japan without Hirohito, he will be tried. Should we feel that the risk of revolt or unrest is too great, he won't be.

(EDITOR'S NOTE: Extremely intelligent conclusion, that. And, of course, it was largely because MacArthur wanted Hirohito's help in implementing the changes he wanted to make that the Emperor was never indicted.)

HONSHU PIONEER – VOL I, NO. 72 – URAWA, JAPAN – DEC. 9, 1945

HEADLINES:
1. USSR ASKS CONFAB (2nd meeting of foreign ministers to be held in Moscow, starting 12/16/45 – main purpose is to get Russia's views on how to deal with the A-Bomb.)
2. STRIKING GMC VETS DEMAND GI BILL PAY (Striking WW2 veterans demand unemployment pay, per the GI Bill of Rights. Local courts rule otherwise.)
3. CHINA'S FATE DISCUSSED (Secret meeting of top Generals and Admirals with MacArthur to discuss disposition of US troops and materiel in all the Far East.)
4. SOLONS DISAGREE ON BRITISH LOAN ($4.5 billion loan to England being debated in Congress – if conditions are too harsh, Britain may reject the loan.)
5. PRECUT HOUSES FOR VETS ($190,000,000 requested to build 100,000 prefab houses for unemployed veterans.)

EDITORIAL:

In New York the conservative Herald-Tribune attacked American policy in China: "American officials explain that the Chinese Communists are being attacked merely because they interfere with the surrender of the enemy. In the case of Shanhaikwan and Manchuria, however, this explanation is not valid. The Chungking troops who besieged Shanhaikwan and broke into Manchuria were not looking for Japanese.

"The sole purpose is to engage in a contest for possession of one of the richest agricultural and industrial areas in the Orient. How would Americans react if the Russians supplied training and guns, and transferred Communist factions in Canada? What would Washington do if the Reds tried to use their military power in a civil war in Cuba?"

Five U.S. Senators have started a campaign to get all American troops out of China, and many organizations are backing them.

In China, the Chinese Democratic League asks why the U.S. is giving lend-lease to China after the common enemy Japan has been defeated.

With general opinion against keeping our troops there, and our professed policy that of getting out, there is good reason to believe that now is the best time to do so.

SUNDAY SUPPLEMENT
12 in Jeopardy – as reviewed by Mr. Arthur D. Thomas, Jr.

(The following story is a sidelight into the life of Mrs. Bertha Fitzelwitz Scott, celebrated author and social worker. Mrs. Scott's latest book, Twelve in Jeopardy, takes a high place in the field of social novels. Chapter XII is reprinted by special permission of the publisher, W.W. Moot, Chicago.)

Chapter XII

Daddy did nothing but sit off to one corner of the pitiably small front room, his head between his hands, his hair unruly, his patched frayed coat pulled up around his neck for the little warmth it afforded.

We children, eleven of us, huddled together in the center of the room, looking helplessly at our father. There were: myself (Hilda), aged seventeen; Bertha, sixteen; Mark, fifteen; Norman, fourteen; the twins, Sally and David, thirteen; Ellen, eleven; Jack, ten; Susie, nine; Alan, eight; Mildred, seven; and the baby of the family, Tony, two. (The missing member of the family, Sammy, aged six, was out trying to steal a loaf of bread for supper.)

Mommy, who up until last week had been considered a member of the family was in Reno, suing poor Daddy for divorce on the grounds of nonsupport. Mummy had borne up under twelve children surprisingly well, but her gentle nature finally acceded to the pressure of the modern tempo. Her whole trouble had been the insidious soap operas and too many fifteen-cent copies of that infamous magazine, "Lurid Love Tales".

Bertha and I were doing everything we could to keep the family together, but Father's depression was too much for our immature years.

Dad's trouble all started with the strike at the Jacob Grant curtain rod factory. The union had called a strike for a two cent an hour increase in wages, but the curtain rod business had built up a considerable backlog, and Mr. Jacob Grant (the employer) was in a position to hold out for an indefinite period. With each day of enforced idleness, Pop became more bitter. It wasn't surprising then, when he came home from the graveyard shift on the picket line with a nasty gash on his head. I'm always so squeamish about such things, but Bertha fixed Pop right up with a piece of plaster. And now he sat, hour after hour, brooding over the fact that he was out of work and Ma had left him.

Bertha could see that something was bothering Father, so in an effort to pull him out of his lethargy, she walked to the window and lifted the green shade on the curtain-less pane, hoping to find something entertaining going on outside in the stockyards.

It was then that the mailman delivered Pop's letter. It was a special delivery letter and carried a Reno postmark. I signed for the letter, since Pa had so much trouble writing. The envelope was a large affair with a firm name in the upper left-hand corner. I anxiously tore the letter open. Across the top was the firm's name again, "Brownall, Brownall, Smith and Brownall – Attorneys at Law". Then I read, "Dear Mr. Fitzlewitz: This is to advise you that your wife, Mrs. Mathilda Thistlewitz, was today granted a divorce in the Superior Court for the State of Nevada".

"Mr. Jacob Grant, resident of your city, engaged the services of our firm for the business of securing the aforementioned divorce.

"Mr. Grant and your former wife were married in the Reno County Recorder's Court. The new Mrs. Grant wishes the custody of her twelve children, products of your marriage.

"If you wish to contest the custody of your children, would you be so good as to wire us immediately. Sincerely, J.P. Brownall"

I looked from the letter to Pop. He had taken the news surprisingly well, and now drew himself up to his full height and said, "Hilda, get me that coupon from the Daily Worker on the International Correspondence School, and mark off that I wanna study Household Fixtures Design. I'll show her an him...".

His head was bloody but unbowed.

(End of Chapter XII)

(EDITOR'S NOTE: I would bet anything that Dad just sat down at the typewriter and typed until the space was full, with no particular plan in mind.)

HONSHU PIONEER – VOL I, NO. 73 – URAWA, JAPAN – DEC. 10, 1945

HEADLINES:
1. NORTHERN HONSHU **RICE RIOTS** (Farmers in Tohuko visit Prince Higashikuni to beg the Emperor to visit them to dispel confusion and prevent rice riots. The rice crop will be the lowest in 45 years, according to the National Agricultural Society.)
2. ATTY GENERAL INVESTIGATES GMC PRACTICES (Strike enters 19th day – no agreement in sight – Attorney General Thomas Clark investigating GM practices.)
3. MARINES FIRE ON CHINESE VILLAGE (B Co., 29th Marine Regiment lays down mortar barrage in retaliation for the deaths of 2 Marines who were hunting rabbits.)
4. PATTON IN AUTO CRACKUP (General George C. Patton 15th Army Commander, was critically injured last night when his Packard turned over several times.)
5. BOEING PLANE SETS NEW US RECORD (Boeing X-432 Mixmaster covers 2,932 miles [NY to Frisco] in 5 hours, 27 minutes and 34 seconds. Plane can carry 48 people – eclipses the record of 6½ hours, set by a P-51 Mustang.)

(EDITOR'S NOTE: "MIXMASTER"? Really? Actually, I flew to California once in a propeller plane, and that name would have been pretty appropriate, now that I think about it.)

FROM A 6-HOLER – BY ROADBLOCK 4 & 20 BLACKBIRDS T:
NO RED POINTS ON NEW GUINEA

Manila has been in the spotlight for the last few weeks as the scene of the Yamashita trial. The Manila dateline has been reserved a corner on the front page ever since the general was indicted. The outcome was pretty well ordained, but no one cared much about that. At least they went to the trouble of having one. As front page trials go, Yamashita got almost as much play as Hauptmann did back in 1933. As sensationalism goes, Yamashita wasn't much. The most spectacular performance was not turned in by the principals in the case, but by occasional witnesses.

The guy who stole the show, as far as we could see, was some Jap "Dog-face" named Ichida, telling how he made dinner of an English soldier. Ichida said things were pretty rough on New Guinea, and they could not always tell where the next meal was coming from. In this particular case it came from a certain Welsh Grenadier Regiment.

Commenting on his dinner, Ichida's friend had this to say: "Human flesh taste very good, please".

Ichida hastily added that they hadn't had much but rice for several days' rations.

The tribunal was unsympathetic, however, and looked with some repugnance on the Jap soldier's unorthodox eating habits.

Now that Yamashita's been sentenced to hang, we can look forward to some trials right here in Tokyo.

The guys who were close to the Emperor should have some even better tales.

(EDITOR'S NOTE 1: for younger readers, the "Hauptmann" reference above refers to Bruno Hauptmann, who was convicted of the kidnapping and murder of Charles Lindbergh's infant son in probably the most sensational American trial of the 20th Century.)

(EDITOR'S NOTE 2: The mention of the name "Ichida" inspires me to tell you about my favorite Professor at the University of Michigan. This has nearly nothing to do with our story, but I am the one writing this, so I can do as I please. Dr. Sakio Ichida taught statistics during my student years at the U of M, and I was fortunate enough to have a class from him. His English was not perfect, but I understood him well enough to know that he was probably the most remarkable man I would ever meet. He was one of <u>nine</u> qualified Judo referees in the <u>world</u> at that time. ["I can kirr you and nobody know how it happen!"] He had flown in the Japanese Air Force during World War II. ["Every day they are asking for vorunteers to fry Kamikaze. Every day I am stepping to the rear!"] He had an amazing sense of humor, and an IQ that was off the charts. All of his sample "experiments" involved the administration of repeated doses of "Japanese saké" to a subject who was jumping rope against the clock, acted out by himself – totally hilarious. I was his favorite student, because I could sometimes explain things to the class better than he could, due to his accent and the fact that he simply couldn't understand how anyone could fail to grasp mathematical concepts that were so obvious to him.)

EDITORIAL:

The Foreign Ministers of the Big Three are going to have a get-together in Moscow on the 16th of this month.

Their last meeting, which was also attended by the Chinese and French ministers, ended in complete failure. After several days of haggling and disagreement over anything of a concrete nature, everyone packed up and went home.

According to the State Department announcements, the talks scheduled for next week between

Byrnes, Molotov and Bevin will be on subjects of a more general nature.

Recent events in China, the Dutch East Indies and Iran have shown us that all is not well with the world, and unless a method of solving such problems peaceably is worked out, there will be grave danger of a major outbreak.

We are getting tired of these discussions of general policy. The joint statements which say absolutely nothing, the gay banquets with their numerous toasts and other such manifestations of diplomatic parleys make good newspaper copy, but something more is needed to prevent further wars.

It is time that these men face the important issues and stop arguing over petty matters.

They don't seem to realize that the fate of millions of people hinges upon their moves, and that many thousands are dying while they drink vodka and pose for news photographers.

(EDITOR'S NOTE: In this regard, very little has changed since 1945.)

HONSHU PIONEER – VOL I, NO. 74 – URAWA, JAPAN – DEC. 11, 1945

HEADLINES:
1. CONALLY DEFENDS STATE DEP'T "CAREER MEN" (Dean Acheson singled out for defense by Sen. Conally and Sec'y. Byrne – Hurley's criticism was "unwarranted".)
2. HOSPITAL REPORTS PATTON PARALYZED (Mrs. Patton on her way to visit – Patton is partially paralyzed, but his condition is otherwise satisfactory.)
3. 200 NAVY SHIPS TRANSFERRED TO MERCHANT MARINE (Recruited from Third Fleet, ships are freighters and troopships.)
4. IKE PROPOSED AS '48 GOP NOMINEE (Sen. Arthur Capper [R-Kans.] proposed Gen. Eisenhower as the 1948 GOP nominee for President.)
5. MAC ORDERS AGRARIAN REFORM (To abolish absentee landlords by providing low-interest loans for tenant farmers to buy their land – intent is to "destroy the economic bondage which has enslaved the Jap farmer for centuries of feudal oppression".)

FROM A 6-HOLER – BY ROADBLOCK CALL OF THE WILD THOM.:

NORTHWARD TREK

"K" Company will add 200 more miles to their already impressive itinerary after our Wakatu move.

Little is known about the area to which we're moving.

Guide books with their customary exhaustiveness have described the goldfish industry, the scenic splendor of the province, the dress of the aborigines and the number of Christian churches within a radius of twelve miles.

One particularly fine item worth mentioning concerns the warrior ceremony at nearby Lake Nikou. A drive or dog sled trek of twenty or thirty miles is necessary.

The Lake Nikou ceremony is performed on the beautiful lake-shore. Players in the performance all stand facing the shore and fire two arrows into the water, to the "tumultuous shouts of all spectators". It might all sound pretty tame, just reading it from the guide book, but for those of you who will be in the vicinity on the day of the festivities (February 4th), drop in on the revelers for the shooting exhibition, and add your wild shouts to those of the multitude.

For sightseers who can't wait to see the Warrior Festival, drop in on the fish hatchery at nearby Asemaru for a good close-up on how goldfish are bred.

Asemaru is the goldfish capital of the world. From here come the goldfish that eventually find their way to big fish bowls in Woolworth's and pet stores throughout the States and the whole goldfish world.

(EDITOR'S NOTE: As usual, it's hard to separate truth from fiction here, but Google could not tell me anything about the places referred to above, so I am taking the position that this entire column is a complete fabrication, down to the last detail — a goldfish hatchery? That's usually a good initial position to take with these writings, until evidence to the contrary is produced.)

HONSHU PIONEER – VOL I, NO. 75 – ENROUTE – DEC. 12, 1945

HEADLINES:
1. YENAN ASSAILS GOP BOSSES (General: There's no reason for Russia to have designs on Manchuria, or for an alliance between Yenan and the USSR – Hoover, Vandenberg & Hurley are entirely wrong about this.)
2. NATIVES PREPARE BATAVIA ATTACK (Natives massing north of the capital – Dutch & English sending out heavily armed patrols – Britain to send every man at her disposal, until Dutch sovereignty has been restored in the East Indies.)
3. GENERAL MOTORS BREAKS CONTRACT WITH UAW (Canceled 5 months before expiration – 250,000 still on strike – GM: union trying to usurp management powers.)
4. NEW ATOM FINDS REVEALED (In dedicating new cyclotron, Dr. Robert Stone predicts 30 common elements may be used as cancer preventatives.)
5. EX ARMY SGT HELD AS SPY (Fred Bauer caught by FBI – ex-lieutenant in the German Army – sent to US as a Nazi spy.)
6. NISEI FIND NEW HOMES (Only half of the 111,000 Japanese-Americans evacuated from the West Coast will be returning to their prewar homes.)

FROM A 6-HOLER – BY ROADBLOCK OLEROCKINCHAIR THOMAS:

```
ON HAVING YOUR CHAIR PULLED AWAY
  This has been one of the busiest moves in "K"
Company's long history of moves.
```

Complications were forthcoming from 386th Reg't, who have been our hosts while we have been in this prefecture.

Shortly before H-hour, it was decided the Japs of the neighborhood weren't to be deprived of their overstuffed furniture, so arrangements had to be made to see to it that luxury-loving Nipponeses were returned Day-Room equipment.

We hardly expected such reluctance at letting furniture go from a people who get along so very well squatting on their haunches, kneeling, or sitting cross-legged. It's nice to know they do appreciate chairs, even if the only object in their having them is to provide some sort of shrine for emperor worship.

Now we should like to take ten, and thank the Urawaborites for their cordiality and chairs.

The Gizmo hymn chronicles the travels of the Marine Corps in glowing phrases.

"From the halls of Montezuma to the plains *(sic)* of Tripoli", but how about the saga of travel-minded "K".

Given a specified amount of time, we could outstrip the prize nomads of the Marine Corps. The best competition from the Corps would probably come from the 1st Marine Div., who at present are holding the Chinese Communists at bay near Tientsin. Although they might surpass us in Oriental travels, we make the world our home.

HONSHU PIONEER – VOL I, NO. 76 – WAKAMATSU, JAPAN – DEC. 13, 1945

HEADLINES:
1. SENATE DROPS STATE DEP'T INVESTIGATION (Triumph for Truman administration – Hurley's charges dropped for lack of evidence.)
2. BOWERS ADMITS BAD JOB BY OPA (Clothing shortages are a result of a bad job of rationing, OPA admits – returning vets having difficulty buying clothes.)
3. ANTI-LABOR BILL DEFEATED (House defeats anti-Wildcat strike bill, 200-182.)
4. EINSTEIN WARNS ATOM RESEARCHERS (Principles of the Atlantic Charter not being followed by Big 3 – we face "unspeakable disaster" if another war occurs.)
5. COMPANY SECURITY FOR FORD (Ford wants to fine workers who strike without UAW approval ["Wildcat" strikes] $3 to $5 per day.)

FROM A 6-HOLER – BY ROADBLOCK MME. BUTTERFLY THOM.:

"GOODBYE LITTLE YELLOW BIRD"

In the midst of the hubba connected with getting set up in a new location, time should be taken to breathe a sigh for that place that was Urawa.

The townspeople were a little slow in catching on, but they're slow in everything they do. You'll get the idea if you've ever seen any of them get out of the way for an onrushing Jeep.

By the time we were ready to depart, they had provided us with a Bazaar and beer hall. Other recreational facilities were more on the ball in getting under way, but the "Row" is more a part of a world-wide institution than anything restricted to Urawa, and so it's difficult to give the entire population of Urawa all the credit.

If the greatest industry in Japan before the war was silk culture, it seems entirely possible that tourist concessions may easily outstrip silk.

Since September the Japanese have shown considerable resourcefulness in preparing places for Yankee soldier to spend his yen.

There's some likelihood that the Jap towns occupied by American soldiers will look like some of the camp towns in the southern United States, with every other store being either a souvenir shop or a bar.

The most touching sight connected with our departure was the poor little Geisha girls' farewells to the American soldiers, as the train pulled out. Powdered cheeks were stained with honest tears, and it is more than obvious to K Co. that even the members of the "oldest profession" can suffer emotions.

(EDITOR'S NOTE: In the "Fred Stark Appendix" of this book there is an excellent cartoon about this move.)

HONSHU PIONEER – VOL I, NO. 77 – WAKAMATSU, JAPAN – DEC. 14, 1945

HEADLINES:
1. IKE WANTS AO CUT (In his first meeting with President Truman, Gen. Eisenhower requests a drastic reduction of occupying forces in both Germany and Japan. Over 2 million to come home in December and January.)
2. LABOR BOARD PROBES GMC (Truman appoints fact-finding board, headed by Newton Eisenhower [Ike's brother], to dig into the 24-day-old strike.)
3. BYRNES LEAVES FOR MOSCOW (Atomic power tops the agenda for Big 3 talks.)
4. CHIANG'S TROOPS ENTER MUKDEN (Nationalist troops encountered no opposition – advance troops also flown to other Manchuria towns evacuated by Russians.)

FROM A 6-HOLER – BY ROADBLOCK "PINKHAM NOTCH" THOM.:

WAKAMATSU, RALLYING POINT

Like a Veteran's Convention, the various members of the 3rd Bn. Have been making their way to the winter resort area of Wakamatsu.

Spurred on by the glowing tales of winter sports and extravagant living conditions, Third battalion men were herded into waiting trucks and whisked off to their new home.

For men of Teakettle Blue, a new home is as eventful as corned beef hash.

Advance parties take a lot out of any move. By the time this Battalion has moved as many times as it has, you know pretty much how exaggerated are the preliminary reports of any area.

It's hard to say what the dreams of each particular man were in regard to this area, but nothing short of indoor showers, lush lounges and six ski tows were expected from this quarter.

Barracks are barracks, whether they be in Ft. Leonard Wood, Missouri, or Wakamatsu, Honshu; whether they be for the elite Kamikaze or the prison compound.

It's a good bet that whoever occupied these quarters first were GI's and not skiing enthusiasts.

The barracks look to have been built for the Japanese way back in the days when the Emperor was on the right side.

There's a "Gay Nineties" look about the construction of honorable new home. Not that there's much that is filigree or incidental, but the architecture couldn't go all out on military quarters. The only extravagance they permitted themselves was height in the ceilings, which would accommodate behemoths, and certainly must have seemed massive to the bandy-legged original possessors.

EDITORIAL:

Beginning today, the Pioneer becomes the official daily of the Third Battalion.

For the present, at least, we number among our readers those members of the 27th Division who are still in Aizu-Wakamatsu.

By way of explanation for our new readers, we would like to give a short history of the Honshu Pioneer.

The paper was founded at Kazo, Japan, just two days after K Company arrived on Honshu. For the first eleven issues it was called the Kazo Kurier. When the unit moved to Kumagaya, it was decided to call it the Honshu Pioneer, thus saving a change in name every time we changed billets.

Since Volume I No. 1, late in September, the paper has been published daily, in spite of the fact that we have moved three times since then.

Due to the small format, we are unable to print all the news. It has been our policy to carry those items which are of most interest to men sweating out a boat-ride home.

This issue, as well as all previous ones, was printed with a Jap mimeograph - a gift of the now inactivated Imperial Home Army.

Nearly all of our equipment, except for the typewriter, is strictly oriental.

We encourage your criticisms and comments, as well as letters to the editor.

(EDITOR'S NOTE: This is indeed a fateful day for the Honshu Pioneer. Its readership is expanding from the 200-250 range, to something on the order of 1000-1200. We need to be alert for changes that may come about because of this increased exposure. Will the very outspoken and freewheeling [and usually liberal] editorial opinions be muzzled? Will Art Thomas and Fred Stark still be able to poke fun at just about anything, with reverence toward none and sarcasm for all? Or will some form of censorship emerge?)

HONSHU PIONEER – VOL I, NO. 78 – WAKAMATSU, JAPAN – DEC. 15, 1945

HEADLINES:
1. ENOUGH SHIPS FOR JAN QUOTA (In response to public clamor for speedy return of veterans, Gen. Wiley says space for 490,000 Pacific veterans is available, but War Department discharge plan is for only 300,000 to go home in January.)
2. AZERBAIJAN REBELS CAPTURE TABRIZ (Insurgents in northern Iran captured the capital city of Tabriz and threaten 2 more – Iran: arms are coming in from Russia.)
3. GOV'T MOVES IN ON CLOTHING BLACK MARKET (Many vets still wearing O.D. Months after discharge – shirts impossible to get – FBI, OPA, A.G. cracking down.)
4. BIG THREE MAY MEET IN SPRING (Truman instructs Byrnes to propose Washington as the site for the third meeting – second meeting is in Moscow now.)
5. FOREIGN BRIDES U.S. BOUND (60,000 foreign brides of U.S. servicemen will start being imported in January – only hospital ships will be used, to allow baby care.)
6. NAVY COURT BARS JAP WITNESS (Navy Tribunal trying Capt. McVay for loss of the Indianapolis and 880 lives refuses to allow Jap submarine commander Amika Hashimoto to testify in his behalf, denouncing all Japs as "untrustworthy".)

(EDITOR'S NOTE: Regarding #6, if you saw the movie "Jaws", you should remember Quint's monologue about serving on the cruiser "Indianapolis" - the ship that delivered the Hiroshima and Nagasaki A-bombs, and was sunk by Japanese torpedoes on its return journey. Only 317 of the 1,196 men aboard were eventually rescued, after floating without lifeboats for 4 days and nights, making it the worst naval disaster of the war. In probably the most shameful episode in the history of the U.S. Navy, the Admirals

that actually bore responsibility for this tragedy decided to court-martial the ship's captain for "failing to zigzag", thus presenting an easier target to the Japanese submarine. He was convicted and eventually committed suicide. He was the only commanding officer of a warship in the history of the U.S. Navy court-martialed for negligence resulting in the loss of his ship during wartime. I would love to explain in detail what a monstrous miscarriage of justice this was, but I refer you to Wikipedia, where you can read all about it. Until I read this <u>Honshu Pioneer</u> report, however, I had been unaware that the Japanese commander who sank the Indianapolis was prepared to testify on McVay's behalf, but was prevented from doing so, because he was "untrustworthy" by way of being Japanese. Hashimoto did eventually testify [to no effect] that zigzagging would not have mattered, and years after his death, McVay was completely exonerated of any wrongdoing in a 2001 resolution, passed by Congress and signed by President Clinton.

FROM A 6-HOLER – BY ROADBLOCK CLOSESHAVE THOMAS.:
CREDULOUS INSPECTORS GENERALLY

```
   Standard Operating Procedure for IG inspec-
tions was always to lay out on your bunk those
items authorized and tuck the remaining items
into a duffel bag under your bunk.

   Every IG inspector below the grade of first loo-
ie (and we've been under the presumption that's
as high as they ever got) was always compliant
and even downright helpful.

   Anyone unfamiliar with the procedure of an
Inspector General inspection might expect the IG
to cause embarrassment to the GI by asking that
his dirty laundry and extra pair of tailored OD's
be unceremoniously revealed, but this is the last
```

thing an inspector would do. Usually the IG gives a self-conscious little chuckle, winks at the soldier, and says knowingly, "Personal belongings, eh, Soldier?"

Either the GI is offended for having been asked, or he simply says, "Why – uh, yessir."

Somewhere in the welter of brass that must go with anything as pretentious sounding as Inspector General's Office there must be a man who takes his work seriously, and is zealous in his execution of orders. 3rd Battalion has met up with just that sort of man.

This is not your run-of-the-mill legman. This is the real thing. Ace investigators are on the job. The long arm of justice is reaching its hand into the remotest sections of Honshu to put its fingers on the 3rd Battalion, 303rd Infantry.

(EDITOR'S NOTE: I would love to know who Dad was talking about here, and what triggered this outburst. His tendency toward straight-faced sarcasm makes it hard to know how seriously to take this. My guess is that his readers were well aware of recent changes in inspection protocol, so he didn't feel the need to describe them. Fred Stark devoted several cartoons to this harassment, so it had to be general knowledge for the men, and despised by all, I would guess.)

HONSHU PIONEER – VOL I, NO. 79 – WAKAMATSU, JAPAN – DEC. 16, 1945

HEADLINES:
1. LOSS HEAVY IN POST FIRE – TWO BARRACKS LEVELED BY EARLY MORNING BLAZE (Defective stove – 200 homeless – S/Sgt. Dossen heroically raced through the fire arousing sleeping men – no loss of life – 4 injured jumping from 2nd floor.) *(EDITOR'S NOTE: Fred Stark made drawings of this event, which are included a bit further on. His note says that the drawings were made at 3:30 AM on December 16.)*
2. MARSHALL LEAVES FOR CHINA POST (New Ambassador to China faces decisions: 1) Removal of 325,000 Jap troops, 2) Withdrawal of US Marines, 3) Power rivalries in China, 4) Policies foe development of China.)

FROM A 6-HOLER – BY ROADBLOCK CLOSESHAVE THOMAS.:
"GARRATROOPERS"

The newest army installation is Fort Unknown Soldier, Wakamatsu, Japan.

If the 3rd Battalion complies explicitly with every Directive and Poop Sheet out of Regiment (and to date there's no reason to believe they won't) this station has all the earmarks of becoming a model I.R.T.C. Camp.

(EDITOR'S NOTE: Infantry Replacement Training Center)

Since GHQ has never been quite able to make up its mind on what sort of occupational duties are entailed, it's not at all unusual that we should go back to the thing at which the 303rd has had the most practice: Namely, the occupation of areas set aside by the United States and designated as areas for the temporary garrisoning of troops. These areas are more generally referred to as installations, posts, cantonments, forts, or camps.

The 303rd Infantry Regiment has seen a good many of these government reservations since its inception at Camp Swift. Garrison soldiering here takes a practiced hand, and the men are here that can do it.

To the casual observer the idea of going back to garrisoning might seem too big a task for an outfit that has had almost a year's vacation. The fine start that the 3rd Battalion has made, however, is indicative of a rousing success.

After one day of garrisoning, we've had a parade, and plans are under way to have a PX in which to spend trash detail afternoons, and a post theater as a consolation prize for nights without a pass.

EDITORIAL:

The day before yesterday, a lowly Private First Class in the Army of the United States testified before a Senate Committee, which was studying a proposal which would make compulsory a system of peacetime military training.

After he had finished his testimony, there was little doubt in the Senators' minds concerning the PFC's opinion of conscription and the Army in general.

Although we don't necessarily agree with him on his vehement opposition to peacetime training, we were more than pleased to hear that an enlisted man had the brass hats squirming in their chairs at the Senate hearing.

This soldier no doubt represented a sizable majority of the Army's lower caste when he lashed out at the "aristocratic phoneys" and the "Pentagon boy scouts".

Probably the case for the enlisted man has been stated more eloquently on various occasions, but seldom has it had such an excellent press coverage.

It is regrettable that Congress and the people have not had more opportunities to get a glimpse of our feelings on subjects of importance to the nation.

(EDITOR'S NOTE: I wish we had a complete transcript of this fellow's remarks to Congress, but it sounds like he was speaking for the vast majority of enlisted men in the Army at that time [or any other time, most likely].)

HONSHU PIONEER
PAGE 5
"L" AND "M" BARRACKS ABLAZE—DEC. 16, 1945
WAKAMATSU HONSHU STARS
ARROW INDICATES DIRECTION OF COOKS' QUARTERS, WHERE FIRE IS REPORTED TO HAVE STARTED. SKETCHES WERE MADE AT 0330–16 DEC
(SOME OF THEM HAD HOSES, TOO)
Jap firemen—40 min. late.
SMASHING CONNECTING CORRIDORS
Blakeman from the 27th Div.
Capt. O'Brien (in trenchcoat) surveys "L" Company's disappearing "billet".
IF THIS GARAND MAKES YOUR MOUTH WATER, COME UP TO THE OFFICE & SEE OUR B.A.R.!
An M1 "salvaged" from the rubble on the afternoon of the 16th —

HONSHU PIONEER – VOL I, NO. 80 – WAKAMATSU, JAPAN – DEC. 17, 1945

HEADLINES:

1. KONOYE COMMITS SUICIDE (Prince Fumimoro Konoye said goodbye to friends and family and died by his own hand [poison] – was to report to prison today, to be tried for war crimes – Suicide note: "I cannot stand the humiliation to be... tried by a US court... a country with which I wanted so much to cooperate.")
2. TRUMAN REVERSES CHINA STAND (Calls for free, strong and independent China – recommends cease fire and peace talks.)
3. SCAP ABOLISHES STATE SHINTO (All state support of Shinto schools and churches must end - "nationalistic elements" must be expunged from the religion.)
4. BRITISH GOV'T IN GMC MIX-UP (UAW asks British Labour Government to intercede on its behalf in GM strike – Britain owns 475,000 shares of GM stock.)
5. TROOPS JAM WEST COAST RAILROADS (Troops arriving in West Coast ports face delays of 4 to 6 days, due to lack of port facilities and train capacity.)

FROM A 6-HOLER – BY PROF. ROADBLOCK NIPOLOGY THOMAS.:

THE NIP

Too many long-haired theorists have written about the inscrutability of the Oriental for just anyone to dispute the weight of so much material. The facts are, however, that these erstwhile educators are passing off the word "inscrutability" in an effort to cover up for shoddy investigation.

Regardless of how repugnant the idea of carrying on research work in Japan must be to the scientists, they owe it to posterity to carry on a more thorough investigation.

This is no way for a supposedly meticulous scientist to write informatively of Honshu aborigines: (From Dr. Matthew Modolsky's book, <u>A Beginner's Course in Asiatic Anthropology:</u>)

"The Jap is a queer duck. In fact in the words of my eminent colleague, Dr. Mortimer Smythe, the Jap 'defies intelligent description'."

If the Jap defies intelligent description, is that any reason, Doctor, why some sort of description should not be given?

The Japanese are a peculiar lot, but not above or below having anything said about them.

Aside from the very evident fact that the Japanese are a treacherous bunch, and not beneath sneaking up behind someone on Sunday mornings, the Jap personality varies from one locale to another.

The Jap around Tokyo is a repentant character (either by design or in fact) and is abject enough to give his Yankee overseers a fair amount of cooperation.

Not so his northern brethren. The Wakamatsu is a specie whose vocabulary begins with "sonabitch" and thinks making honorable 'melican soldier PO'd is best sport possible.

(EDITOR'S NOTE: Do I really need to tell you that Modolsky, Smythe and the anthropology book are all inventions of my father's fertile imagination? Didn't think so.)

EDITORIAL:

One of the last representatives of Japan's militarist regime to be indicted by the War Crimes Commission died by his own hand yesterday.

He was Prince Fumimoro Konoye, thrice Premier of Japan and one of her most ambitious war-hawks.

In 1937, during his first premiership, the "incident" occurred at Nanking's Marco Polo Bridge, which touched off a war of eight year's duration.

It was Konoye's second term that saw the forging of the Rome-Berlin-Tokyo Axis.

He brought Hideki Tojo into his cabinet in August, 1941, and shortly thereafter bowed out to the Pearl Harbor mastermind.

After the surrender, Hirohito appointed the Prince as his chief adviser on Constitutional reform.

The American press immediately set up a loud clamor for Konoye's arrest, and many people began to ask why such an out and out militarist should be assigned to a post which would be a guiding factor in the future of Japan.

Not long after that, the Emperor dumped Fumimoro like a hot potato, and turned to men of more liberal leanings.

Konoye was no good. His suicide only hastened the work that would have no doubt been done in a few weeks by an Allied gallows.

HONSHU PIONEER – VOL I, NO. 81 – WAKAMATSU, JAPAN – DEC. 18, 1945

HEADLINES:
1. ACTION DEMANDED ON G.I. BILL AMENDMENT (Would remove the requirement for VA approval to get a loan and increase the maximum loan from $2,000 to $4,000.)
2. YENAN LAUDS TRUMAN'S NEW CHINA POLICY (Advocates a coalition government and nationalized army – Neutral sources hope US policy will hasten peace.)
3. AZERBAIJAN ASKS UNO RECOGNITION (Insurgents ask UNO to recognize Azerbaijan as a sovereign nation – Iran's governor: "Province seems definitely lost".)
4. JAPS TO USE OWN TROOPSHIPS (To free more US ships for demobilization, SCAP allows Japan to get its merchant fleet back in operation to bring their troops home.)
5. BOEING PLANE IN CRACK UP (Returning from its record-setting coast-to-coast flight, the X-432 Mixmaster crashed near Baltimore yesterday – crew bailed out safely.)

(EDITOR'S NOTE: I hope they disposed of that Mixmaster name after this mishap.)

FROM A 6-HOLER – BY PROF. ROADBLOCK OYSTERBAY THOMAS.:

JAPANESE RETREAT

The "thing" to do if you amount to anything in the Japanese social world is to spend some time at the quiet little retreat of Sugamo.

The popularity of this little resort comes neither from its famous waters that made Baden and Ems the European "spots" of the 19th Century, nor are the skiing facilities good.

Sugamo provides all the seclusion of a monastery along with accessibility, for Sugamo is just on the outskirts of Tokyo.

The retreat's register reads as if it were the Tokyo Social Register of 1942. Present visitors include the names of Marquis Kido, big-shot governmental blue-blood and Seizo Kobayashi, former Governor General of Formosa.

Prince Fumimoro Konoye, close buddy of the Emperor, had a reservation for yesterday, but a meeting with his ancestors has made the visit impossible.

Sugamo is not an attractive Swiss chalet, nor an oriental Shangri-la. It's a collection of buildings resembling a munitions factory more than anything else. Around the buildings is a wire enclosure, making goings and comings a rather rough job. So far no one has tried to get out.

The United States has assumed the responsibility of allocating space at Sugamo. Getting in is pretty much a matter of what you did for the Japanese war effort. Of course, a gang of lesser fry, social climbers, is bound to have crept in for having done nothing more than refuse American PW's a glass of water.

(EDITOR'S NOTE: As you may have guessed, my father is actually describing a real place, for a change. Sugamo Prison is where Japanese suspected of war crimes were held while awaiting trial. Seven of them were actually hanged there.)

HONSHU PIONEER – VOL I, NO. 82 – WAKAMATSU, JAPAN – DEC. 19, 1945

HEADLINES:
1. CHINA PEACE IN SIGHT (Fighting has slackened in last 3 days – peace talks to start in 7 to10 days – Chiang prepared to form coalition government.)
2. PACIFIC COAST TROOP BACKLOG REACHES 40,000 (Train and housing shortages are keeping many men on board the ships that brought them home.)
3. STALIN RETURNS TO MOSCOW (Was on a doctor-ordered vacation in the Black Sea area for two months, while Molotov handled both foreign and domestic matters.)
4. HOUSE ARGUES SANCTIONS BILL (Tempers rise as Congress debates Presidential power to send troops to the UN, and to impose economic sanctions on aggressors.)

EDITORIAL:

Reports are arriving daily from both Washington and Pacific Coast cities, telling of the railroad tie-up which is preventing the unloading of troops returning for separation.

Not only is the present propaganda subtle, but its artistry threatens to surpass some of Joseph Goebbel's masterpieces, which explained the failure of the German Army's frequent offensives on the Russian front.

Some of the recent stories have been tear-jerkers. One can picture thousands of Pacific vets gazing listlessly from portholes of ships, which have been anchored for days in West Coast ports,

Naturally, when the folks at home read something like this, they'll assume that homecoming troops are pouring into the States faster than was originally anticipated. Thus Congressional mail from irate wives, mothers and sweethearts will be cut down, and the solons will turn the heat off.

It is interesting to note that in the dark days when the nation was in danger, there was no lack of facilities with which to send men to foreign lands, so that they could protect those who stayed behind.

Now that these same men are waiting to get back to that for which they fought, it's a different story.

(EDITOR'S NOTE: I think this piece is likely Mr. Hanratty's work. I have been expecting something along these lines as I read through these issues in chronological order. The recurring themes are: Why are we here – We have nothing to do – We want to go home – People at home are screaming for our return – Oh dear, there aren't enough ships, crews, replacement troops, ports, trains, jobs, housing, or whatever, so the whole process is being delayed – Ain't that a shame, etc. This has smelled funny to me for quite a while now, and this editorial seems to be saying the same thing: It was not a lack of anything except the will to bring them home that kept the troops in Japan. I suspect that the big-wigs were still afraid that those "untrustworthy" Japanese might get up to something without a large occupation force to keep tabs on them, and re-enlistments were not keeping up with their idea of "large".)

HONSHU PIONEER – VOL I, NO. 83 – WAKAMATSU, JAPAN – DEC. 20, 1945

HEADLINES:
1. COMMITTEE APPROVES GI BILL AMENDMENT (House Veteran's Affairs Committee approves amendments to increase loan amounts, add loan uses, extend repayment time, include correspondence courses, make all ages eligible for education, & include Americans who fought for Allies. Still to be voted on by Congress.)
2. FACT BOARD BEGINS GMC STRIKE STUDY (Despite protests from both sides, Truman-appointed board begins investigation of strike – UAW votes to continue strike – GM threatens force to get non-striking workers through picket lines – Ford workers reject 12.4% pay hike.)
3. WEDEMEYER UNDER STATE DEPT (State Dept. asks War Dept. to curtail US troop movement in China beyond that necessary to demobilize remaining Japanese troops.)
4. US SHIP LANDS DUTCH MARINES (The USS Winchester, manned by an American crew, delivered a large number of Dutch Marines to Batavia, East Indies today, while 60 ships stand idle in West Coast ports for lack of crews.)

FROM A 6-HOLER – BY GUNDAR SWENSEN OLAFENSEN:
MUTTERRECHT

   World Wars, in spite of their being horrible, inhumane, and the most destructive of man-made catastrophes, have usually left a certain amount of progress in their wake. Atomic energy, without the catalytic effect of the war, would possibly have waited until 2100 A.D.

   But this last idiocy added to its destruction by turning the historical clock backward in many ways.

Neuropsychiatrists tell us now that returning Vets should be and are marrying the motherly type when they are finally discharged.

They say, "Exposed repeatedly to dangers and frustrations of Army life he can do little about, it is natural for a soldier to feel utterly abandoned. Also, naturally, he then builds up the most fantastic wishes and desires for love.

"In his attempt at self cure he tries to recapture a feeling of security by unconsciously turning towards women of the maternal type."

Anthropologists write that beside being the actual bosses of families, women at one time were the bosses of primitive cultures.

Families revolved around the mother, and it was the mother's brother who was the head of the family, and not the father. From here one might easily deduce who ran the entire establishment.

Modern women are still loud in their cries that this is a "man's world", and no doubt there is justification for this gripe.

On the other hand, we can still see remnants of "mother-right" cultures, so caution is the watchword.

(EDITOR'S NOTE: Say what? Gundar Swensen Olafensen? *Is he actually worried about a post-war matriarchy? Considering his own marriage to the aptly named "Sarge", that could have been a legitimate concern, but it's more likely an attempt at humor that I am somehow not appreciating properly.)*

HONSHU PIONEER – VOL I, NO. 84 – WAKAMATSU, JAPAN – DEC. 21, 1945

HEADLINES:
1. IKE WANTS DEMOBILIZATION **SLOW-DOWN** (Two months at full manpower are needed to weatherproof and box up equipment to be sent back to the U.S.)
2. SCAP DELAYS JAP ELECTION (MacArthur delays elections until an eligibility list can be prepared – a "death blow" for Japan's former militaristic leaders.)
3. TRUMAN NAMES DELEGATES TO U.N.O. MEET (U.N. Appointees: Eleanor Roosevelt, Sen. Tom Conally, Sen. Arthur Vandenberg, Edward Stettinius.)
4. POINTS DROP ON JAN 1ST (Enlisted men: 50 points or 3½ years; officers: 70 points or 4 years, to be eligible for discharge.)
5. SOLONS PASS NEW GI BILL (Congress passes the improved bill – it now awaits Truman's signature.)

EDITORIAL:

One of the latest examples of the Chinese Nationalist brand of democracy was the revelation that many representatives of the American press have been placed on blacklist by the Chiang regime.

Some months ago, Pepper Martin of the United Press was refused admission by Chungking. This action was not effectively opposed by the US Embassy, and since that time many other prominent newsmen have been barred, on the grounds that they were "unacceptable to China".

Among those whose applications for visas were refused were Jack Belden, Vincent Sheehan, Leland

Stowe, and other correspondents accredited to the CBI Theater during General Stillwell's command.

Also denied the right to report the activities of US Marines in China was Edgar Snow, associate editor of the Saturday Evening Post and noted author of several books on China.

It would seem that the situation in Chungking is such that only those dispatches to America which either praise or ignore the fascist government in power there are allowed to enter the Chinese "Republic".

It is no wonder that the people of the United States have been kept in the dark on recent events in China, which have been responsible for the injury and death of many US Marines.

(EDITOR'S NOTE: Hindsight is 20-20, they say, and everything I know about the Chinese Revolution has been learned from the headlines of the <u>Honshu Pioneer</u>, so I am basically ignorant here, but I can't help wondering what China would be like today if we had stayed out of this conflict, or even helped the Communists. I have been told that Ho Chi Minh approached the U.S. at about this time, asking for help in gaining independence for Vietnam, and the "Pacific Wing" of our State Department wanted to support him. However, the more powerful "European Wing" refused to turn against France, our WW2 ally, so we opposed him instead, and he went to the Communists for help. That decision by the U.S. has taken its rightful place in history's Hall of Shame. Were similar choices available in China at this time? The editorial tone of the <u>Honshu Pioneer</u> seems clearly to favor the Communists over the Fascists, and similar feelings were being expressed in the U.S. at the time. Maybe this was the question that fueled my father's fascination with China for the rest of his life.)

HONSHU PIONEER – VOL I, NO. 85 – WAKAMATSU, JAPAN – DEC. 22, 1945

HEADLINES:
1. CHINA FIASCO DELAYS US TROOP RETURN (Gen. Wedemeyer: US forces must stay in China 1) to repatriate Japanese troops, 2) to protect American property. Marshall, hailed by Chinese press, meets with Chiang to "clear up internal affairs".)
2. PATTON DIES (With his wife beside him, Gen. George C. Patton died of his injuries in a Heidelberg hospital.)
3. COMMITTEE TO INVESTIGATE RAIL TIE-UP (Thousands of vets trapped on West Coast for Christmas – CIO will entertain them – Congress asks for investigation.)

FROM A 6-HOLER – BY ROADBLOCK ROUGHING-IT THOMAS JR.:

N, W & K RR

The Niigata, Wakamatsu and Koriyama Railroad has the distinction of being the sole connecting link between the various units of the 303rd Inf. Reg't.

The mode of transportation adopted by the N W & K Railroad is steam locomotion. It seems to work pretty well, but not as efficiently as the catalogs always lead you to believe.

The trains that the locomotives pull closely resemble the coaches used on the Serviceman runs made by the Southern Pacific RR. The principal difference being that N W & K RR uses electricity for illumination.

Riding on the Japanese railroad is a memorable experience, but trying to go anywhere on the road has all the characteristics of an expedition.

The trains run anywhere from twenty minutes to four hours late. The three hour and forty minute difference in train times make forecasting train arrivals something like predicting meteor appearances.

Preparation for a ride on the NW&K includes several blankets and rations for three days.

Keeping the northern Honshu RR on a schedule would present a knotty problem to the Office of Defense Transportation, who already have their hands full with figuring out how they're going to get some 40,000 servicemen jamming West Coast ports home for Christmas.

The newest angle is to provide the returning servicemen with a Christmas party, replete with Santy Clauses and other goodies.

How about stocking the local RTO's with gum drops?

EDITORIAL:

Over sixty million tons of American equipment is rusting in supply dumps in the European Theater because demobilization is reportedly moving at such a fast pace.

If these many tons of Army paraphernalia compare in content to that which has already been turned over to the Surplus Property Board for disposal, at a fraction of its purchase value, a great percentage of it won't be worth the paper it's wrapped in.

The flotsam and jetsam salvaged from a wartime army is seldom worth much in the days of peace. "Swords into plowshares" is a little out of date.

Without a doubt, it is absolutely necessary that this mountain of junk be returned to the US as soon as possible. We are wondering what is going to be done with it after it is waterproofed, packed and shipped.

Even granting that this materiel is worth its weight in gold, it wouldn't seem that it was essential that our soldiers be used to expedite its removal.

It is difficult to understand why men should be kept overseas for such a task when the vast manpower potential of the conquered nations is available.

Equipment is in danger of rusting, but we are no longer fighting a war. Once again we must consider individual rights.

(EDITOR'S NOTE: It seems that the Editor is not buying Eisenhower's excuse for holding U.S. troops in Europe. Neither am I. As previously discussed, the real reasons for the delays in the demobilization program may have been quite different from the ones given publicly.)

GUEST EDITORIAL from the States:
MINISTERS CONDEMN COMPULSORY SERVICE

Despite newspaper "polls", the people of this country are emphatically opposed to compulsory military training in peacetime. A splendid illustration of this was given in Washington within the last few days.

The Washington Ministerial Union is made up of practically all the pastors of Protestant churches in the Capitol. At the last meeting of the union, Rev. Custer Cromwell, pastor of Lewis Memorial Methodist Church, offered a resolution condemning "enactment of any law by Congress which would provide for COMPULSORY MILITARY TRAINING FOR THE YOUTH OF OUR NATION." It was adopted almost unanimously.

(EDITOR'S NOTE: I was not aware of this controversy before my recent education by reading these pages, but it is heartening to know that there was so much opposition to our becoming a militaristic nation, even after such a traumatic war. Of course, the militarists won anyway, as they have ever since, despite Eisenhower's warning in his farewell speech. At least we don't need the draft any more, thanks to high-tech military automation and the lack of decent job opportunities for kids coming out of high school or college.)

HONSHU PIONEER – VOL I, NO. 86 – WAKAMATSU, JAPAN – DEC. 23, 1945

HEADLINES:

1. JAP OCCUPATION'S FIRST PHASE FINISHED – MAC (No more directives from SCAP - demilitarization of Japan nearly complete – challenge now is democracy.)
2. PACIFIC COAST BOTTLENECK CONTINUES (Everything possible is being done – striking Greyhound bus drivers propose a truce to help get vets home.)
3. OPTIMISM AT MOSCOW MEET (Preliminary Big 3 meetings going well – Stalin arrives, celebrates 66th birthday – Byrnes considering concessions in Balkans.)
4. UAW-GMC TALKS TO OPEN (Reuther: GM should be more receptive now to 30% wage hike – UAW will make sincere effort at collective bargaining.)
5. ICKES FAVORS HAWAIIAN STATE (Sec'y of Interior Ickes lauds Hawaiian war record, sees no reason for further delay in granting Statehood.)

EDITORIAL:

A bill was introduced in Congress in the last day of this year's session which would solve the problem of the 60 million tons of US Army equipment said to be rusting 'neath European skies.

It was proposed that all surplus property now stored in territories belonging to our wartime allies be sold to these countries on a credit basis.

The credit derived from this transaction would be placed in an education fund, which would be used to finance the exchange of students between the United States and other nations.

This is an excellent method of promoting good will and understanding in a world which is growing more and more compact.

Such an arrangement would also prevent a slow-down in demobilization – which is said to be necessary in order to have men available to aid in the preparation of these odds and ends for shipment to depots in the USA.

Meanwhile, the bill will lie in the Congressional hopper until our solons conclude their holiday spree and traipse back to Washington for another round of speeches and investigations.

(EDITOR'S NOTE: Our Editor seems to realize, with some irony, that this bill sounds too good to be true, and that the rusting equipment problem is likely a smokescreen, anyway.)

SUNDAY SUPPLEMENT
Lost in the RICE LATITUDES – THE FIRST OF 378 ARTICLES BY A CELEBRATED AUTHORITY ON JAPAN. NEXT WEEK: JAPANESE DANCING
• A. D. THOMAS •

The expression Samurai Sword is a misnomer. That is, the Samurai sword is a sword all right, but it's not a kind of sword. A Samurai sword is any old sharp object that a Samurai might have carried, with which to run his adversaries through.

The flower of knighthood bloomed in Japan as well as Europe. The knights in Japan were called Samurai, and like all good knights, they carried swords, with which to pursue Holy Grails and rush to the aid of fair damsels.

The knights in Japan differed a lot from their Western counterparts, in that more of a premium was placed on power and authority than on virtue and honor, hence the idea of the sword as a symbol of authority.

The Samurai controlled Japan for many centuries before they were superseded by the Black Dragon Society, and in that time they very much popularized the sword. This accounts for the reason Samurai is seldom mentioned without tacking on the word "sword".

At the time of walking-battle the Samurai carried monstrous stickers, some of them six feet long. The popularity of the long sword was short-lived, however. The Nip knights found their short stature was more easily adapted to the Katana, the sword in vogue with present day policemen and firemen.

An enterprising Samurai hit on the idea of the Katana roughly a thousand years ago, when he decided that a horse was a good thing to be on in combat, and wielding a six foot sword was out of the question.

The Katana has a moderate curve and a ridge in the middle of the blade, which gives added strength and prevents breaking and bending.

Another popular model which found pretty general use in olden times was the Tsurugi, a short dirk which has archeological value, but the sword authorities can't find many practical uses to which the Tsurugi could be put. The fact that it came in handy for sticking into someone's back should be sufficient reason for consideration.

Everyone is pretty well decided then that the Katana is the sword best suited for generally getting rid of an opponent.

The popularity of the relatively new sword caused a big splash in sword circles, and everyone decided it was just the thing for settling personal grudges. The market for the Katana was tremendous in Japan, and all the good Samurai felt at a loss if they were without their trusty curved blade with the middle ridge.

Ironmongers throughout the Island flooded the market with blade after blade. The hurry, in modern times, to provide the Samurai with his sword has meant a cheapening of the manufacturing process, but for a symbol of Jap feudalism, hang onto your "Samurai", whatever its workmanship.

HONSHU PIONEER – VOL I, NO. 87 – WAKAMATSU, JAPAN – DEC. 24, 1945

HEADLINES:
1. CHINA FIGHT CONTINUES (New Nationalist attacks reported in Inner Mongolia – US lands more Central Chinese troops in Manchuria – Marshall has nothing to report after meeting with Chiang on peace proposal from Chou En Lai.
2. BRITISH TROOPS JAPAN BOUND (18,000 British troops left Singapore for Kure.)
3. SIAM TO DELAY BRITISH TALKS (Britain, per US request, postpones demands on Siamese government.)
4. MINISTERS IN 7 HOUR PARLEY (Cordial Big 3 atmosphere includes repeated toasts – discussion centers on Turkey.)
5. SEVEN MEDICS DIE IN BLAZE (Fire in a Kyoto barracks kills 7, severely injures 22.)

FROM A 6-HOLER – BY A. ROADBLOCK DELONG THOMAS:
TOKYO SIGHT-SEERS

This time of year Tokyo becomes quite depressing, and it's nice for the GHQ boys to get away from the drudgery of their desks in the Finance Building.

Wednesday two members of GHQ received permission of their boss to take a ¾ ton truck on a tour of northern Japan.

The two tourists didn't take any precautions for their trip. They started without any reconnaissance of the Koriyama, Wakamatsu area.

The leisurely trip north came to an abrupt end five miles north of Koriyama (home of the 1st Bn.)

when their truck piled into a particularly large snowdrift.

The Provost Marshall of the 1st Bn., accustomed to pulling GHQ joyriders out of ditches, came to their rescue and put them up for the night at 1st Bn. Hdq. Co.

You might think the GHQ EM would have been grateful for the hospitality accorded them by their Teakettle Red hosts, but the fare and quarters only upset their delicate digestive tracts, and gave then a nasty old case of the sniffles.

The GHQ Commandos explained that they are unused to the barbarity of sleeping on army cots and having to eat spaghetti.

They were sure that the Koriyama dwellers would understand that long months of sleeping on beds with mattresses in steam-heated rooms had made them particularly easy prey to drafts and rations out of a can.

They suggested that a GHQ agency be established to warn unsuspecting travelers of primitive conditions in the north.

HONSHU PIONEER – VOL I, NO. 88 – WAKAMATSU, JAPAN – DEC. 25, 1945

HEADLINES:
1. STIFF UPPER LIP MARKS THIRD BN'S CHRISTMAS (Activities limited to religious observance, special dinners, and a party at HQ Co.)
2. CHINA TO GET US SHIPS (Admiral Barbey: An undisclosed number of ships have been transferred to the Chinese, including LST's, Liberty ships and more.)
3. BRITISH DRIVE INTO SEMARANG (BBC reports: fighting continues in Indonesia – British tank attack drives into Semarang in central Java – poorly but bravely defended.)
4. DEC 7 PROBE TO REOPEN (Admiral Stark to testify on Monday, followed by Admiral Kimmel and General Short.)

'TWAS THE NIGHT BEFORE CHRISTMAS

It was the night before Christmas, and all through the barracks,
Most of the GI's were in a state of hysterics.

Not because they were lonesome and blue,
But just because of the lack of brew.

A case for each man was ordered and bought
And stacked in the storeroom to be almost forgot.

They tell us tomorrow we'll have a can or two,
And maybe the next day it'll be two times two.

But tonight is the time for which we paid our sen,
To bring peace on Earth, good will to men.

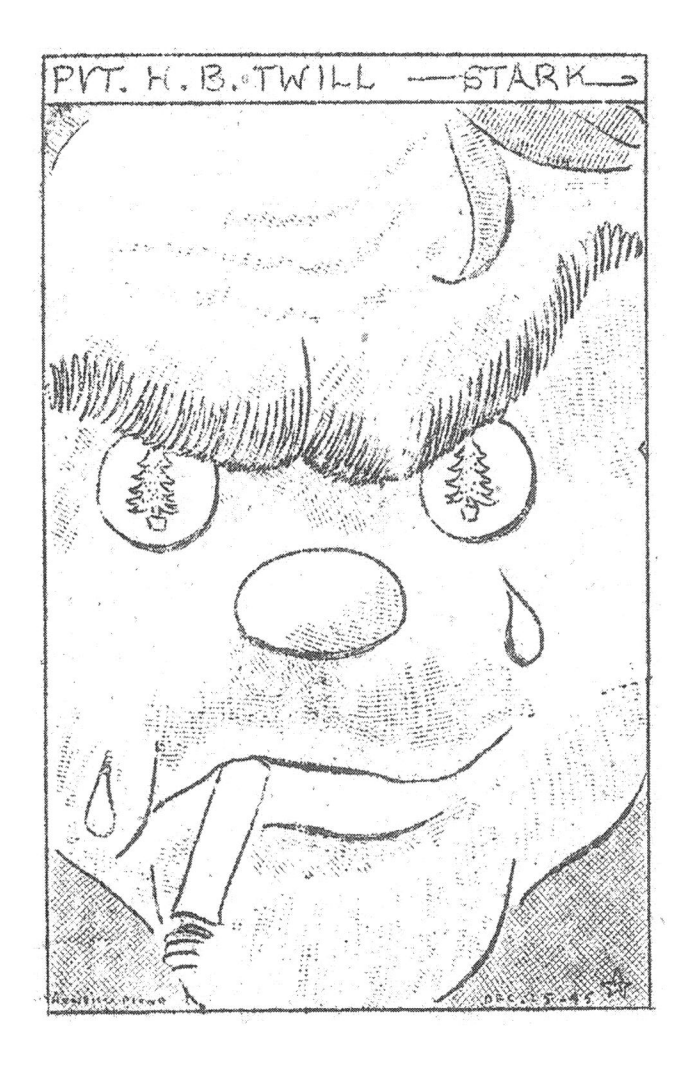

(EDITOR'S NOTE: Although to date very little "poetry" has appeared on the pages of the <u>Honshu Pioneer,</u> outside of Dad's "6-Holer" column, I am reluctant to attribute this unsigned masterpiece to him. Somehow, it doesn't sound like his voice, but who knows? The Fred Stark drawing above was directly beneath the poem, so probably it was his work.)

HONSHU PIONEER – VOL I, NO. 88 – WAKAMATSU, JAPAN – DEC. 26, 1945

HEADLINES:
1. PROGRESS REPORTED ON MOSCOW DISCUSSIONS (Talks slow, but good results expected – peace treaties agreed for Finland, Italy, Rumania, Hungary – A-Bomb to be discussed next – meetings expected to continue past the holidays.)
2. BRITISH AGREE TO INDONESIAN PROPOSAL (Disarming of remaining Japanese troops will be left to the Indonesians, per their proposal.)
3. US SPAIN BREAK HINTED (US talking with exiled Republican Government, who are awaiting Franco's downfall to take over as a caretaker government.) *(EDITOR'S NOTE: I hope they weren't holding their breath while they waited.)*
4. BEER HALL OPENS TODAY (Members of 3rd Bn. can now get their daily ration of 3 cans at the new hall, which also features 3 ping-pong tables and a billiard table.)
5. TRUMAN PARDONS SERVICE CONVICTS (All men who were serving jail sentences and joined the service after 12/7/41 have been pardoned, as a Christmas gesture.)

FROM A 6-HOLER – BY A. ROADBLOCK "GOODIES" THOMAS:
"MAY THE MERRY BELLS KEEP RINGING"

Happy Holiday! Greetings from the American Red Cross! A message from your Commander-In-Chief on the occasion of Christmas 1945! A gigantic electric "Merry Christmas" sign has been erected on the Dai Ichi Building in Tokyo.

Let's not forget our men overseas on this, the first Christmas of what is hoped to be a new era of peace.

Tons of turkey, Red Cross packages and other "goodies" have been pouring into Yokohama for the past six weeks.

Everyone is beside themselves with providing the men overseas with a good time on Christmas.

But all these tons of benevolence from interested parties and people whose job it is to be interested, are just mementos of another world.

Christmas could have been nothing more than a time for a furtive prayer that a boat show up within the next few weeks, but we had to be coaxed into thinking that we were being let in on a good thing.

We were touched by the Christmasy gestures; that's the big trouble. There was just enough of Christmas there to have made us very conscious of other Christmases. We got close enough to breathe in a nostalgic lungful.

We've had a long time in which to feel sorry for ourselves, and yesterday we were given the coup-de-grace to our bitter cup.

It would have been better if the Red Cross had sent rock salt to aggravate our inflamed wrong sides.

(EDITOR'S NOTE: I guess you might call that "black humor".)

EDITORIAL:

Overshadowed by recent events in other parts of the world, the situation in French Indochina has not decreased in seriousness.

The native provisional government has stated that the Anemites will fight for their freedom with "Independence or Death" as their slogan.

A UP correspondent in Hanoi expressed doubt that the French will be able to assume full control of the country without a full-scale military campaign against the insurgent forces led by Ho Chi Minh.

Hatred for France is so great that the appearance of a Tricolor is enough to create a disturbance.

Some of the more fanatical groups have announced that a French attempt to assume control by force would result in a massacre of the 15,000 French citizens now living in Hanoi.

Leaders of the movement have protested to the United States that France has violated the principles of the Atlantic Charter.

The plea, as well as those made by Indonesian Republican spokesmen, has placed the US in a very embarrassing position.

Although we shouted loud and long about the Four Freedoms during the war, commitments made to the French and Dutch governments now prevent us from aiding the cause for which the war was fought. The idea of an America which favored right over might is fast disappearing.

(VERY LARGE EDITOR'S NOTE: Wow! We've seen some pretty good editorials in this little Army rag, but this one goes to the top of my list. I could write several chapters of my own on this subject, but I will refrain from saying more than this – I had good friends that died in Vietnam, and others whose lives were changed forever. At the time, I thought that the war was a complete waste, based on lies and sustained by more lies. To now see that really intelligent people were writing about the roots of that war 20 years before we were deeply involved, but with nobody listening, makes we want to smash something.

But instead I will attempt to elucidate a couple of points to my younger readers [as if anyone young is ever going to read this]. We have heard previous mention of the Atlantic Charter, but given no explanation of what it was. It was a 1941 agreement between the U.S. and Britain that was later agreed to by all the Allies. As always, we turn to Wikipedia for some details:

> *The Atlantic Charter acted as clarification that America was supporting Britain in the war. A key American aim was to force a change of British policy in regard to its Empire. The eight principal points of the Charter were:*
>
> 1. *no territorial gains were to be sought by the United States or the United Kingdom;*
> 2. *territorial adjustments must be in accord with the wishes of the peoples concerned;*
> 3. *all people had a right to self-determination;*
> 4. *trade barriers were to be lowered;*
> 5. *there was to be global economic cooperation and advancement of social welfare;*
> 6. *the participants would work for a world free of want and fear;*

> 7. the participants would work for freedom of the seas;
> 8. there was to be disarmament of aggressor nations, and a postwar common disarmament.

Sounds pretty good, doesn't it? If all the Allies had stuck to that, we'd have a different world today, wouldn't we? I especially like the bit about "postwar common disarmament".

I guess I might also need to explain the "Four Freedoms" mentioned above to the Peanut Gallery. [Oh crap! Do I need to explain "Peanut Gallery", too? No – look it up!] In his 1941 State of the Union Address, President Roosevelt stated that people everywhere in the world should enjoy these four freedoms:

> 1. Freedom of speech
> 2. Freedom of worship
> 3. Freedom from want
> 4. Freedom from fear

These are engraved on his Washington D.C. Memorial, but more memorably they became the subjects of four oil-on-canvas masterpieces by the late artist Norman Rockwell, which now form the centerpiece of his museum in Stockbridge, Massachusetts. It is pretty nearly impossible to look at them without crying. In 1943, they were put aboard a train that toured the country to promote the sale of War Bonds. They were directly responsible for $130,000,000 of such sales, or in 2013 dollars, eleven fantasticrillion [or 1.7 billion].

Sorry to be nostalgic here, but when I was growing up in these United States, I thought ideas like those expressed in the Atlantic Charter, the Four Freedoms and the Bill of Rights defined us as a nation. I wish I still thought so.)

HONSHU PIONEER – VOL I, NO. 89 – WAKAMATSU, JAPAN – DEC. 27, 1945

HEADLINES:
1. SCAP ORDERS WEEKLY **JAP BUSINESS REPORT** (MacArthur orders weekly accounting reports on all Japanese economic activity – prices, production, etc. - rather than monthly or more – close check on her ability to rejuvenate her military capacity.)
2. US OBSERVERS AT GREEK POLLS (US, British and French troops have been asked to act as referees in upcoming elections in Greece.)
3. INDIES TO GET CONSTITUTION (Dutch Commissioner arrives in London to confer with British parliamentarians on a constitution for the Indonesian Republic.)

EDITORIAL:

The success or failure of the occupation of Japan depends upon, and is the responsibility of, the individual American soldier. Beneath the morass of official directives, the attitude of Pvt. Joe still remains the one great democratizing force.

Recently there have been incidents which have tended to prejudice the Japanese public against us. Black market dealing and a general lack of fair business transactions on our part rank high on the list of offenses.

Within America we lived in a society based upon the legal concepts of fair enterprise and the inviolability of personal property, yet here we have shown a reluctance to conduct ourselves as Americans. The actions of free men are more than a democratic code conformed to within a democratic society – they are the every day principles of free living which we are privileged to carry to the unenlightened corners of the earth.

The Japanese still look upon us with respect, and to us for guidance, so it would seem that a renewed sense of purpose on our part as individuals might yet bring these islands into the family of free nations.

Let us not lose the advantage we won by force of arms in the field of human relations.

(EDITOR'S NOTE: I've been waiting for something like this. Up to this point in the Honshu Pioneer archives, you might get the idea that, aside from some occasional high-jinx, the U.S. occupation was being done by a very large troop of well-behaved Boy Scouts. Any group of 400,000 men with not a lot do to is bound to contain some bad actors. If their misdeeds were confined to swindling the natives on some black market deals, as this would suggest, it would seem to qualify as a pleasant surprise. Something tells me there were also more serious incidents that were not reported here. The tendency of men to misbehave when they are far from home and think nobody is watching has been documented for ages.)

HONSHU PIONEER – VOL I, NO. 90 – WAKAMATSU, JAPAN – DEC. 28, 1945

HEADLINES:
1. JAP WAR FILES FOUND (Trials of thousands of alleged war criminals have been delayed by lack of evidence and witnesses – 72 cases of documents found by GHQ should solve this problem.)
2. GI'S EXEMPT FROM JAP LUXURY TAX (SCAP orders removal of tax from all items sold to occupation troops, to return the cost of occupation to the Japs.)
3. TURKS FEAR RUSS GRAB (Georgian SSR has demanded 150 miles of Black Sea coast be returned to Soviet sovereignty – Turkish foreign minister complains.)
4. MARINE MORALE LOW IN CHINA (American sources reveal Marine morale very low – Dean Acheson says Gen. Marshall is keeping informed of meetings with both sides.)
5. HOUSING PLAN UNFAIR TO VETS (Rep. G. Outland [D-Cal] suggests lower-income GI's be included in housing plan – not everyone can afford a $10,000 house.)

FROM A 6-HOLER – BY A. ROADBLOCK EGGSINHISBEER THOM.:

DOUGHNUT DUGOUT

Extreme patience, a good sense of direction and a sloppy march of one mile down poorly lighted streets pays for admission to the Third Bn.'s own Service Club.

Standing in the midst of Aizu squalor, the Service Club stands out like P.S. 51 in all of its 1890 ugliness. The Club building is tall, red, and full of 19th Century doodads.

The most deceptive thing about the Third Bn.'s recreation spot is that the doughnut, coffee, library ping-pong, writing room and latrine are not housed in the big red structure, but in the roughly thrown together wooden structure tacked onto one side.

The big building, however, has been put to use. It's here that the Battalion holds its basketball games. The gymnasium is known as Gym No. 2. No one has yet found just where Gym No. 1 is located or whether it is any better heated or provided with any better facilities, but it's our guess that the "2" business is just another attempt to awe the highly impressionable Nip.

Wakamatsu's Service Club is not as well stocked with feminine entertainers as its regimental counterpart in Fukushima. There's never any more than one or two around, and they always have dishrags in their hands.

On the credit side of the ledger, may we recommend the Service Club's coffee as the best in all Honshu – the black potion served would make the most discriminating Brazilian coffee connoisseur's heart jump.

(EDITOR'S NOTE: Although he must have been aware that today was his first wedding anniversary, nothing in his column would betray it. However, I am having a bit of trouble tying the "eggs in his beer" in his daily alias to anything in the column itself.)

EDITORIAL:

The recent Allied directive abolishing state Shintoism as a practice in Japan shows definite promise of ushering in a new era of liberalism.

This ancient religion, or "way of the Gods", with its thirteen sects and 110,000 shrines, completely dominates the political and cultural life of some seventeen and a half million Japanese. While this figure does not represent the majority of the populace, it is nevertheless extremely significant from a nationalistic viewpoint, as the sect deifies the imperial household members, as well as many important national figures.

During her drive for world dominance, the imperial line revised Shinto to meet the fanatical nationalistic qualities needed to bolster the home front and successfully prosecute the war. At the same time they insured the perpetuation of their political and economic dynasty.

It is obvious then that the malignant roots of such an outmoded national policy must be destroyed before the Japanese mind is capable of grasping the principles of a democratic restoration.

This directive is not expected to change overnight into an adherent of westernized government, but it shows promise of giving the Japanese the opportunity of adopting free choice toward that end.

(EDITOR'S NOTE: Of course, Shinto did not disappear from Japan after this, but perhaps "State Shinto" did, whatever that should mean. Today a large majority of Japanese are not religious at all, and Shintoism is said to have about 4 million adherents, although more might observe some aspects of its rituals at certain times, just as many non-religious Americans "celebrate" Christmas.)

PRICE CONTROL CAMPAIGN

Several members of the battalion have brought an undesirable situation to the attention of this paper. Prices of commodities in the Wakamatsu area are ridiculously high.

After investigation by individual members of the Pioneer staff, this accusation was found to be correct. So, it was decided that the matter should be brought before the eye of Military Government in order that a suitable solution could be found – one desirable to both the occupation troops and the Japanese.

After a discussion with the AMG, in which close cooperation was a keynote, the following tentative plan was formulated:

A non-buying period of approximately a week should be put into effect. During this time, no EM or officer would buy any article from any shop in Wakamatsu. A commission should be formed to conduct a survey of prices in stores all over town.

After extensive study, the commission would submit a report to both AMG and Battalion. In order that the plan be made successful, this paper deems it necessary that these points meet the approval and receive the complete cooperation of every man in the battalion.

HONSHU PIONEER – VOL I, NO. 91 – WAKAMATSU, JAPAN – DEC. 29, 1945

HEADLINES:
1. BIG THREE MINISTERS AGREE ON JOINT POST WAR POLICY (Russia to join Far Eastern Advisory Commission – All Axis peace treaties done by May 1 – Korea to be independent in 5 years after UN administration – Russian and US troops to withdraw from China as soon as possible – Use of the A-Bomb is outlawed.)
2. CHIANG GETS WRITTEN PEACE BID (Chou-En-Lai offer: 1) Cease fire, 2) Talks to be scheduled, 3) Non-partisan observers to investigate allegations at fronts, 4) Forces hold present positions. Chungking reply expected today.)
3. BRITISH VACATE JAVA MARCH 1 (Withdrawal date established after 3 days of meetings with Dutch officials in London.)
4. NATIONS FORMALLY SIGN BRETTON WOODS PROPOSAL (23 nations sign the monetary agreement and share in $18 billion fund for war rehabilitation.)

(EDITOR'S NOTE: I will spare you several thousand words that I would like to write about the last item, and limit myself to this: 1. Bretton Woods, although well-intentioned, was one of the most important mistakes ever made; 2. The greatest economist of the 20th Century, John Maynard Keynes, presented a plan that was vastly superior to the American-dominated gold standard plan that was actually adopted, but it was swept aside by American hubris and greed; 3. We are still paying the price for this catastrophe, and we will continue to do so.)

STATESIDE - BY A. HAMBURGER

PREVIEW??

Eleanor Roosevelt writes in her daily column, "The history of Europe proves that curtailment of labor's rights is a danger signal of impending fascism. Current demands for labor regulation are the results of failure to provide for workers during reconversion, while corporation earnings are protected by legislation passed in wartime to get their full cooperation for production."

Anti-labor propaganda among servicemen has served its purpose, and conversations on the present strike situation in the States can be frequently heard condemning unions and their demands.

Sec'y of Commerce Henry Wallace revealed a report from the division of Research and Statistics of the Commerce Dept. showing industry generally can afford a 10% wage increase and the auto industry can afford a 15% increase, followed by 10% more in 1947.

Reconversion Director John W. Snyder withheld from the public, with President Truman's consent, a similar report drafted for his Industry-Labor Advisory Committee by his own staff – a report showing that industry could raise wages by 24 percent without suffering.

Returning to civilian life armed only with the distorted view of the labor situation as presented in the overwhelming proportion of the press, and ignorant of such facts as presented above, will lead the vets of this war to support just such legislation as Mrs. Roosevelt warns against as the prelude to an impending Fascism.

(EDITOR'S NOTE: Well, labor did have its day after the war, but if Mrs. Roosevelt can see what is going on in the 21st Century, she must be spinning in her grave.)

HONSHU PIONEER – VOL I, NO. 92 – WAKAMATSU, JAPAN – DEC. 30, 1945

HEADLINES:
1. **OPA TELLS JAPS – SLASH PRICES** (After meeting with Battalion OPA: All items to have 2 price tags: with and without luxury tax – A supervised [by OPA] bazaar to be opened by Wakamatsu merchants – prices to be lowered across the board.)
2. **TRUMAN SIGNS GI BILL** (Amended "GI Bill of Rights" provides $65/mo. to single vets, $90/mo. to married vets for college, removes age restrictions.)
3. **BYRNES REPORTS MOSCOW PARLEY** (Sec'y of State returns in "optimistic mood", meets with President Truman aboard his yacht to brief him.)
4. **PATTERSON PLANS ETO-ASIA TOUR** (Sec'y of War to visit Army installations around the world to check on living conditions, shipping and demobilization numbers.)

FROM A 6-HOLER – BY A. ROADBLOCK DELONG THOMAS:

WAKAMATSU SOCIAL CLUB

In front of the 3rd Battalion's Service Club, a matter of 200 yards through a labyrinth of Japanese back yards, stands the Wakamatsu Social Club.

Any week night the Social Club rocks to the rhythms of the hottest bands by way of V-disks. To make atmosphere cosmopolitan Joe, the record changer, spices things up with an occasional Japanese number. The GI's are a little nonplussed by the woodblock and zither music, but the manageress gets a whoop out of them.

We wouldn't want to say the Social Club is thriving under false colors, but the facilities hardly live up to the grandiose name. The dance floor is the approximate size of a squad room, and a waltz looks pretty much like a stampede. No one has thought to try the jitterbug.

The Club runs on a 12-hour basis, the 20 hostesses exchanging their Jap partners for GI's from 7 to 9PM.

The girls have learned a lot from American movies, and all affect Western dress with varying degrees of success. The predominant motif is a long white, on the shoulder gown, with a gathered blouse that goes a long way toward showing off the gals' faces and not much else.

The girls are a little dead on their feet, but that's understandable when you consider that they have been standing on them since noon.

The price of two hours entertainment is 15 yen, but the big deal is to wait until your Co. goes in free.

(EDITOR'S NOTE: At this time ¥15 = $1. By early 1947 a dollar was worth ¥50; by 1948 it was ¥260; by 1949 it was ¥360. Runaway inflation had not yet begun, but was just around the corner.)

EDITORIAL:

The practice of Jap beating which has shown an alarming increase in the last two weeks, not only contradicts the accepted standards of human decency, but also is a disgusting violation of the principles of Americanism.

Whether or not we wish to admit it, the principle of "man's humanity toward man" is as old as the Declaration of Independence and as American as a three base hit. Since when has the American soldier had to resort to the tactics of Yamashita and the Little Glass Eye? Since when has Yankee ingenuity had to substitute brute force for the orderly processes of law? If these Japanese workers committed offenses either of a private nature or against the American Army (and there is no proof to that effect) there are still legal agencies before which they may be taken, capable of administering justice in an intelligent and democratic way. EXPEDIENCY IS NOT AN EXCUSE FOR BRUTALITY.

The purpose behind our occupation is not to flaunt our individual or collective power before a defeated people, but rather to prevent a future world conflagration through national understanding.

History has given us a moment in the consciousness of man, in which to build a new world based on the concepts of democracy. We won a war as good soldiers. We can win the peace as good men.

(EDITOR'S NOTE: *Ah, so a little bit of black market swindling was not the only wrongdoing that American troops were responsible for, as I suspected. Still, it's good to hear that this wasn't considered much of a problem until the last two weeks. Just a few months ago, the Japanese were using every suicidal trick in the book to kill as many Allied personnel as possible before their inevitable defeat. It is hardly surprising that a few American GI's might still harbor some ill will toward them, in spite of the peaceful mission they were engaged in.*

I was unfamiliar with the "Little Glass Eye" reference, but research revealed that this was the nickname of Tsuchiya Tatsuo, an infamous prison camp guard, who was sentenced to life in prison for exceptional cruelty, in part for slowly beating to death an American prisoner, who he had first stripped and left outdoors in the middle of winter, after said prisoner had caught him stealing the Red Cross parcels intended for prisoners.)

GUEST EDITORIAL – FROM THE <u>SAN FRANCISCO CHRONICLE</u>:

Chiang-Kai-Shek is no more democratic than Hitler, Lt. Colonel W. J. Peterkin, who spent two years in Central and Communist China as a military observer for General Joseph Stilwell, said today.

"The Nationalist Government is graft-ridden beyond belief", the officer said. "In a single instance, one Nationalist Chinese General received $2,000,000 of the $3,000,000 paid on a contract...".

He said that while Chiang's program for China appears only on paper, the Communist Government plan is in actual operation and is almost completely free of graft.

Peterkin is credited with having spent more time with the Chinese Communists than any other US officer.

(EDITOR'S NOTE: Again we see the Communists getting better press than the Nationalists, but was there perhaps some bias at work here in the selection of Stateside op-ed content?)

HONSHU PIONEER – VOL I, NO. 93 – WAKAMATSU, JAPAN – DEC. 31, 1945

HEADLINES:
1. JOINT CONTROL PLANNED IN OCCUPATION OF JAPAN (Marshall and Chiang meeting in Shanghai – Russia, China and US to share occupation duties.)
2. INDIES IN TRUCE AS DUTCH-NATIVE PEACE TALKS OPEN (No new outbreaks of fighting – peace talks under way to end 3-month-old conflict.)
3. MARINE AIR ARM TO LEAVE CHINA (Brig. Gen. George Thomas announces that all 7,500 men will leave for the US in January.)
4. TURKEY REQUESTS CONFERENCE (Tensions increase in Levant and Black Sea area – Turkish minister asks for assurances from Soviets that they will expand there.)

EDITORIAL:

The strong-arm tactics of some members of this battalion toward the civilians of Wakamatsu are invoking vicious reprisals. We refer more specifically to the assault made on Pfc. Lester Bevins the other night by an unknown assailant.

According to Bevins no incident occurred which could have prompted the slugging, so this paper suggests that he received a blow meant for some other party.

Lately, predatory looting parties, with an utter disrespect for the sanctity of women and the home, have shown an arrogance which has made the streets of Wakamatsu unsafe for American soldiers after dark.

As a result, reprisal is inevitable. Then what? A counter-reprisal by us, touching off an era of bloodletting? Such an incident could blast the purpose of the occupation and forever prejudice the Japanese people against us.

Being an American doesn't mean just coming from there. It means living by American principles, and in that light we should like to mention TOLERANCE, which would go far in correcting this situation.

This paper calls to your attention today's letter to the editor, in which eleven men plead for more tolerance towards the Japs. One of them was Pfc. Bevins.

LETTER TO THE EDITOR:

The undersigned are of the opinion that some members of this battalion, without perhaps realizing it, are busily engaged in making the city of Wakamatsu a place which no American soldier would care to visit after dark.

We'd like to know just what some GI's think they're accomplishing when they go out in gangs and rub snow on the heads of Japanese civilians. Exactly what good is being done the cause of lasting peace and the ideal of "freedom from fear" for which we fought, when some brave "conqueror", backed up by a mob of buddies, hits an inoffensive man and shoves him into a snowdrift?

Is he avenging the "sapping" of an American soldier by an unknown Jap the other night? If so, it won't work. It is just such acts of unthinking arrogance on our part which will bring on repetitions of that incident and lead to a vicious cycle of reprisals back and forth.

To the guys who've been pulling this sort of black-shirt stuff, we'd like to suggest: Sure, the Nips are getting a lot better deal under us than we'd get if they were occupying our homes, but that doesn't make it right for us to behave as they might if the situation were reversed. Not right, or practical, either. Most of us have seen enough fighting and anger and suffering this past year. We'd like to be able to spend what time we must in Japan in peace and friendliness, without being afraid that a local citizen, p.o.'d because his grandpop was beaten up by a bunch of "Yanqui" toughs, is going to stab us in the back some dark night.

(EDITOR'S NOTE: Well, international relations have certainly gone downhill in a hurry. The surprise to me is that it took over 3 months for this kind of incident to surface on these pages. I suspect that part of the problem is that new troops have been arriving right along, and I would bet that the troublemakers are among the newest arrivals. I'm hoping their more seasoned comrades are going to help them see the folly of their ways, as they are certainly attempting to in the above writings.)

HONSHU PIONEER – VOL I, NO. 94 – WAKAMATSU, JAPAN – JAN. 1, 1946

HEADLINES:

1. BIG 3 DECISIONS IRK MACARTHUR, KOREANS – KOREANS REACT TO MOSCOW (Mass strikes, riots, stoning of US occupation forces in southern Korea in response to Big 3 decisions.)
2. MACARTHUR TO MAKE BEST OF AGGRIEVED SITUATION (AP dispatch: MacArthur's directives subject to revision by advisory board may undo his good work.)
3. 600,000 ELIGIBLE FOR DISCHARGE THIS MONTH (Attempts being made to discharge all 50-pointers in January – shipping schedules say it may be possible.)
4. SCAP REVISES JAP SCHOOLS (Minister of Education ordered to prepare new texts, courses – all nationalistic teachers fired – all militaristic courses suspended.)
5. CHIANG'S SON ARRIVES IN MOSCOW (Chiang-Ku-Fuo, son of Chiang-Kai-Shek, visits Stalin to discuss Manchuria – Kremlin: Russians want peace in China.)
6. TRIALS REVEAL NAZI DISSENSION (Himmler & Goebbels were kicked out of Nazi Party for trying to seize control – Hitler had plans to continue the Party after defeat.)

FROM A 6-HOLER – BY ROADBLOCK GALL TOMAS: *(EDITOR'S NOTE: This pseudonym thing is getting out of hand. He has forgotten how to spell "Thomas".)*

```
RING IN THE NEW
   While New Yorkers jostle each other in Times
Square and merry-makers generally throughout the
world carry on the first peacetime New Year's fes-
tivities in too many years, Wakamatsu is morbidly
quiet under a newly fallen snow.
```

There's nothing out of the way in the manner the 3rd Battalion celebrated their seeing-in 1946.

Teakettle Blues starts in with a clean slate. Short-arms and showdown inspections characterized the program in many companies.

NEW YEAR'S CHEER

Any holiday that receives universal recognition in the States is an unusually bitter day for redeployed sweater-outers in the Fukushima area. Any holiday that is so universally in song and drink as that of New Years is really a raw dose.

Things were made little better by a last minute beer delivery. Each frothy mouthful of three-point-two was a bitter reminder of things that were – or things that might have been.

SUPPLEMENTARY BREW

For those of you who thought the only Stateside brew this side of the Pacific was brown stuff in cans, rest, our lot isn't as bad as all that. The big commissary in Yokohama announces that enterprising Coca-Cola manufacturers are going to make possible a bottle of Coke to every stranded GI in the islands of Nippon. Our tummy is already turning flip-flops for that maroon potion with the hourglass bottle.

(EDITOR'S NOTE: I haven't bothered to mention it until now, but for those of you reading in your sleep, yes, that is the same Fukushima where many years later the earthquake and tsunami created a huge nuclear power disaster, whose effects have since contaminated most of the Pacific Ocean and have now even reached the shores of the U.S.)

EDITORIAL:

As the last sands of 1945 dropped silently into the glass, there came from Moscow the first long-awaited signs of world accord. The conference of foreign ministers, which had been unable for so long to agree on the major issues of peace, at last found the common ground necessary for discussion.

One of the most hopeful signs for peace in Asia was the proposal of an advisory council in Washington to handle Far Eastern affairs, and a four-power commission in Tokyo to more democratically administer the Japanese problem. The question of foreign troops on Chinese soil was discussed, and there was complete accord on the part of the United States and Russia to withdraw all units as quickly as possible.

The great news, however, was the decision of the Big Three to form an international atomic control commission, for the purpose of giving the physicists of the world the necessary basis to rationally study the subject. While America will not immediately release the secret of atomic energy, certain phases of it will be at the disposal of the commission for research.

It would seem that out of the blood and suffering of the past few years, man has come to realize that in this atomic era it must be one world... or no world at all.

The success of the Moscow conference, indeed heralds a HAPPY NEW YEAR.

(EDITOR'S NOTE: As I read these pages, I am continually struck by the basic "goodness" of the people that produced this paper. When Tom Brokaw entitled his book about them "<u>The Greatest Generation</u>", he hit the nail on the head. The principles that they fought for were WORTH fighting for. The lack of cynicism, the integrity, the sacrifice, the unselfish pursuit of a better world are all breathtaking, when seen in the light of today's jungle of lies, greed and corruption. The naiveté of the above editorial may seem laughable now, but I find it inspiring and heart-warming in a way. If people like this were actually in charge of the world, how much better off would we be?)

HONSHU PIONEER – VOL I, NO. 95 – WAKAMATSU, JAPAN – JAN. 2, 1946

HEADLINES:
1. 'BAMA BEATS USC; A&M OVER ST. MARY'S (College football bowl results seem to be the most important news available today.)
2. 26,000 EXTRA BUNKS IN 8TH ARMY JANUARY QUOTA (It appears that shipping space is available for men with less than 50 points to leave in January, but so far no action is being taken to make this happen.)
3. TRUMAN APPOINTS BOARD TO STUDY STEEL STRIKE (Despite failure to make GMC reveal wartime profits, Truman appoints a 2nd board to study the steel strike that may idle 800,000 on Jan. 14, if they don't get the $2/hr. Wage hike they demand.)

EDITORIAL:

The article in last Sunday's Stars and Stripes, in which Miss Sharon Rogers vented her zealous fury at the personal relationships between GI's and Japanese women, didn't quite ring the bell.

Miss Rogers is the leader of an all-girl orchestra currently on tour in Japan, and as such she no doubt feels that any opinion offered by an exponent of "what the boys want to get home to" will be promptly heeded by the homesick dogface.

Specifically, it is the tootsie-wootsie relations that she so vehemently objects to, and she infers that all soldiers are cads, because back home the ladies are just wasting away awaiting their return. She even offers statistical proof, claiming that her girls date 75% soldiers. Who the other 25% associate with, and where Joe the war worker spends his evenings, she doesn't cover.

Miss Rogers states that she was utterly shocked upon learning the other day that she was playing in a VD ward, and on what she termed as "shacking up" she was particularly bitter, implying that it was too good for the Japanese women, and something to be hoarded for the joyous day of our homecoming.

It is public knowledge that traveling girl bands are not Campfire Girlish by nature, and we feel that in the case of Miss Rogers, an outraged sense of maidenly virtue was not tempered with discretion.

(EDITOR'S NOTE: Not wishing to take sides in this "skirmish of the sexes", I will admit that Miss Rogers must have fallen off the turnip truck rather recently if she thinks that a few hundred thousand young men, trapped far from home for months on end, with no females of their own race anywhere about, are not going to "shack up" with whatever local women make themselves available. Equally naive would be to expect that Japanese women, having lost huge numbers of their men during the war, and literally starving in its aftermath, would not be throwing themselves into the path of American GI's in great numbers. Having said that, I still find the "Campfire Girl" crack about all-girl bands to be uncalled for, sexist, and offensive.)

HONSHU PIONEER – VOL I, NO. 96 – WAKAMATSU, JAPAN – JAN. 3, 1946

HEADLINES:
1. HITLER AIDE BELIEVED FOUND (Missing since last April, and tried in absentia at Nuremberg, Martin Borman was picked up on a farm road near Ems.)
2. DUTCH INDIES ADMIRAL OUSTED (Admiral Helfrich had stated that Indonesian independence would menace peace in the Pacific. He was recalled by Premier Schermerhorn, who recently stated in London that he would welcome UN arbitration.)
3. G. BRITAIN, SIAM IN AGREEMENT (Siam makes small concessions – US helped scale back British demands, after Siam asked them to intercede.)
4. RUSS APPOINT GROMYKO TO FAR EAST COMMISSION (Believed to be a sign or USSR sincerity – Russian forces out of Manchuria by 2/1/46.)
5. HST SPEAKS TO US TOMORROW (Expected to promote Full Employment Act, Army-Navy Merger, and compulsory military training. His SOTU address on 1/13/46 to be televised for the first time ever.)
6. LAST LAUGH ON LORD HAW-HAW (William Joyce, known during the war as Lord Haw-Haw [English voice of Nazi Germany], will be hanged Tuesday morning as a traitor to Britain. His defense that he was not a British subject was not upheld.)

FROM A 6-HOLER – BY ROADBLOCK CEILING THOMAS, JR.:
ORIENTAL PRICE ADMINISTRATION
    Wakamatsu's tradesmen and merchants have learned to dread the name Oriental Price Administration. Two hundred shopkeepers thwart recalcitrant children

with the threat "The OPA will get you if you don't behave".

Throughout mercantile Wakamatsu the initials OPA mean business – mean continued business or no business at all.

A mighty man is the OPA agent. Calm, authoritative, of the highest integrity, he passes down out-of-the-way alleys, ever on the prowl for a yet undiscovered black market operator.

The words Oriental Price Administrator have leapt like Old Faithful through the hushed back streets of Wakamatsu.

"Your pipes are selling for nine yen, instead of the agreed-upon seven yen? Sorry, but I have no choice but to close your shop."

And the plaintive cries of the offending tradesman mean nothing to the not-to-be-trifled-with OPA investigator, who has heard this tale of woe before.

Should you begin to feel sorry for the carefully scrutinized shopkeeper, belay your tears. Every yen-thirsty merchant of Wakamatsu has been invited to participate in an OPA sponsored bazaar, where souvenirs of local craftsmanship from 50 sen lacquer ware to 600 yen kimonos will go on sale.

Two floors of a comparatively large store will be given over to cooperating merchants this Saturday.

(EDITOR'S NOTE: *It should be remembered that Americans had been living with wage and price controls, not to mention rationing, throughout the war. This OPA business might seem a bit* *heavy-handed, but it was no worse than what was happening back home.)*

EDITORIAL:

By now it should be quite clear that while the Pacific war was caused by the imperialistic aims of Japan's militarists, its prosecution would have been impossible without the support of the Japanese people. But to condemn the masses, who had only a superficial knowledge of Americans and were utterly ignorant of their underlying characteristics, is an injustice on our part, because they were unable either to discredit or contradict the assertions and insinuations of the military.

Today there is a splendid opportunity for the army permanently to cement Nippon-American relations through sponsored organizations designed to promote social and intellectual intercourse with the Japanese. To date we know of no such organization, but it would seem that individual relationship in kindred fields of interest, with the viewpoints of the individuals discussed on an equal basis, would go far in breaching the almost impassible chasm of nationalism. We suggest as a starting point, mixed study groups in the fields of art, music, literature, and language, with permission for the soldier to have healthy social contact within approved Japanese homes.

Diplomatic procedure has seldom impressed the masses, but the word of Pvt. Joe, who split a pot of tea with mama-san one night, will remain unchallenged.

HONSHU PIONEER – VOL I, NO. 97 – WAKAMATSU, JAPAN – JAN. 4, 1946

HEADLINES:
1. MAGIC CARPET CUT BY THIRD (Pacific fleet of 352 ships cut by 105 – reason: crews should have been out long ago – will not seriously affect Pacific vets getting home.)
2. COLLABORATION CHARGES HURLED AT PI GOV'T (Senate President Manuel Roxas, a suspected collaborator, to run for Philippines President – Alexander Uhl: US should punish collaborators and act to prevent return of a puppet regime to power.)
3. CRIME WAVE TERRORIZES JAPAN (Organized crime has become huge in Tokyo – 9 murders in 3 months – radical measures needed.)
4. ZAIBATSU FALSIFY REPORTS (Tokyo newspaper: Wealthy are whitewashing reports from Manchuria & Korea to clear themselves of blame for postwar chaos there.")
5. Approximately 10,000 GI's in China have been told that their return to the US will be delayed for an indefinite period.

EDITORIAL:

Tucked away in an obscure corner on Page 3 of the Nippon Times of January 1, is an article regarding the illegal hoarding of quantities of war materials by high Japanese officers of an air division formerly stationed in Shimonosaki. Just why the Times was reluctant in giving front page space to such obviously "hot news" has caused much discussion among readers of the article.

These materials, hoarded in direct violation of an Allied order to deliver such equipment to the Home Ministry, included 5 motorcycles, 21 radio sets with batteries, 139 parachutes, communication equipment, 27 cannons and 12,000 rounds of ammunition, vast supplies of powder and staple foodstuffs, and 110,000 yen in cash.

The manner in which the materials were cached in civilian houses of the neighborhood indicated a premeditated attempt to maintain some of Japan's war potential, yet the officers involved, after arrest and cross-examination on November 3 of last year, were released on December 20 to carry on the business of Japanese demobilization.

This paper regards the situation with extreme alarm, and suggests the possibility of a connection between the obvious "playing down" of an important news story by the press, and the release of these criminals to continue their subversive activities.

(EDITOR'S NOTE: One wonders whether the six-week investigation may have determined that these malefactors were merely black marketers, rather than a secret subversive group intending to fight another war, or stage an armed revolt against the new government. Whatever the case, it is certainly questionable why the whole affair was kept so quiet, as the editorial points out. I wonder if we are going to hear more about this incident in the future.)

HONSHU PIONEER – VOL I, NO. 99 – WAKAMATSU, JAPAN – JAN. 5, 1946

HEADLINES:
1. TRUMAN CALLS FOR ACTION ON STRIKES, JOBS – ASKS PEOPLE TO SPUR CONGRESS ON IMPORTANT BILLS (Sen. Johnson [D-Col] calls on President to use his wartime powers until Congress can act.)
2. CHIANG STUDIES YENAN REPLY (4-point Communist proposal "being discussed" - Democratic League accuses Chiang of delaying peace and "undemocratic methods".)
3. MAC PURGES LAST JAP WAR HAWKS (MacArthur orders Japanese Diet to oust all who aided the war effort – calls on American educators to come to Japan and help remodel schools along non-military lines.)
4. Army & Navy: Atomic bomb tests will be made on Japanese & American ships.
5. CNS NEWS FROM THE STATES (Cost of living up 33% for everyday goods – 6 million to be unemployed by spring – Price controls choking auto production – All POW's to be withdrawn from US work force – Gov't has $10 billion worth of ships to get rid of.)
6. WELL STOCKED PX OPENS TODAY (Most items limited to 1 per customer – Boycott of local merchants will probably end tomorrow.)

FROM A 6-HOLER – BY ROADBLOCK DELONG THOMAS:
```
PLANS AND TRAINING
   Convention and organization are jeopardizing
progress of the United States Ground Forces.
   The development of the atomic bomb, the ap-
plication of radar and jet propulsion are making
```

ridiculous advancement in other fields of Army endeavor.

In 1919 those doughboys who had the misfortune to be caught in demobilization snarls occupied their day hours with classes on Interior Guard and Care & Cleaning of the '03. Twenty-seven years later GI's in the same unfortunate position are spending their time doing the same sort of thing their fathers did.

The question is: Has war technology advanced so far over war plans and training (as integral a part of the Army as the A-bomb) that G3 must resort to the same thing they did in 1919?

The solution to the problem is to make the most of training facilities they have on hand.

We're in Japan. Japan declared war on the United States. It is important to the citizen of the United States and to a prospective citizen of a family of nations to know what goes on in a country that has been such a menace to the world.

Prophylaxis and the prevention of war should now be the consideration of everyone, and not the care of a weapon used by an army in a war already won.

Let the men of the occupation study Japan at first hand, not by closeting them in Americanized army barracks with a musty outdated field manual, but let them out into Japan, where they can see for themselves the forces which contributed to the most devastating war in the world's history.

What a significant democratizing potential could be realized by the release of 500,000 barracks-confined occupees. Half a million men who had the benefit of spending from twenty to twenty-five years in the most completely free nation in the world would be a far better advertisement for democracy than the prosecution of a few obscure war criminals.

The people of Japan should be made to see how Americans live and act, that they might realize a life entirely within their grasp.

(EDITOR'S NOTE: Whoa! Does anyone see a potential downside to turning loose 500,000 soldiers to mingle freely with people they were trying to kill (and vice versa) just a few months back? What could possibly go wrong? I believe that this entire column is one big deadpan joke, although it starts out sounding like a serious critique of Army training procedures. He knows perfectly well that this is an absurd suggestion, and wonders if anyone will take him seriously. If anyone did, I suspect that Hanratty heard from them the same day.)

EDITORIAL:

The failure of the Allies in assuming the responsibility of directing Italy along the lines of democracy, is in our opinion a glaring example of international lethargy.

Today in starving and impoverished Italy, the era of the dictatorship is becoming by comparison "the good old days". It is no longer a case of ideological principles for the great mass of Italians, but the pressing question of liberty versus food. It is true that Italy is free, but in the homes of Naples and Milan free men are starving. In the streets boys are stealing and looting and girls are selling themselves for a crust of bread.

WE ASK, where are the principles of the United Nations and the UNRA? And where are the builders of world peace, who spoke so glibly of a family of nations?

WE'LL TELL YOU WHERE THEY ARE.

They are busy putting the ideals of peace on worthless bits of paper, while at the same time pursuing a policy of international laissez-faire. They are sitting behind mahogany tables dreaming up new ideas of how the world should be run, while right now a part of that world is dying.

Italy has put aside the bloody black shirt of fascism and is now rummaging among her rags, but some say she may again put it on, exclaiming, "This time it will deliver me from my woes".

(EDITOR'S NOTE: Although I have visited Italy several times, both on business and as a tourist, I do not have a deep understanding of her politics. However, I have the distinct impression that democracy, as we understand it in the U.S., is a foreign concept there, and that organized crime plays a somewhat more significant role than it does in the U.S., unless you include large international corporations in your definition of organized crime.)

HONSHU PIONEER – VOL I, NO. 100 – WAKAMATSU, JAPAN – JAN. 6, 1946

HEADLINES:
1. CHINA ARMISTICE SIGNED (Chiang and Mao sign armistice, ending civil war in China – neither side will interfere with railways – Gen. Marshall acting as arbitrator.)
2. DEMOB. SLOW-DOWN ASKED (Gen. Collins: Lack of re-enlistments means men must be kept overseas – 3-month delay should be worst case.)
3. JAVA FIGHTS; PEACE NEAR (Dutch forces in Java to execute 344 political prisoners – fighting continues near Soerbaja – Dutch ex-Governor appeals for independence of all colonies of all nations.)
4. JAP MERCHANTS FEEL OPA WHIP (Citing failure to delete luxury tax, OPA orders all stores with GI clientele to cease operations until all OPA directives are agreed to.)

SUNDAY SUPPLEMENT
Lost in the RICE LATITUDES – THE SECOND OF 378 ARTICLES BY A CELEBRATED AUTHORITY ON JAPAN. NEXT WEEK: BIACCO

• **A. D. THOMAS** •

EARL CARROL'S AND SAM GOLDWYN'S conception of an Oriental dance is not received enthusiastically at the Studio of Far Eastern Dance, Uwi-Gawa, Tokyo.

The Tokyo dance studio run by Mr. Kyonoshi Wagashima and his wife have on their staff a group of purists, when it comes to Japanese dance.

Mr. Wagashima feels that dances by Betty Grable, Eleanor Powell and Ann Miller are misrepresenting the hallowed institution of the Oriental dance.

It's not the brevity of the costume worn by the Hollywood danseuse that causes Mr. Wag so much concern – it's this business of debasing art for expediency.

Mrs. Wagashima is even more outspoken on the subject of American "Nautch" girls. "It's a prostitution of art," says the old girl.

In consideration for the concern shown by this quaint old couple, here is the real low-down on the business of the Japanese dance.

The Japanese are old hands at the dance game. There are records of the Japs dancing around their rude huts and caves back when Buddhist missionaries were converting the people in 300 AD.

The cavorting around fires was only a prelude for things to follow.

When the missionaries began converting the heathen Jap, they decided to liven up their ministry with a little dance routine. But you know how ministers are when they unbend – they only enter into the frivolity half-heartedly.

The dance that developed out of the missionaries' teachings has come to be called No drama.

The name No drama is rather paradoxical, since the participants put on more of a drama than they do a dance.

Each movement, gesture and grimace is symbolic, and the whole thing moves slowly for the Western observer who is accustomed to the voluptuous bouncings of scantily clad cuties.

There is more than one kind of dance put out by No dramatists. They are: Dengaku and Kagura.

Both dances, however, are conventional and unclimactic. The Columbia Encyclopedia says they are "highly stylized... its keynote is harmony - the harmony of movement, music and expression."

The dances at best are pantomime of static nature. The Japanese Terpsichores have a tree dance, a lake dance, a mountain dance; but snake dances, fire dances require too fast and furious a pace for the Oriental.

Secular dancing in Nippon has been the first calling of all the nicer Geisha girls. The Geisha girls have been partially successful in livening up the old feudalistic Kagura and Dengaku. The wrinkles the Geisha have given the dance are still a far cry from jitterbugging or even ballet.

The United States occupation will do a lot toward bringing the Jap dancer out of his institutionalized church and put him on the stage.

(EDITOR'S NOTE: Oh dear! This is a completely new type of column for Dad. He apparently sets out to actually educate his readers about a serious aspect of Japanese culture, and then throws in a bunch of total nonsense, so you can't tell truth from fiction, and you would probably conclude that he made the whole thing up, as usual. Here he is apparently deliberately [and somewhat humorously] misleading his readers about the actual nature of Noh.

A few facts about the classical Japanese dance theater, called "Noh": It started in the 14th Century – not 300 AD – and missionaries had nothing to do with it. Only men may perform, using masks for female roles. There are about 250 highly codified plays that may be performed. Traditionally, several are performed in a sequence that may last all day. It was based on earlier folk dance forms, one of which was indeed called "Dengaku". It has nothing whatever to do with social dancing. Most Geishas were trained in dance, but, of course, could not dance in Noh dramas, being female.

"The Nautch Girl – or the Rajah of Chutneypore" was a comic opera from the late 19th Century, which had an Oriental setting, much in the style of Gilbert and Sullivan's "Mikado". Nautch girls were popular dancing girls in northern India, who performed scantily clad.)

HONSHU PIONEER – VOL I, NO. 101 – WAKAMATSU, JAPAN – JAN. 7, 1946

HEADLINES:
1. SOLONS, NATION, GIS – **PROTEST SLOWDOWN** (Congress, citizens, families of GI's and GI's themselves all outraged at "poor management by the Army" slowing the return of overseas troops.)
2. NEHRU PREDICTS INDIA REVOLT (Nehru: When Indian Congress reconvenes, now that the war is over, it will take up its campaign for Indian independence again.)
3. REIGN OF TERROR IN POLAND (Premier Morawski: Terrorist acts in Poland are being fomented by Gen. Anders, former commander of the Polish Army.)

FROM A 6-HOLER – BY ROADBLOCK DELONG THOMAS:

```
1 ACT PLAY
  Scene: The gentleman's room of the Pentagon
Building, first floor.
  Time: The present
  Characters: Brig. Gen. Warren P. Pancretius
and Col. Mortimer Frost
  WARREN: (Drying his hands before an automatic
dryer) There are still quite a number of troops
over in Japan, aren't there, Mort?
  MORT: (doing the same with his hands) Well,
sir, I should suppose there would be the custom-
ary number.
  WARREN: Howzat? The customary number, you say?
  MORT: Yes sir, you know, whatever is necessary
for the interest of the United States and the
preservation of peace.
```

WARREN: I don't want you to think I'm pinning you down, Mort, but I have to turn in a report to the old man next week on the number of troops in Japan. Oh, say, Mort, while we're in the wash room there's no reason for you to address me as sir.

MORT: That's very decent of you General, and as for the exact number, I should say it is around six or eight brigades, you know how it is.

WARREN: Thanks, old man. Could you tell me what sort of duties the troops of the occupation have?

MORT: They serve as sentinels for a watchful and reawakened America and as the personal envoys of the United States for the democratization of Japan.

WARREN: Thanks, old man. I'm glad of this opportunity to talk with you and get the real lowdown on the story of the Japanese occupation.

(EDITOR'S NOTE: Just good clean fun, at the expense of a couple of clueless [and imaginary] officers.)

EDITORIAL:

For the last day and a half, we have been trying to figure out the angle on the Army's announcement to slow down demobilization by fifty percent because of the difficulty in getting overseas replacements. Now there must have been a good reason for such a reversal in policy: it's just that we like to keep abreast of such interesting little tidbits of news as wars, demobilization, etc.

Maybe it is because Congress believes it has reduced the number of long-term servicemen overseas to a point where they are no longer a large enough group to be a political menace.

<u>Maybe</u> some new "obstacle" was encountered, making it impossible to send replacements for occupational troops as quickly as they were sent to combat zones.

<u>Maybe</u> public-spirited pressure groups are needling Congress to keep the peach-fuzzed eighteen-year-olds and the ex-war workers away from the evil influence of the Army.

<u>Maybe</u> the Army, in discharging its <u>low-point excess in the States</u>, believes it has won civilian popularity.

OR MAYBE, JUST MAYBE, IT IS TOO MUCH TROUBLE TO DRAFT, TRAIN, EQUIP AND TRANSPORT REPLACEMENTS, WHO IN TURN ONLY WOULD HAVE TO BE RETRANSPORTED TO THE STATES IN A FEW MONTHS TO UNDERGO THE COMPLICATED PROCESS OF DEMOBILIZATION.

(EDITOR'S NOTE: Sounds a bit angry, doesn't he? However, I believe he hit the nail on the head, and is just sick of all the obfuscation and prevarication coming from official channels.)

HONSHU PIONEER – VOL I, NO. 102 – WAKAMATSU, JAPAN – JAN. 8, 1946

HEADLINES:
1. **MANILA GI'S IN PROTEST MARCH** – DEMONSTRATORS ASSAIL PATTERSON, BRASS HATS (Over 2,500 GI's marched into Manila City Hall to protest the demobilization slow-down. Later MP's broke up a 2nd march on General Scyer's HQ.)
2. MARSHALL TO MEDIATE WAR (Gen. Marshall to preside over a 3-man commission to meet next week to arrange a cease-fire in the Chinese civil war.)
3. ARMY SAYS INF MOST DANGEROUS (Analysis of Okinawa casualty numbers shows 87 out of every 100 were infantrymen. 1 of 2 infantrymen became casualties, and 1 of 4 died. It was 10 times more dangerous to be in the Infantry than in the Artillery.)
4. SOLON SCORES BRITISH LOANS UNRAA AID (Rep. Reid Murray [Wisc]: No aid should be given to nations carrying on "Imperialistic wars to destroy humanity" - specifically Britain – to make "bombs and bullets to take the lives of innocent people".)

(EDITOR'S NOTE: Re. #4: I was unaware that such protests against our closest ally were taking place at this time, but I am in complete agreement with Rep. Murray, and I suspect that the editors of the <u>Honshu Pioneer</u> were as well, since they put this story on the front page.)

EDITORIAL:

```
   Today China is in a state of chaos.
   The shooting war between the Communist and
Nationalist forces has stopped, but there is
```

still a lot of war within the tattered boundaries of China.

It's a bitter war, too, complete with secret police, terroristic censorship, and jails filled with political prisoners.

So far things have been all in favor of the Generalissimo, but the whole situation appears to be dangerously bizarre when one considers that the Chinese people understand and accept the iron fisted methods used by the Nationalists in suppressing their opposition. After nearly fifteen years of fighting, the Chinese still look upon the Communist-Nationalist friction not as a major political issue affecting them and their country, but as a fight between rival political gangs.

In the past, US Far Eastern policy has never been too firm, and the recent State Dept.-Murray fracas ended without any visible results, but through it, it has become apparent that peace in China is almost as necessary to us as it is to the Chinese.

The avowed purpose of the Marshall mission to referee the dispute and end the civil war, will, if successful, again put the US in its announced position of leading the world to peace.

HONSHU PIONEER – VOL I, NO. 104 – WAKAMATSU, JAPAN – JAN. 10, 1946

HEADLINES:
1. **TRUMAN LAUDS DEMOBILIZATION** – DEMOBILIZATION IS SPEEDY IN FACE OF OVERSEAS NEED (President Truman, responding to a flood of telegrams and protests: This is happening as fast as possible "with justice to all concerned".)
2. YENAN ACCUSES CHIANG OF TRUCE VIOLATIONS (Peace negotiations postponed pending verification charges that Central troops have refused to lay down arms.)
3. 97TH GUARDS KILL JAP THUGS (2 killed, 3 wounded trying to break into boxcars filled with food intended for the Japanese people – Guards commended.)
4. SENATOR JOHNSON BLASTS OVERLY OCCUPIED ZONES (Johnson [D-Colo.]: Slow-down is unnecessary – Congress should investigate need for occupation troops.)
5. SMALLPOX CLAIMS SIX (31 GI's in Korea diagnosed with smallpox – 6 have died.)

EDITORIAL:

In the Comment and Query column of yesterday's <u>Stars and Stripes</u>, Chaplain Edmund P. Kielty publicized certain declarations made by the 24th Division Chief of Staff, regarding The Army Educational Program.

The declarations were as follows:

(1) Enlisted men haven't the mental stature to understand world problems and never will. It is useless to try to inform them.

(2) Asking E.M. What they want to study under A.E.F. Is "bunk". We'll train them for our job

shortages. We'll get our work out of them. Their civilian future is no concern of ours.

We answer this man, whoever and wherever he is, with another declaration. This declaration was not conceived in the cesspool of fascism and disseminated for the perpetuation of an unjust caste system, but came into being as the unanimous expression of the principles by which Americans have lived – and died – since 1776:

"We hold these truths to be self-evident, that all men are created equal, that they are endowed by their creator with certain inalienable rights, that among these are life, liberty and the pursuit of happiness."

(From Declaration of Independence, Thos. Jefferson, 1776)

Times have changed since Jefferson soldiered.

(EDITOR'S NOTE: This report beggars belief. My hope is that Chaplain Kielty, if this is indeed what he said, was taking considerable liberties with the actual words spoken by the unnamed Chief of Staff, in an attempt to attract attention to a perceived problem. I can't imagine any senior officer, no matter how hard-boiled by the war, defending or even tolerating statements such as those.)

HONSHU PIONEER – VOL I, NO. 105 – WAKAMATSU, JAPAN – JAN. 11, 1946

HEADLINES:
1. **EXCESS GI'S TO GO – IKE** (In an apparent response to protests, Eisenhower orders all occupation commanders to immediately release all non-essential troops to the US. - High-pointers to be given preference – 840,000 Pacific troops to be cut to 375,000 by May instead of July – discharges down to 2½ years in April, 2 years in June.)
2. NO FREEDOM, SAY S&S MEN (26 enlisted men sign statement that <u>Stars and Stripes</u> has become a War Dept. organ, after GI's letter is censored by officer in charge.)
3. PHONE STRIKE MUZZLES NATION (50 phone companies in 32 states shut down – strikes are in sympathy with American Communications Association strike.)
4. SENATOR ASKS WACS BE KEPT (Sen. Thomas [D-Utah]: Up to 6,000 volunteers should be kept in the regular Army - "They are a Godsend.")
5. ASK AIR MAIL COST CUT (Air transport spokesman asks for 5¢ per ounce vs. 8¢.)

FROM A 6-HOLER – BY LESH-SHELLABWATER THOMAS:

```
HAPPY SINNEN-ENKAI
   No people are so holidayily blessed as those
whose home is Japan.
```

Any labor union in Japan conducting a strike to have all holidays off would laugh collective bargaining out of the picture. The laborers would spend more time feting various and sundry holidays than they would attending their place of business.

Yesterday was Fair day, and in the eyes of Wakamatsuites as much a holiday as Labor Day in ours.

The Japanese have made a fetish of holidays, and anyone who wanted to take the trouble could find a holiday in progress in some sector of Japan every day of the year.

For a start the Japanese begin the year by celebrating Siho-hai (or erecting of pine tree fete); on Jan 3rd the Japanese observe Gensi-sai (or drinking of Toso sake fete); the Shinnen-Enkai is a holiday pretty much reserved for the Imperial family, but there's nothing against carrying on a private celebration of your own.

Anyone who hit on the Holiday Inn idea in Japan would have their hostelry so often filled with guests that it would be necessary to set them up as permanent residents.

Our favorite holiday, though, is the Kawa-Biraki (or River Fete), "an ancient festival, held on the water usually on the third Saturday of July. It has no religious significance, being merely designed to attract people to the river to enjoy the cool evening breezes..."

That's the spirit, no pretense – just another day for which work can be knocked off.

(EDITOR'S NOTE: I can find nothing about "Siho-hai", but the other holidays mentioned are quite legitimate and accurately described [more or less] – very unusual for Dad. You may have even seen videos of "Kawa-Biraki" [or Kawabiraki], famous for its beautiful floating lanterns drifting down the river in the dark. "Holidayily" is a

nice word, don't you think? English dictionaries may have been in short supply in Wakamatsu.)

EDITORIAL:

We got a good paper in Europe. It was called Stars and Stripes.

The name became a legend as an honest expression of the men... no holds barred.

When we arrived in the Pacific, we found out we were going to have an S&S there, too. We expected something pretty good, because we had a lot of gripes. We figured they'd be taken care of.

The first copy puzzled us a little, though. The Pacific S&S looked like a glorified news sheet drawing its ration from 8th Army I&E.

But the paper got a little better and they started a column called COMMENT AND QUERY.

Then we found the trouble.

The boys on the paper knew who was getting the raw deal, but they weren't allowed to print it. They were not censored, they were stepped on.

Last night, over WVTR, Tokyo, the guys in the Pacific found out how Col. J.B. Parks, Jr., officer in charge, had kept his staff from printing WHAT THEY KNEW TO BE THE TRUTH.

In a blanket accusal, 26 members of the editorial staff charged, over the radio, that Parks suppressed letters from GI's to COMMENT AND QUERY and deliberately distorted the issue of demobilization; adding that S&S had never been a free press, but merely an organ of the War Dept.

We insist, along with our fellow journalists of S&S, that such an important voice in Pacific affairs should have complete freedom of expression.

(EDITOR'S NOTE: Once again, I am impressed by the moral courage demonstrated by these guys [and apparently by some of their superior officers]. Censorship of a military newspaper would hardly be newsworthy in today's world, but these fellows were clearly outraged by it. It is interesting to see how much bigger the <u>Stars and Stripes</u> staff was. I assume the format their paper was also much bigger than the <u>Honshu Pioneer</u>.

Unfortunately, the same kind of censorship may be awaiting this paper, and it would not surprise me to learn that this particular editorial was the straw that broke the camel's back, with its direct attack on a Colonel, by name. As much as I admire their courage and integrity, calling out a senior officer by name and in print seems foolhardy and even arrogant to me, and almost certain to have consequences.)

HONSHU PIONEER – VOL I, NO. 106 – WAKAMATSU, JAPAN – JAN. 12, 1946

HEADLINES:
1. **CONGRESS INVESTIGATES DEMOB** (Special panel of Senate Military Committee asks Eisenhower for a complete review – War Dept. has broken its promise that 2-year men would be out by March – Protests are "near Mutiny".)
2. CHIANG OK'S COMMUNISTS (Final cease fire order issued – Chiang: All political parties to be legalized, including Communists, and "four freedoms" to be honored.)
3. BOARD AGREES TO WAGE HIKE (Fact-Finding Board recommends 19½¢ per hour wage hike in 50-day-old GM strike – Will either side agree?)

EDITORIAL:

The demolization SNAFU still has most of us on the ropes. The rumors are coming hot and fast, so take time to analyze them. And that goes for the news releases too, which in most cases turn out to be War Department or theater command "snow jobs".

Take for instance the latest figures offered by General Eisenhower. They state that the occupational strength in the Pacific at this time is 840,000, and that by May it will be cut to 375,000. It was further announced that to meet this schedule 30,000 fresh troops would have to arrive here every month.

Up to now it doesn't look too bad, does it? Well... take another look and then sharpen your pencils and do a little figuring. The 375,000 figure represents 44% of the troops in this theater at present. If replacements arrive for five months at a rate of 30,000 a month, there will be a 39% turnover of the minimum 44%... and we just don't think there will be the needed 225,000 over and above the replacements.

So, why not pick out the lowest of the low right now, and send the rest home on the first available ships. American policy in the East has already been formulated, and we hardly feel that it is likely to change within the next few months. If 375,000 soldiers can do this job in May, when things should obviously be better organized, they can do it RIGHT NOW.

(EDITOR'S NOTE: While I certainly sympathize with everyone's desire to get home as soon as possible, the logic of that final paragraph escapes me. If things will be better organized in May, wouldn't that be an argument that more troops might be needed before then?)

HONSHU PIONEER – VOL I, NO. 107 – WAKAMATSU, JAPAN – JAN. 13, 1946

HEADLINES:
1. **MIDPAC POINTS CUT** (Armed Forces Radio: All men in Pacific Theater [except for Japan] with 48 points or 38 months proceed immediately to Replacement Depots to be sent to the States. - Sec'y Patterson: 400,000 to be sent home by May 1, regardless of number of replacements sent – Further action from our command believed imminent.)
2. LABOR NEGOTIATIONS FAIL (700,000 steel workers to strike tonight – GM rejects Fact-Finding Board proposal.)
3. BIG 5 DISAGREE AT UNO MEET (Split is over non-permanent members of the Security Council – vote may be postponed – Soviet to head A-Bomb committees)
4. GI PAPER CHARGES PRESS INTERFERENCE (Staff of the <u>Daily Pacifican</u>, GI paper in Manila, report that a new officer has arrived in their office to delete any articles that might reflect poorly on the War Department.)

FROM A 6-HOLER – BY THUNDERHUG THOMAS:

```
HOUSING CONDITIONS
   Landlords and real estate men should not be
given much trouble by prospective home buyers who
have spent any amount of time with the forces of
occupation.

   Maybe we've lost a discriminating taste for
homes, but the most exacting GI can't fail but be
impressed by a promise lavish enough to include
inside toilets and radiators in every room.

   The first question put to anyone fortunate enough
to get away from Wakamatsu on whatever kind of
pretense (pass or hospital sojourn in Niigata)
```

is: do the bowls flush; and are there radiators? You might expect them to ask about shrines or scenery, but we're products of an age of central heating and flushable toilets – caught in a world inhabited by North Japan primates.

ROUND THE WORLD WITH A CAN OF NUTS

The redeployed 97th Division has circled better than half the world, has been stationed on three different continents within four months time, and for all the shifting scenes one item has managed to tag along with a lot of persistence, and that is the familiar red or blue can of Mr. Planter's peanuts.

Wherever the 97th goes, Planter's Peanuts go too. From a breakdown of "200" rations, from the shelves of orderly Stateside PX's, from behind the wicker cages of Ship's Stores the Planter's can stares out with a mocking leer, as much as to say, "Too bad you can't dodge our haunting familiarity, but I'm going where you go. Try and get rid of me."

(EDITOR'S NOTE: Whoa. "North Japan primates"? I have watched enough 1940's cartoons to know that the general American view of the Japanese during that time was as sub-human "monkeys" or worse [not an unusual way to characterize the enemy in any war, of course], but somehow I was not prepared to hear that view from my father. In later life he was anything but a racist, and was usually pretty careful to speak respectfully of just about everybody. But again, I guess I have to try to transport my mind to a different time, place and situation.)

STATESIDE – BY A. HAMBURGER:
CLARIFICATION

The <u>New York Times</u>, which many herald as the world's greatest and best newspaper, is betraying the faith so many GI's have in it as a purveyor of "All the News That's Fit to Print".

Overseas GI's are the potential unemployed which the Government speaks of when it warns of six to eight million jobless by Spring.

The Times has had a subtle campaign going over the recent months, in which it complained about the "too speedy demobilization" in its editorial and feature columns.

Hanson Baldwin, its military expert, at first expressed great concern lest the US become too weak to conduct any major campaigns. Of course, it was not exactly clear just what such a campaign would consist of, at the very moment the world was seeking ways to get together on a way to peace. Hanson did hint that we should protect our financial interests in China and in any other corner of the earth where his friends might have invested some money.

Two weeks ago, the Times revealed some very interesting information, which may or may not have some bearing on the recently announced slowdown.

Although not disclosing exactly whom it was speaking for, the Times stated that the troops now overseas and still in the Army should be kept there. There were no jobs to be had, and they would only become an additional burden on the state. Therefore, why all this rush to demobilize the Army, which is the only secure place these future unemployed can be housed, fed and controlled most cheaply and effectively?

(EDITOR'S NOTE: At last we see in print some arguments favoring the slowdown of demobilization. How important these arguments may have been to decision-makers at the time is hard to judge [for me, anyway], but I have learned over the years that trusting the "official" versions and explanations of events and decisions is very risky.)

HONSHU PIONEER – VOL I, NO. 108 – WAKAMATSU, JAPAN – JAN. 14, 1946

HEADLINES:

1. **MAC ORDERS BUNKS FILLED** – MEN WITH 38 MONTHS OR 48 POINTS NOW ELIGIBLE (No ship to leave with an empty berth – Excess troops to be sent home regardless of points – Panama Canal to be used to relieve West Coast congestion.)
2. IKE PROMISES DEMOB SPEED (Warns Canadian audience of post-war pitfalls – Blames Army unrest over demobilization on discord in the States – Promises to return troops as fast as possible.)
3. GI TO DIE FOR CHRISTMAS EVE MURDER (Killed 2 Japanese civilians while drunk on Christmas Eve – Was to be sent home on points Christmas Day.)
4. CIO POSTPONES STEEL STRIKE (Pres. Truman orders 700,000 back to work, pending negotiations – Fact-Finding Board to propose a compromise solution.)
5. HALF A MILLION DRAFT DODGERS (FBI has investigated 525,756 draft violations – 12,789 convictions so far – sentences total over 34,000 years.)

EDITORIAL:

A world unorganized for peace is a world continually on the red side of the ledger. When confronted by lawless and deliberate aggression, even the most peaceful nations must defend their sovereignty by the total mobilization of all their resources, and this costs money... staggering sums of money.

Although the actual cost cannot be computed, because as yet no one has dared stand before mankind and put a price tag on human life, certain figures are available, which show the tremendous dissipation of property and resources that came as a result of this war.

Up to January 1945, the total cost of World War II was 730 billion dollars, of which 270 billion, or 39%, came from the pockets of U.S. taxpayers. This figure alone is greater than the combined cost for all countries participating in the first World War.

The figure appears even more overwhelming when viewed in the light of how far it would have gone toward building a better America. It would have paid for the operation of every school and university for 60 years – cost free education for three generations of Americans, built 7 million miles of paved roads, and constructed 44,625,000 six-room houses – a private home for every three persons in the land. All of this plus a 1 million dollar hospital in each of the 3,073 counties of the United States, is what we could have had. This paper figures peace as a GOOD BUSINESS DEAL.

(EDITOR'S NOTE: My hat is off to the writer of this piece, which I admire more than I can say. I did not check his math, and, of course, he may have obtained these calculations from elsewhere, but calculators were not available, so somebody did some serious pencil pushing. The 1945 dollar was worth $12.90 in 2013 currency, so the U.S. portion of this bill would have been 3 and a half TRILLION dollars. As of this writing, we have spent at least 4 trillion dollars in Iraq and Afghanistan [according to Brown University], on top of the base military budget of over 1 trillion per year, when

debt interest, veterans benefits, etc. are all included. The way I see it, the U.S. is spending more on the military now than we did in World War II, adjusted for inflation. This 1946 editorial reminds us of what we are giving up to maintain that spending.)

HONSHU PIONEER – VOL I, NO. 109 – WAKAMATSU, JAPAN – JAN. 15, 1946

HEADLINES:

1. CHARGE ARMY MISUSES TROOPS AND PROPERTY (Soldiers tell Senate Committee that good gear was burned at Batangas base on Luzon – charges immediately denied by officials – soldiers promise to produce 1,000 affidavits.)
2. UNION ACCEPTS TRUMAN'S FACT BOARD PROPOSAL (UAW votes to accept wage hike of 19½¢ - must be accepted by GM before 1/21/46, or 30% demand returns.)
3. ASK ABOLITION OF PRIVILEGE (500 soldiers met in Paris to demand ouster of Sec'y of War Patterson and end of all special privileges for officers.)
4. REDS OPTIMISTIC ON CHINA FUTURE (Troops on both sides laying down arms.)
5. SCAP OK'S JAP ELECTIONS (National elections authorized any time after 3/15/46.)

FROM A 6-HOLER – BY A. HOP-KISSED THOMAS:

FROM A JAPANESE HOP

It's not quite the same. Whatever the grains, whatever the care in preparation, the stuff that flows from the big drab brown bottle to be had in the PX is a far cry from the foamy liquid on tap and in bottles in the United States.

Each bottle here tastes as if it were designed to make the lonely tippler here sign the pledge: – sign the pledge to buy American. But pledges don't mean much to the not-so-stalwart lads of the Army of Occupation.

When the walls begin to close in on a man, and the days and nights begin to be one long day of guard-walking, brew is brew.

When General Order Number Six, point-adding and calendar-watching become one endless jumble of snow and soggy hotcakes, we'd be the last ones in the world to inquire as to whether our particular tank of brew bore the kiss of the hops.

When the cold Northern blast bounces off the PX door, and the arguments of the group huddled about the fire get louder and louder, Mr. Suzuki's stuff does the job as well as any. It would be hardly fitting and proper to question whether that particular brand was the one that made Wakamatsu famous.

So drink up, me lads, and we'll buy the next one. If you're not thirsty, pass it on to your buddy. They say it spoils with the cap off.

EDITORIAL:

In Manila yesterday, the rumblings over Army misadministration became a roar. Led by Sgt. Emil Macey, a committee of nine EM representing 175,000 troops in the Luzon area charged that:

1. Army officials at Batangas Luzon burned great quantities of usable shoes, blankets and clothing.

2. That thousands of unneeded troops HAD BEEN, and WERE BEING retained in the Philippines.

In answer to charge one, the base officials said that the equipment was mildewed beyond salvage. To charge two they gave an emphatic no.

However, Sgt. Macey, a former official of the CIO, revealed that if he were granted congressional immunity from Army courts martial, he was prepared to submit 1,000 sworn affidavits from men of the base to bear out the charges, plus evidence that the railway battalion was being held as potential strike breakers against four native unions.

In the past this paper has taken a stand against the misuse of government property by Army officials. In that respect our policy remains unchanged, but to us this case of settling inter-Philippine affairs smells of economic imperialism.

The American Army is a democratic institution. It is the will of the American people as they strive toward a lasting world peace.

It is not, and we hold that it never shall be, a tool of big business and power politics.

(EDITOR'S NOTE: Those last two paragraphs should make modern readers wince and shudder. Again, one almost hopes the writer did not live long enough to see how far we have drifted from his ideals. I am sure he meant "democratic institution" in the sense that the Army is intended to be under civilian control, and since we are [theoretically] a democracy, that means democratic control. He could not have meant that the Army itself is a democracy.)

HONSHU PIONEER – VOL I, NO. 110 – WAKAMATSU, JAPAN – JAN. 16, 1946

HEADLINES:
1. CONGRESS TO HEAR IKE, NIMITZ ON DEMOBILIZATION (Sen. Johnson: GI complaints against the slowdown are justified – Ike & Nimitz to speak informally.)
2. 1,000 TROOPS MEET WITH WAR SEC'Y IN SHANGHAI (Patterson arrived yesterday – troops want specifics of demobilization policy.)
3. NATIONWIDE G.E. STRIKE THREAT (200,000 workers demand 16¢ more per hour- 75 plants in 16 states would be affected.)
4. SOLONS TO PRESS FACT BILL (Waiting for GM is respond, 2 Senators press for immediate action – Walter Reuther: Truman should force GM to accept.)

EDITORIAL:

Last night after his tenth beer, Pvt. Joe got philosophical on the question of world peace. "Always gotta be wars", he said. "people is greedy. It just ain't in the cards... all this world peace stuff."

Well spoken Joe. We can see that while your buddies were dying in an attempt to create a decent society, you were giving a lot of serious thought to the question. You're a thinker Joe, and that's what we like about you. You always keep an open mind.

Yes... it's open all right – open for all the poison that you hear and read every day to seep in... and twist and distort the real meaning of what you fought for. Open so that the many unscrupulous veterans organizations which wrap themselves in the American flag and promise jobs, government bonds, and just about everything for nothing in an attempt to get power, can enroll you as a member in good standing.

But sooner or later your beery defeatism will catch up with your son, Joe. It will catch him, and at some remote spot on this earth... it will kill him.

Right has just won a great victory over the dark forces of evil, but as yet they have not been entirely destroyed. They lie in waiting, ready at the first sign of weakness to poison again the lives of free men.

We don't profess to know all there is about world peace, but we do know that there is no choice. Peace is an indivisible thing. We must have one world, or no world at all.

We'll drink a beer with you any time at all Joe, but let's make up our minds right now that we're going to drink it in a free and peaceful world.

(EDITOR'S NOTE: I feel stupid that it took so long, but I had a small epiphany reading this one. The 97th was an Infantry Division. They fought valiantly in Germany before being sent to Japan. Large numbers of them were wounded or killed. <u>Of course</u> they had to believe that it was worth it, and that the world had been permanently changed for the better. This little "dialogue" is intriguing because both sides were correct, in a way. Pvt. Joe's prediction about future wars of greed has come true many times. The author's prediction about Joe's son dying in Vietnam [or wherever] also came true many times, I'm sure.)

HONSHU PIONEER – VOL I, NO. 111 – WAKAMATSU, JAPAN – JAN. 17, 1946

HEADLINES:
1. **IKE REVEALS DEMOB PLAN** – SOLONS' OPINION DIVIDED AFTER INFORMAL TALK (Ike: further GI demonstrations are pointless – All men with 45 points or 30 months to be out by 4/30/46; 40 points or 24 months by 6/30/46 – Senators: Protection of property not a reason to tie up so many; We want a hearing to explain why 1,500,000 men will still be needed after July.)
2. **TRUMAN WANTS US TRUSTEESHIP OF ESSENTIAL ISLES** (Many of the islands won back from Japan should remain under US control for a long time.)
3. **MEAT PACKERS TO WALK OUT** (Demand closure of 2 independent packing houses in Evansville, IN – little hope seen to avert strike.)

FROM A 6-HOLER – BY IF-T'WILL-CAN-DO-IT-SO-CAN-I THOMAS (A.D.):

```
OH SHIP OF STATE SAIL ON AND ON
    Nnnangn-n-n-n, Nnangn-n-n, -n, chug-chug-chug,
the sound of the fog horn and the splash of surf
against the ship sides is beginning to creep into
our dreams. Flotsam and jetsam provide an anath-
ema for the hours of insomnia between taps and
reveille. Little boats, big boats, boats with
sails and boats with oars; boats manned with pix-
ies and derelicts have been a deliberate campaign
of driving us nuts.
    Mouths hanging open, stupor gazes at the squad
room's stove soon will be taking its toll in some
good knocked-out cases of insanity.
```

Meanwhile, things back in the States ramble on with their accustomed regularity. Psychologists are worried that returning veterans will have difficulty adjusting themselves to civilian life.

HINTS TO THOSE WHO SEND PICS ABROAD

There has been a lot of criticism lately from GI's and interested persons in the welfare of soldiers that overseas Joe is not getting the best that Hollywood has to send.

There is talk that the grade "A" movies are held too long in the States, that the movies sent over here are for the most part grade "B" and western thrillers.

To put an end to adverse criticism and recommendations for the improvement of the GI's movie fare, a group in Hollywood have come up with a practical suggestion.

Their recommendation: Send all movies in which the heroine appears more than once clad in an abbreviated bathing suit or a flimsy negligee to troops overseas.

(EDITOR'S NOTE: I didn't bother to search for a record of this "Hollywood group". You are welcome to try, if you like. Please let me know if you find anything. The pseudonym for the day has me intrigued. "IF T'WILL CAN DO IT SO CAN I"? What can it mean? Private Twill was Fred Stark's cartoon character – an imaginary member of K Company. Did Fred have him doing something about boats? The only thing I could find was the cartoon of Twill rowing to San Francisco in his helmet, but that was six weeks ago – pretty far-fetched.)

HONSHU PIONEER – VOL I, NO. 112 – WAKAMATSU, JAPAN – JAN. 18, 1946

HEADLINES:
1. JOHNSON SAYS – **4F'S FOR AO** (Senator Johnson [D-Col]: Use 4-F's and single men up to 45 as Army replacements overseas – Army plan for 1.5 million men by July 1 is at least 500,000 too many – Conscription will be needed past its May 15 expiration date.)
2. IKE ON NATIONAL HOOKUP (Eisenhower to explain demobilization slowdown to national radio audience on 1/21/46.)
3. SURPLUS US PROP. ARMY HEADACHE (Sec'y Royall: Many men still required to guard millions of dollars worth of gear left around the globe – Sen. Revercombe [R-W.Va.]: Give us a complete list. - War Dept. promises to supply it.)
4. BRADLEY RULES STRIKING VETS GO PAYLESS (Gen. Omar Bradley: Vets are not entitled to unemployment pay if participating in a strike.)
5. AGE IN STATES OUT AT ONCE (Army bases in the US are ordered to discharge all men with 45 points or 2½ years of service immediately.)
6. US MEAT SHORTAGE LOOMS (Packer strike averted, but issues not resolved – OPA alerts investigators to be on watch for black markets.)

HONSHU PIONEER – VOL I, NO. 113 – WAKAMATSU, JAPAN – JAN. 19, 1946

HEADLINES:
1. **IKE FORBIDS MASS MEETINGS** (Eisenhower: Complaints by individual GI's are OK, but mass protesters are subject to court martial – 650,000 Pacific troops to be cut to 375,000 by May 1.)
2. SENATE FILIBUSTERS FEPO BILL (Southern Senators reading fiction aloud to prevent vote on Fair Employment Practices bill, which ends discrimination due to race.)
3. HST CONFERS ON STRIKE SITUATION (Truman proposes own formula to prevent walkout of 800,000 steel workers on 1/21/46 – CIO Pres. Murray left in a bad mood.)
4. MASARYK ASKS UNO ARMS CONTROL (Czech Minister Masaryk asks UN to take control of all arms industries – Security Council meets for first time.)
5. BEVIN TO MAKE AFRICAN BEQUEST (In response to UN colonial mandates, Britain offers southwest Sudan to UN control – New Zealand cedes Samoa to UN.)

FROM A 6-HOLER – BY ROADBLOCK DELONG THOMAS:
HEAVEN HAS TWO SONS

A fresh theme of an old, old story cropped up yesterday, with the announcement that there was a competitor for the rather dubious distinction of being the Japanese Emperor.

Old Hiromichi, an obscure shopkeeper who has bided his time in relative obscurity, is now openly vying with Hirohito for custody of the sacred mirror, sword and jeweled necklace, and the right to ride the white horse.

We realize that dozens of operas and romances have been built around the business of restorations of monarchies, but in this age of democracies and self-expression, it's not often that the real thing comes along.

The story of Emperors Hirohito and Hiromichi should delight anyone addicted to the operettas of Gilbert and Sullivan, or even Met devotees of Prince Igor. The potential cast is all there. The usurped throne kept secret lo these many centuries is restored to its rightful owner Prince Hiromichi (an unpretentious shopkeeper) through the efforts of General MacArthur (a handsome, dashing soldier) who defeats the soldiers of the imposter Hirohito (a wicked fellow) on the field of battle.

There you have it. Of course, the soprano part is very noticeably missing, but then if Hiromichi has a sister the cast is complete. In the absence of Hiromichi's sister, perhaps a WAC, a shapely impish WAC could be found, who by her beguiling intrigue could thwart the Hirohito crew on the home front.

(EDITOR'S NOTE: Hiromichi was only the first of about nineteen men who put themselves forward as Japan's rightful Emperor at this time. It didn't work. Dad's concern for a soprano part in his imagined operetta was likely inspired by watching his sweetheart [and later wife] sing the lead in "HMS Pinafore" at Dearborn High School. Sarge had a beautiful soprano voice and great stage presence, and both she and Art were lifelong fans of Gilbert and Sullivan.)

EDITORIAL:

Yesterday Congress passed a motion to resume discussion on the fair employment practice bill. The bill provides for the establishment of a commission with the power to prevent discrimination in employment – regardless of race, creed or color.

Hot on the heels of this motion were the diehard moss-backed southern senators, who took the floor immediately after the motion was passed. The southerners declared that they would keep talking until the bill was dead. Today a full blown filibuster is in progress.

THIS CALLOUS DISPLAY OF DISCRIMINATION IS IN ABSOLUTE CONTRADICTION TO THE PRINCIPLES OF DEMOCRACY OUTLINED IN THE CONSTITUTION OF THE UNITED STATES.

It is an example, vividly clear to all thinking Americans, of pressure politics used to guarantee minority domination in exchange for political support.

We ask these senators, "On the battlefields of Europe and the Pacific, did the blood your sons run any redder than the blood of a Catholic, a Negro, or a Jew? Did any one of these groups pay any less than the total price asked for the protection of your liberties?"

Today you stand in Congress lending your weight to measures which deny the principles for which the American soldier fought... and all to stay in office.

We brand you as worse than a ward-heeler. You're the ward-heeler's dog, yapping for the ward bone."

(EDITOR'S NOTE: Well, that's telling 'em! Again we are seeing the passion for a better world that grew out of the incredible sacrifices that these men made in this war. If only there were some way to recapture that purity and passion now, when we need it more than ever. I was unaware of this particular bill, which sounds more like something from the Great Society era of the 60's, but the use of the filibuster to maintain the status quo, when a sizable majority of the public wants change... now that <u>has</u> grown and prospered since 1946.)

HONSHU PIONEER – VOL I, NO. 114 – WAKAMATSU, JAPAN – JAN. 20, 1946

HEADLINES:
1. DEMOB HEARINGS CLOSE (Ike gives Army's revised demobilization schedule: "We must secure the peace". Congress: GI complaints should be heard and answered.)
2. HERSHEY AIRS PLANS (Gen. Hershey to Senate: Extend the draft beyond May 15 expiration, and require all inductees to serve 18 months.)
3. STEEL STRIKE SCHEDULED TODAY (U.S. Steel rejects Truman's proposed compromise – 800,000 to strike today, demanding a 25¢ raise.)
4. NZ PREMIER SCORES UNO VETO POWER (Fraser denounces great powers for insisting on veto power over UN actions.)
5. SENATE FILIBUSTER ON FEPC CONTINUES (Southern Democrats bring Senate to a halt to prevent Fair Employment from passing – threaten to keep talking for a month.)

SUNDAY SUPPLEMENT – VOL I, NO. 13 – JAN. 20, 1946

Lost in the RICE LATITUDES – AIZU HONORS THE NINETEEN GALLANT YOUTHS WHO PERFORED HARAKIRI, RATHER THAN FORSAKE THE BUSHIDO PRINCIPLE.
• A. D. THOMAS •

IN THE NORTH COUNTRY BEYOND THE Kans of Ibaraka and Totugi rises lofty majestic Higashi Yama. From the hills clustering about the mountain comes a tale of heroism, both tragic and incredible.

The people of Aizu once lived under a proud and noble ruler. Almost four centuries ago Masiuki Matsudaira founded the most famous of all Bushido schools – the school if Nisshin Kan. Nisshin Kan was more than a school – in it the sons of leading Aizu families were taught the code of Japanese knighthood. The Samurai sons were taught to revere honor above life itself. In all Japan the knights of Nisshin Kan were respected and feared. For three centuries graduates of this school were held in high esteem, and tales of their swordsmanship, riding skill, their integrity and allegiance to their ruler were told in all Japan.

In 1868 Japan was in the throes of a new era. Over all the dominions of Japan the new Mikado, Emperor Meize, was integrating and centralizing the islands. One after another, the Shoguns of the various Kans resigned their autonomy to take allegiance to the new Emperor. Everywhere Meize was acclaimed and honored, everywhere except in remote austere Aizu. In Aizu the people still looked to their own ruler for authority. The titular head of Asizu Kan and the direct descendant of famous Samurai Masuiki Matsidaira was Katamori Matsidaira. As Shogun of Aizu, Katamori was also the head of the Nisshin Kan.

When Emperor Meize was told of the arrogance of the people of Aizu, he dispatched 200,000 of his best troops to subdue the proud Aizuites and bring them under the central authority of Tokyo. His reasons for sending such a large force were due in part to the stories of the incredible Nisshin Kan bravery.

The government forces marching north from Tokyo deployed in a wide encircling movement, and in a matter of a few days had completely surrounded the area of Aizu, from Higashi Yama on the southeast to Onohara Valley on the southwest. Shogun Katamori ordered his little band of 10,000 men strung out as pickets as the only opposition to the Tokyo hordes. Minor skirmishes characterized the early phases of the action. Finally the government troops were thought to be making a large scale offensive through Onohara Valley. Baron Katamori, wishing to be in the thick of things, decided to ride a short way south to the village of Takezawa and see how his troops were making out.

Before going to Takezawa, Katamori was approached by 16-year-old Naiki Hinata, who offered the services of hiss Nisshin Kan schoolmates in the defense of Aizu.

Katamori was very much impressed by the offer, but decided the boys might better stay behind for a last ditch defense of Aizu castle, should things be going really badly at the front.

The boys didn't much like being dismissed by their ruler, and being asked to perform a task they considered beneath their soldierly dignity, so they marched in the direction of Onohara, hoping to get in the fun. When they reached the valley, things were pretty slack. There were no government troops in sight, and they thought their disobedience had been in vain.

By the time the schoolboys had reached Onohara, the day was pretty well on, and their leader, Hinata, turned over his command to Gisaku Shinoda and went to look for something to eat. Hinata hadn't been gone half an hour when from out of the hills came the ear-splitting cries of "Banzai", and a whole raft of Meize troops was on them. The government forces, thinking the disturbance in the valley was due to an extra large concentration of Aizu troops, decided this was a good moment to attack.

The Nisshin Kan band fought valiantly, but they were hopelessly outnumbered, and headed back in the direction of the Wakamatsu castle. On their way back they passed Mt. Eimori, where they caught first view of the city and the castle. There, in the center of the town, they saw what they thought to be the castle burning. Shinoda and his band of 19 troops were pledged to defend this castle, and now it looked to them as if disaster had overtaken the Aizuites – the castle was on fire and their esteemed leader presumably dead.

The school of Nisshin Kan indeed taught its lesson well. When the nineteen survivors of the Onohara battle saw their Aizu world smoldering away, they did the last honorable thing, the first principle of the Bushido code, they ended their lives by the act of hara-kiri. Facing the castle on their knees, the last class of Nisshin chanted aloud their Seiki-no-uta (last requiem of Samurais) and departed their lives in an orgy of blood.

A short time later a mother out looking for her small son found the nineteen youths on the slopes of Mt. Eimori, their bodies twisted in agony and their katanas still protruding from prostrate forms. Each of Katamori's soldiers was gone over by the old woman, and finally she was rewarded for her efforts by finding one who still breathed - youthful Teikichi Inuma. Although his stomach was rent and blood escaped from a wound in his throat, Inuma was miraculously alive.

The old woman must have been badly informed on the code of the Bushido - otherwise she wouldn't have taken the pains to save his life. The greatest dishonor in the eyes of a good Samurai is the failure in the masterful art of stomach-splitting. Inuma had failed. If the woman had known the shame and dishonor that were to dog the footsteps of poor Inuma, she would have done him the good favor of leaving him on the Eimori field of honor to die a hero's death. As it was, she carried the youth to the house of a friend in nearby Shiokawa, where his wounds were staunched and he was nursed back to health.

Teikichi Inuma died in 1942, in an obscure home in Sendai, where he worked as a telegrapher. Inuma was renounced by the people of Wakamatsu, and so bitterly did he feel his shame that he was never able to bring himself to visit the shrine at Eimori.

(EDITOR'S NOTE: Ignoring some minor disagreements in the spelling of Japanese names, this story is absolutely accurate. My father apparently wanted to share it unblemished by his usual inventions, exaggerations and sarcasm. I would state with some confidence that the reason was his love of the truly dramatic and the truly heroic, which lasted throughout his life. Of course, the term "hara-kiri" refers only to the belly cutting method, not the correct name for a ritual Samurai suicide, which would be "seppuku". The names of all 20 members of this band are inscribed on the memorial [or "shrine, as Dad would have it], along with this poem by Matsudaira Katamori, which translates as:

"No matter how many people wash the stones with their tears, these names will never vanish from the world."

Fred Stark, who was probably my father's closest friend on the paper, provided an excellent illustration for this story. It's not Fred's usual style, but as I read through these issues, I discovered that he was a master of many artistic styles.

The castle burning in the background is a nice touch. However, this was not the only illustration that Fred provided, and the other one seemed to have no bearing on the text. I had to do some research to explain this discrepancy, but what I learned was the following:

The Italian fascist dictator Benito Mussolini heard the story of the Byakkotai members who committed suicide, and was deeply impressed by their loyalty to their lord. In 1928, he donated a column from Pompeii to be erected by the graves at Iimori [or Eimori] Hill. This column remains there to the present day.

My theory is that Art and Fred visited the memorial together, and then returned to the office to work on this story independently. Fred thought that Mussolini's column from Pompeii was very impressive, and that Art would surely include a reference to it in his story. Art probably intended to do so, but ran out of time and/or column-inches before he got around to it. They included Fred's drawing of the column [at right] anyway, but their readers must have been mystified by its presence, and Fred's title block – FASCISTA "PRESENTO" – could not have helped much.)

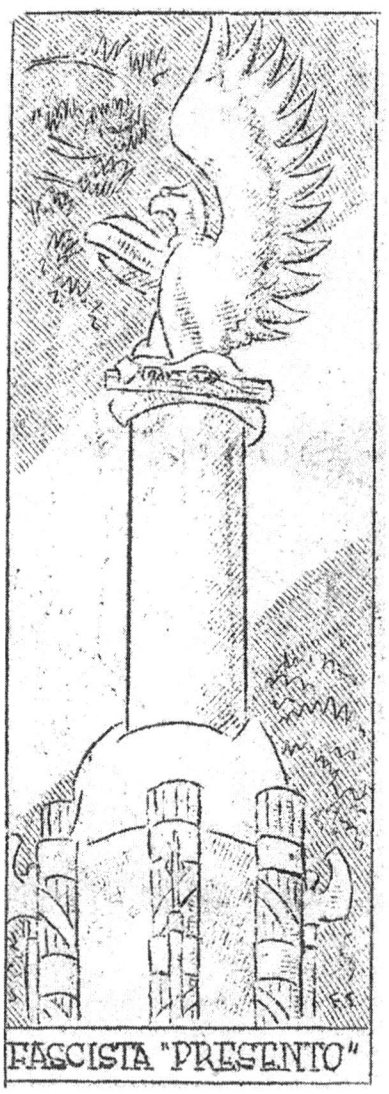

HONSHU PIONEER – VOL I, NO. 115 – WAKAMATSU, JAPAN – JAN. 21, 1946

HEADLINES:
1. KAISER ACCEPTS HST OFFER (Henry J. Kaiser accepts Fact Finding Board proposal to increase wages 18¢ per hour. His 4,000 men will be the only steelworkers working.
2. MANILA GI'S RENEW PROTESTS (After drawing up proposals to get 400,000 men home, Chairman of Manila Council of GI's resigns. Proposals to be sent to Congress.)
3. DPS RETICENT TO GO HOME (271 Russian prisoners, held in the U.S. as traitors, attempted suicide rather than be returned to the USSR for trial. 12 succeeded.)

FROM A 6-HOLER – BY ROADBLOCK OLD SALT THOM.:
WATERMANSHIP

It's been suggested that an effort be made to refresh all those men of the Battalion with thirty months service or more with a few facts of marine life.

If you'll think back to the classes on Watermanship held in San Luis Obispo it will be remembered that they were none too successful. The spirit wasn't there and the flesh was always getting wet.

Rather than hold regular classes, higher echelons have suggested a refresher be incorporated in unit newspapers. It might be that Plans & Training didn't want to subject those with fewer months of service and lower points to material ostensibly for the men about to go home.

Remember while aboard ship the life belt is a soldier's best friend – keep it with you at all times. Aside from its being such a good friend, various watches (port and starboard) are asked to admit no man to the chow line unless he has it with him.

Another important matter to navy personnel is keeping the ship clean. "Keeping the ship clean" is pretty matter of fact and requires no special knowledge of nautical jargon to know what is meant by the term. The word "ship" generally means the boat on which you are traveling. (Caution – when referring to the boat with sailors around, always speak of it as a ship. The Seamanship Manual says a boat is smaller than the thing ordinarily used for troop transport.)

Perhaps the whole business of Watermanship would be brought back if we reminded you of the sea anemone. The sea anemone is a soft-bodied, non-poisonous marine animal.

(EDITOR'S NOTE: Travel in the homeward direction is clearly the leading topic of conversation, even for something as silly as this column.)

HONSHU PIONEER – VOL I, NO. 116 – WAKAMATSU, JAPAN – JAN. 22, 1946

HEADLINES:
1. **STEEL STRIKE BEGINS** (More men will be idled than any strike in history — UP estimates 1,625,000. Truman's 18½¢ compromise was rejected by both sides.)
2. DEGAULLE QUITS AS FRENCH HEAD (DeGaulle has fallen out with leading political factions in France – will address nation tomorrow to give his reasons for leaving.)
3. FIRST GERMAN VOTE SINCE HITLER (Elections took place in towns under 5,000 population in the American zone – 90% turnout.)
4. UNO MACHINERY FACES TEST OVER IRAN-RUSS DISPUTE (UN leaders not worried by Iran's complaint of Soviet interference – request is only for investigation, not action.)

FROM A 6-HOLER – BY ROADBLOCK DELONG THOMAS:
MISSION TO SHANGHAI

Everyone was quite willing to let George do it a month ago. By George was meant our former Chief-of-Staff and now special envoy to China Gen. George Catlett Marshall.

A month ago China was at disastrous odds with herself. The Reds were mixing it up with the Kuomintang troops of Generalissimo Chiang-kai-shek in a fratricidal war that seemed to be chiefly concerned with the priorities of railroad travel. The Communists were holding out for free, impartial rail travel for all; the Chiang government insisted space should be allotted first to troops headed for the occupation of Manchuria.

And then, as so often happens in cases of Civil War, one thing led to another until other issues became bandied about and the whole fiasco of name calling culminated in the expose of the State Department by former Ambassador Patrick Hurley. Hurley claimed that certain "career" diplomats were subjecting the professed foreign policy of the US to expedient ends of their own. There was a big Senate investigation (the stock conditioned reflex of our legislators for anything that smacks of being SNAFU), and the upshot was the appointment of Gen. Marshall as ambassador and conciliator extraordinary.

Things looked bright for a while. It seemed that the old army man was going to get things straightened around in fine shape. He was hailed by both free railroader and privileged railroader as a peacemaker.

Now we read that a trusted lackey has run off with General's wardrobe and the Communists and Chiangists have gone back to saying naughty things about each other.

(EDITOR'S NOTE: Somewhere hidden in this web of sarcasm, I think there might be a nugget of genuine political commentary – not something usually found in Dad's columns. I get the impression that he thinks all of the U.S. actions and pronouncements regarding China are a bunch of window-dressing, and generally without substance or real purpose.)

EDITORIAL:

Within one week of its first assembly, the United Nations Organization has found itself confronted with a major problem that may challenge the actual power of the Security Council.

The problem is that of alleged Russian interference with the internal affairs of Iran.

The Iranian delegate, Nastrullah Entezam, charged that Russian officers and troops were instrumental in inciting the recent revolution in Azerbaijan province, which resulted in the Teheran government's loss of sovereignty over a large section of northern Iran. As a result Iran has appealed to the United Nations Security Council to investigate the state of affairs within her country.

Although the Iranian appeal did not request that the Council take action against the Soviet Union, as it might have done under the UNO charter, we feel that if this organization is to avoid the same mistakes that led to the eventual ineffectiveness of the League of Nations, it must act on small matters of organization importance immediately.

The situation in Iran is not so much a question of local independence as it is a test of whether or not the UNOSC is sufficiently dynamic to deal with the internal problems of its members... and make its decisions stick.

HONSHU PIONEER – VOL I, NO. 117 – WAKAMATSU, JAPAN – JAN. 23, 1946

HEADLINES:

1. **LABOR MANAGEMENT CRISIS** – STEEL STRIKE SPREADS IDLENESS TO OTHER JOBS (1,680,000 on strike – Many more jobs at risk – CIO's Murray: Industry must accept President's decision – Government seizure of steel plants seems possible.)
2. OPINION DIFFERS ON HST SPEECH (President urges general wage hikes & extension of price controls – Republicans want more spending cuts.)
3. UNO SETS UP A-BOMB GROUP (Unanimous vote sets up Atomic Energy Control Commission – Sen. Connally: Secret of the A-bomb is safeguarded by America.)
4. YENAN REJECTS CHIANG PLAN (Communists reject Government proposal, put forth their own plan for creation of an elected Chinese legislature.)
5. COMMUNISTS FORMING FRENCH GOV'T. (Communists are now the strongest party in France – Attempting a purely left-wing government, they propose Maurice Thorez as president – Other parties are not pleased.)

HONSHU PIONEER – VOL I, NO. 118 – WAKAMATSU, JAPAN – JAN. 24, 1946

HEADLINES:
1. **ANGLO-RUSS AT ODDS IN UNO** (Russia demands UN investigate presence of British troops in Indonesia and Greece; Britain my ask the same, but include Iran and Netherlands in the list.)
2. CONGRESS COLD SHOULDERS DRAFT EXTENSION (No early action expected on draft extension or Army-Navy merger into a single Defense Department.)
3. BRITISH WILL LAND LATE JAN. (News agencies are invited to accompany British troops landing on Southern Honshu – Australia and New Zealand troops to follow.)

FROM A 6-HOLER – BY ROADBLOCK "WOOF!" THOMAS:
MISS ROGERS, PUBLICITY HOUND

If Sharon Rogers has a publicity agent, he must be a happy man at the moment. Sharon either must have a fine publicity agent or a fine flair for the dramatic.

She hadn't been in Japan more than a week before the Stars & Stripes had started personally plugging Miss Rogers. It was Rogers and Yamashita on the front page day after day. It almost got to the point where we didn't know but what Miss Rogers was the star witness in the Manila trials or Yamashita was the first violin player for the feminine swingsters.

Opinion all over Japan was pretty well divided on the girl instrumentalists. Almost all the GI's were anxious enough to hear their performance; and if the GI's didn't like their brand of swing, fifteen girls is fourteen more than enough to insure every theater would be jammed.

Miss Rogers received more notoriety from her opinions on fraternization than she did for musical prowess or lack of it. Indignant letters poured in from all over, attacking her ideas that GI's adopt a strict code of celibacy for their occupational sojourn. It wasn't so much the non-fraternization that bothered the GI's but her blanket accusation against all occupees that their conduct on the streets was deplorable and a black eye to Stateside Femininity.

Whatever were Miss Rogers' motives, the result of her talks with the press had the desired effect. We and a million more like us now know of Sharon Rogers.

Yesterday she surpassed anything she had yet done in the way of publicity; the plane in which she was riding plunked into the Japanese Sea near Shikoku and for the twelfth time in Miss Rogers' Jap stay she made the Stars & Stripes. Hats off to Miss Rogers, who is insured a place in show business for her publicity even if she should forget how to play a note.

(EDITOR'S NOTE: I had never heard of Miss Rogers, but I did find a 2009 posting on the Internet: —Les Brown Jr attended the Military Gala in Branson on November 8 with members of the WWII USO show, the Sharon Rogers Band. Three band members were in Branson to introduce their new book, The Sharon Rogers Band: Laughed Together, Cried Together, Crashed & Almost Died Together.")

EDITORIAL:

After every war there eventually arises the question of reparations. And justly so, for those who follow the course of aggression should be made to pay in some way for the reconstruction of the lands they ravaged. But heavy reparations advanced against a defeated nation, even though that country was an aggressor, does little toward advancing international cooperation. In fact we hold that it retards it, by creating a state of internal chaos within the debtor nation which may be used easily by power hungry politicians for their own ambitious ends.

We feel that the recent statement from Washington urging the Allies to abandon their reparations claims against the Italian government was a realistic approach to the problem, both from the standpoint of business and world peace.

Washington said that it was important that Italy retain her industrial equipment for civilian production and her Merchant Marine, and revealed that the suggestion would be placed before the four-power conference in London this month.

Because of the close integration of Allied relief to Italy, 1 billion of which comes from America, if reparations are paid to all claimants the bill would be footed in reality by the U.S. taxpayer.

America's relief to Italy is proof of her desire for world cooperation; her reparations stand proof of her international business ability.

HONSHU PIONEER – VOL I, NO. 119 – WAKAMATSU, JAPAN – JAN. 25, 1946

HEADLINES:
1. **MAC OUTLAWS FEMALE SLAVERY** (SCAP orders an end to the age-old practice of selling daughters to brothels – Japanese prostitution magnates are alarmed.)
2. CHINA FIGHTING RENEWED (Fighting continues in 5 northern provinces – had been reported ended, but no – Communists attacking on a large scale.)
3. RR UNIONS ASK STRIKE VOTE (Brotherhood of Railroad Trainmen's 215,000 members to vote – Locomotive Engineers' 78,000 members may follow suit.)
4. MIDPAC DEMOB SPEEDED (Gen. Richardson announces a 2-month speed-up of discharges – those eligible by June 30 will be discharged by May 1.)

HONSHU PIONEER – VOL I, NO. 120 – WAKAMATSU, JAPAN – JAN. 26, 1946

HEADLINES:
1. **ENOUGH SHIPS** (500,000 men to be returned from the Pacific by July 1 – ships are available for all January and February discharges – other theaters may be slower.)
2. UNO AGREES ON A-BOMB CONTROL (Big Three proposals for an international commission to control atomic energy were accepted overwhelmingly by the UN.)
3. NAVY PREPARES A-BOMB TESTS (Units of the ship target fleet are westbound for testing – 3 tests planned: above the ships, at sea level, and underwater.)
4. STRIKE FORCES FORD LAYOFF (4-day-old steel strike to idle 40,000 Ford workers.)

HONSHU PIONEER – VOL I, NO. 121 – WAKAMATSU, JAPAN – JAN. 27, 1946

HEADLINES:
1. **PACKERS REJECT GOV'T CALL** (Government seizes packing firms to stop meat famine – striking workers refuse to return – expected to change their minds soon.)
2. CHIANG OK'S STRONG COUNCIL (Foreign Minister calls for more power for All-Party Council, less for the President – up to now, talks were proceeding "very poorly".)
3. UNO TO CONSIDER RUSS COMPLAINTS (UN Security Council will investigate internal affairs of Indonesia, Greece and Iran.)
4. BOMBAY RIOTS CONTINUE (Gunfire, tear gas mark the 4th consecutive day of nationalist rioting – 22 killed, 600 wounded in Bombay province.)

FROM A 6-HOLER – BY ROADBLOCK DELONG THOMAS:
```
VANTAGE POINT
   For an overall view of the passing parade in
the Wakamatsu Military station there isn't a bet-
ter vantage point than the number one guard post,
the sentinel box at the main gate.

   A book might easily be written on the seemingly
singular events that take place at the main gate
in the course of a two-hour hitch.

   The special orders for Post One probably don't
make as entertaining reading as they might have,
had the author wanted to let himself go. For
example, there is no provision on the accepted
procedure for the guard in the case of a Honey
Train's arrival.
```

The Honey Train is quite a caravan. There is no prescribed uniform of the train's retinue. Old favorites are denim shirts with a plain design of Japanese letters, and baggy pants of vertically striped material. The boss of the outfit tries to assume a certain dignity as he approaches the gate, but the procession of the proverbial wooden buckets, the long poles for recovering the last little doubloon at the bottom of our 6-Holers is generally too much for him, and he inevitably gives the guard a chicken sort of a grin.

The Japanese have learned a lot about the Americans in the time that occupees have been in Wakamatsu. The case of a guard, however, is a matter that they haven't figured out as yet.

To the Jap, the man in the box with a rifle is still a staunch symbol of authority and still deserves an obsequious bow as befits a foreign conqueror.

EDITORIAL:

Not long ago, after a War Department spokesman announced that demobilization was to be slowed down, thousands of GI's in Manila, Yokohama, Frankfurt and other cities in other lands marched on their commanding officers and protested.

These men were not so naïve as to believe that their CO's could do anything about the slowdown, but they always managed to have the gentlemen of the press present.

Such action in many armies would be classified as mutiny, and the fact that they were not punished shows the power of the people's voice when it echoes in the halls of Congress.

Possibly the American Army lost face in the more official quarters of these foreign lands.

However, it was a vivid demonstration of American democracy at work – One that no doubt amazed the millions recently liberated from a much different type of government.

It also served to remind anyone with any grandiose ideas about militarizing the United States that he'd have a pretty big job on his hands.

We don't advocate weekly protest marches, but we disagree with anyone who thinks that those held two weeks ago didn't do any good.

The news that the various commands are knocking themselves out to get the eligibles home is excellent proof that democracy works.

(EDITOR'S NOTE: Jeepers! Where to begin? I love the idealism of this author and his staunch resistance to the idea that his country could ever become militaristic, but I think he is confusing the power of democracy with the power of a free press. Clearly it was the newspaper reports about these protests that got people stirred up back in the States.

There are many, many reasons why this entire episode could never happen in today's world, but I will mention just a few:

1. *The U.S. HAS become the most militaristic nation in the world, in spite of the author's hopes. The Military-Industrial Complex that Eisenhower warned us about has become the most powerful and secretive force on Earth.*

2. *The press is completely managed and censored in any area where U.S. troops are deployed overseas, so even if such protests took place, you would never hear of it.*
3. *Even if such news did leak out in some other way, the mainstream media in the U.S. would still never report it. They are owned by the same corporations that are part of or profit from the Military-Industrial Complex.*
4. *Congress is no longer cowed by public opinion – only by the opinions of large corporations and their lobbyists. As long as those guys are happy, legislators have nothing to fear from the managed press.)*

HONSHU PIONEER – VOL I, NO. 122 – WAKAMATSU, JAPAN – JAN. 28, 1946

HEADLINES:
1. **LABOR PEACE IN SIGHT** (Packers halt walkout – Ford & Chrysler grant wage increases – Railroad unions agree to arbitration – Labor Dept. waiting on Steel.)
2. SHORT BLAMES MILES, MARSHALL FOR PEARL HARBOR (General Walter Short. Commander at Pearl Harbor, accuses 3 generals of using him as a scapegoat.)
3. KAISER PLANS STEEL EMPIRE (H.J. Kaiser announces plans to create a steel empire twice the size of any of his other industries.)
4. IRAN HEAD ASKS RUSS TALKS (UN delegates from Iran announce a change in their government. They have been told by the new premier to withdraw their request for an investigation into Russian interference in Azerbaijan. Matter to be settled privately.)

FROM A 6-HOLER – BY ROADBLOCK DELONG THOMAS:

```
W-I-T-T
```

"This is station W-I-T-T on the air." – Tune in on your loud-speaker around 9:30 or 10:00 for the greatest little record session to be had on this island. With no apologies to Tokyo Mose and his gang on Radio Tokyo, let it be said that Cpl Witt and his bunch at the radio shack beat just about anything to be had in these parts in the way of radio entertainment.

No imposing granite structure houses the men of W-I-T-T, there's only an off-color clapboard shack tucked in a remote corner of the compound over near the place our officers call home.

Any tune is yours for the asking. Just drop a line to the radio shack, or better, get hold of a telephone and let them know just which of the many discs you'd like to hear. They have them all.

It's bandstands one, two, three, four, five and ad infinitum as far as the members of W-I-T-T go. At their fingertips are Benny Goodman, Les Brown, Lionel Hampton, Charlie Barnett and as many lesser bands as you'd care to mention – all yours for the asking. You don't have to be a musician to have a piece dedicated to your First Sgt. or platoon leader. If you've an eye on an existing rating in your outfit, let the W-I-T-T boys do the browning for you. They don't care who they dedicate a piece to; why last night they dedicated a piece to the PIONEER.

To Cpl. Witt and non-TO assistants go the choicest of our decaying-from-long-disuse orchids for their aid in bolstering the morale of 303d, 3d Battalion.

EDITORIAL:

History struck an ironic note in Tokyo this week when the first shipment of wheat and flour arrived there from the Philippine Islands.

Only a short time ago, foodstuffs from all of the conquered nations of the Pacific were pouring into the bustling ports of Japan as tribute to the victorious Nips.

Now, the liberated Philippine nation, still suffering from the effects of being twice a battleground in a short span of three years, is sending food to its once proud conqueror. This time payment will no doubt be made in something more valuable than the now worthless occupation pesos.

We are not in a position to know whether the gesture was made out of a desire to aid a Pacific sister in distress or due to a dire need of cash. However, it should not be difficult for the Filipinos to know what the Japs mean when they speak of starvation, malnutrition and hardship. Thanks to their northern neighbors, most of them have a first-hand understanding of these problems, due to an intimate association with Samurai rule.

We doubt that it will make much difference to the hungry Japanese concerning the source of their rations, just so they get them.

It is possible that there is regret – genuine this time – that General Yamashita's men burned so many farmhouses.

HONSHU PIONEER – VOL I, NO. 123 – WAKAMATSU, JAPAN – JAN. 29, 1946

HEADLINES:
1. 22 LOSE LIVES IN U.S. FIRES (Freezing temperatures harass firefighters – KC, NY, Chicago, St. Louis, Charleston all suffer.)
2. **GM SETTLEMENT REPORTED NEAR** – INDUSTRY HEADS EXAMINE CHRYSLER, FORD CONTRACTS (68-day strike to end soon – 1,332,000 still idle in other strikes – Meat packers returning to work for government – Railroad workers agree to arbitration.)
3. MANILA GI'S DISBAND GROUP (Group decides they have accomplished their mission, will obey Eisenhower's order against more mass meetings.)
4. YENAN GROUP OPTIMISTIC (Communist military head: World peace means China needs no large standing army & U.S. troops can go home now.)
5. JAP PAPERS WARNED ON NEWS STORIES (American censors are wise to Japanese attempts to evade censorship, and "are not very pleased". Some papers have subtly hinted that holdups have been committed by American troops.)

(EDITOR'S NOTE: Censorship by an occupying power? Imagine that.)

FROM A 6-HOLER – BY ROADBLOCK DELONG T.:
```
TAKE ME OUT COACH
   Probably the most heart-breaking sight to be
found among the GI occupees of Wakamats' is that
of the lad with enough points or months for dis-
charge, but sweating out those last few days.
```

His daily morale is as varied as the temperature of a GI stove, and every word uttered concerning ships and what the Old Man said to what's-his-name-who-has-31-months-service, is accepted by our eligible friend as indication of his status.

Old timers use all sorts of ruses to avoid these boys, having learned long ago that any analysis of THE situation in the presence of the melancholy crew many times has unfortunate consequences.

Getting cornered by one of them is like having a patch in your bore at Saturday inspection – nothing good ever comes of it.

If one of them buttonholes you – think, and think fast. Tell him you're on guard, that you have a train to catch, or that PTA applications are being made out in the orderly room. (He always has a few hot yen.) In extreme emergencies, shout "FIRE!" and run.

Under no circumstances, however, should you ever attempt to bolster his morale with the latest poop from wherever you happen to get your late poop. You'll only make him more confused.

Even if you have the real poop – be careful. Not long ago a Joe in one of the other battalions told his buddy that he had seen his name on the shipping list. The excited home-bounder thereupon bussed his buddy on the cheek, and they're both in the observation ward at the 91st Field Hospital.

(EDITOR'S NOTE: *No mystery here regarding what was on Dad's mind at this time. Since this was apparently his very last column [the last one I have, anyway], it would seem likely that he had* *seen his own name on the shipping list. I was hoping he would find some way to say goodbye to his readers, but perhaps he thought it might be cruel.)*

EDITORIAL:

The committee of the United Nations Organization which seems to be acting in the best faith of the people of the world is the delegation now in the States trying to find a permanent site for the UNO.

Back in London, where the big agenda of the conference is being threshed out, UNO business is being subjected to the same sort of pressure politics that have always characterized a convention of nations.

Big things were expected of the international congress when the various countries were able to reach a satisfactory answer for the problem of atomic control. Lately, however, the same odious scheme of "balanced powers" and national jealousies, always the plague of international effort, are pervading the goal of world security.

Two weeks ago the Iranian delegates courageously accused Soviet Russia of meddling in its internal affairs. This then was to have been a real test for the UNO. Here was an opportunity for the new international organization to assert itself as a courageous force to which the peoples of the world could point with pride as being more than a mouthpiece of the Big Five. What happened?

After the accusation by Iran, the government of Iran is taken over by a new appeasement government, a government which feels that any differences it

```
might have with the USSR can be handled outside
the jurisdiction of the world court.
```

(EDITOR'S NOTE: Well, there's another element of world history of which I was totally unaware. One cannot help but wonder, however, what forces were set in motion by this incident, and what, if any, impact they have had in shaping present-day Iran. The rather cynical view of the UN presented here, as a champion of justice, as long as no powerful nations are offended, seems to have held up pretty well.

This is also the last <u>Honshu Pioneer</u> editorial that has anything to say. From here on they all read like government press releases. It was 18 days ago, on January 11, that the <u>Pioneer</u> published that editorial expressing outrage at the censorship of the military press, and calling out the responsible Colonel by name. I had the feeling that it was going to have consequences, and it appears that it did. Well, they had a great run, and I'm grateful to have gotten the opportunity to share some of their noble thoughts with a wider audience.)

HONSHU PIONEER – VOL I, NO. 134 – WAKAMATSU, JAPAN – FEB. 11, 1946

HEADLINES:
1. **STRIKES EASING OFF** – WESTERN UNION, GM ELECTRICAL STRIKES SETTLED (Western Union & GM electrical workers end strikes – Steel workers to settle soon.)
2. INDONESIA CHARGES TO BE DROPPED (Charges by Ukrainian UN delegate against Britain will be "quietly dropped".)
3. BAD CONDITIONS PREVENT WIVES JOINING OVERSEAS GI'S (Food & sanitary conditions are not good enough – It will be "some time" before wives can visit.)
4. NEW ATTEMPTS TO HOLD PRICE LINE (Demands of both management and labor making it difficult to stabilize U.S. wages and prices.)
5. CHINA BEGINS RECONVERSION (Both sides want peace – good progress reported in ending hostilities – Communications must be restored.)

(EDITOR'S NOTE: We now have nearly a two week gap between issues, which I would attribute to my father's departure from Wakamatsu. This, of course, raises the question of how he came into possession of these February issues at all. I can only think that some friend who stayed a bit longer in Japan collected them and sent them on to him. My leading candidate for this was going to be James P. Hanratty, who remained as Editor at this time. However, as we will soon see, he did not stay around much longer either. My new guess is A. Hamburger, who became Editor after Hanratty's departure. Given the new editorial policy, I doubt that we have missed much of interest.)

HONSHU PIONEER – VOL I, NO. 135 – WAKAMATSU, JAPAN – FEB. 12, 1946

HEADLINES:
1. **ASK UNO WORLD GOVERNMENT** – NATIONS LEADERS CALL ON HST TO FOSTER UNO MOVE (Civic and cultural leaders: The UN is "the one hope of avoiding atomic war" - UN should be a world government, not a "debating society".)
2. BRITISH BRIDES ARRIVE IN NY (The Queen Mary brought over 2,300 British war brides to New York – 1,100 more expected within a week.)
3. NATION AWAITS PRICE DECISION (Truman to announce new steel prices, stabilization policy – Hopes are that these will reduce labor strife.)
4. 100 MILLION VOTE IN USSR (First election since before the war – Overwhelming vote of confidence for government – One party election.)

(EDITOR'S NOTE: There has been a distinct change in the paper since the end of January. Original cartoons and art work have disappeared, and syndicated cartoons ["Blondie", etc.] have replaced them. Editorials no longer give opinions, strong or otherwise, about current events, but instead provide educational material about the provisions in the "GI Bill of Rights" and how to use them, etc. News coverage of events in Japan has nearly disappeared completely, while wire service reports from the U.S. now dominate the front page. In short, the <u>Honshu Pioneer</u> seems to have become an official organ of the War Department, and a pretty dull read. My guess is that Fred Stark, Art Thomas, and whoever was writing those fiery editorials all shipped out on the same boat.)

HONSHU PIONEER – VOL I, NO. 136 – WAKAMATSU, JAPAN – FEB. 13, 1946

HEADLINES:
1. GM UAW REJECT 18½¢ RAISE AS MINOR STRIKES CONTINUE (Walter Reuther: We will not accept 18½¢ - we demand 19½¢, as previously stated.)
2. COMMITTEE VOTES 22-17 FOR N.Y. CONN. UNO SITE (Site in Westchester County, between New York and Connecticut, chosen by UN committee.)
3. ETO SUPPLY MENACED BY HIJACKERS (Gangs of hijackers are raiding supply shipments to the American zone in Germany.)
4. THIRD ARMY RAIDS UNDERGROUND (Based on reports of Nazi activity from Yugoslavia and Russia, 3rd Army begins raids on underground Nazi cells.)
5. US-BRIT AVIATION PACT SIGNED (Air bases opened up – Numbers of commercial flights agreed to.)

(EDITOR'S NOTE: J. P. Hanratty's name disappears from the masthead today. I would love to believe that he resigned in protest of the new toothless editorial policy, but there is absolutely nothing to suggest that. It's far more likely that he was shipped home, since he was writing letters to my father from California by March. The new Editor is A. Hamburger, a columnist and feature writer who has been with the paper from the beginning.)

HONSHU PIONEER – VOL I, NO. 137 – WAKAMATSU, JAPAN – FEB. 14, 1946

HEADLINES:
1. **CHARGE ARGENTINE-NAZI COLLABORATION** – STATE DEPT DISCLOSES ARGENTINE WAR DESIRES (State Dept: Argentina strove for Axis victory to become strongest nation in Western Hemisphere – UN hears similar charges against Spain.)
2. RUSSIAN SAYS BRITAIN FAILED TO DISARM JAPS (UN Delegate Vyshinsky: British actions in Greece & Indonesia violate Atlantic Charter – Eleanor Roosevelt condemns Russian proposal to return all refugees to native lands – Proposal is defeated.)
3. PARTIES STRADDLE ISSUES = HOOVER (Herbert Hoover condemns both parties for fence-sitting on the most important issues of the day.)
4. TUGBOAT STRIKE BRINGS NY TO KNEES (Little or no progress has been made in resolving this "paralyzing" strike.)
5. RIOTS IN ALEXANDRIA (Anti-British rioting breaks out in Egypt.)

(EDITOR'S NOTE: Apparently, nothing newsworthy is happening in Japan at this time.)

HONSHU PIONEER – VOL I, NO. 138 – WAKAMATSU, JAPAN – FEB. 15, 1946

HEADLINES:
1. **US ARGENTINE BREAK SEEN** – DIPLOMATIC SPLIT SEEMS IMMINENT (Response to Nazi collaboration charges – Expulsion from UN likely for Argentina.)
2. NATION'S STRIKE SCENE CLEARS (NY fuel crisis ends as tugboats go back to work – Truman reports completion of new wage-price guidelines – Steel strike nears end.)
3. UNO CHOOSES NYC AS TEMPORARY HOME (Permanent home still not determined – Motion to investigate Britain's actions in the far east defeated.)
4. PATTERSON TO ASK CONTINUATION OF DRAFT PAST MAY (Current law expires May 15 – 40% of enlistments are for 18 months or less – More men will be needed.)
5. FOOD FOR CHINA (168,482 tons of aid received by UN Relief in China in January.)
6. ICKES RESIGNS CABINET POST (Sec'y of Interior Harold Ickes resigns: "I will not commit perjury for any political party.")

(EDITOR'S NOTE: Re. #6: Ickes felt that Truman was pressuring him to modify his memory with regard to the nomination of Edwin W. Pauley as Secretary of the Navy. Pauley had been the national treasurer of the Democratic Party and allegedly offered Ickes $300,000 [almost $4 million in 2013] in campaign contributions if he would drop Interior Department claims to certain oil-rich lands. Truman accepted Ickes' resignation and gave him 3 days to leave. Pauley declined the nomination, anyway.)

HONSHU PIONEER – VOL I, NO. 139 – WAKAMATSU, JAPAN – FEB. 16, 1946

HEADLINES:

1. ARMY ANNOUNCES – **4-FS TO BE INDUCTED** – 75,000 MEN PREVIOUSLY REJECTED NOW TO BE CALLED (Army lowers physical standards – Only men 18 to 25, who are not fathers will be drafted.)
2. HST PRICE PLAN EXPECTED TODAY (Truman has met with high officials – New stabilization formulas expected – GM and steel firms await results.)
3. HOUSE COMM. OKS 60¢ WAGE MINIMUM (Senate Labor Committee approves minimum wage increase from 40¢ to 65¢ per hour — Bill to reach Senate floor Monday.)
4. HARRIMAN RESIGNS USSR POST (Averill Harriman resigns – Lt. Gen. Walter Smith, Chief of Staff to Eisenhower, nominated as new Ambassador to USSR.)
5. AAF, NAVY, MARINES DROP POINT SCORES (All services are lowering requirements for discharge – Army Air Force will release 500,000 by June.)

HONSHU PIONEER – VOL I, NO. 140– WAKAMATSU, JAPAN – FEB. 18, 1946

HEADLINES:
1. CANADIAN ACCUSES RUSSIAN SPY ACTS (Recently discovered spy ring found to be Russian – Military, economic, possibly atomic secrets stolen – US: no comment.)
2. CONCENTRATION CAMPS? (American League for a Free Palestine: Thousands of Palestinian Jews have been arrested and held without charge in concentration camps.)
3. STEEL, OTHER STRIKES SETTLED (GM and electrical industry strikes to end soon — US Steel grants 18½¢ raise.)
4. ARGENTINE PAPERS ATTACK PERON (Praising US reports on Nazi collaboration, newspapers call for Juan Peron to withdraw from Presidential election.)
5. UNO TO BUILD SUPER NEW HOME (UN committee calls for cooperation from architects everywhere to design a new home, to be located in Westchester County.)

(EDITOR'S NOTE: No mention was made, but it appears that the Honshu Pioneer *did not publish a Sunday edition this week. Number 139 was published on Saturday, and Number 140 came out on Monday. The Sunday Supplement was sometimes published under a different name [MR.], but I have nothing for the missing date [February 17], so it's hard to know what happened. Whatever it was, the lack of Japanese news continues.)*

HONSHU PIONEER – VOL I, NO. 141– WAKAMATSU, JAPAN – FEB. 19, 1946

HEADLINES:
1. **POINTS, MONTHS DROP AGAIN** – 42-44 POINTERS ON HIGH SEAS BY NEXT WEEK (Colonel Shaw of 8th Army: Men with 40 points or 24 months to leave as ships become available.)
2. MAJOR BLACKMORE AIRS VIEWS (New 3rd Battalion Commander: Every GI is an individual salesman for democracy – a great deal depends on our contact with Japs.)
3. DELAY SEEN IN GM SETTLEMENT (New issue of promotions and transfers needs to be resolved – Threat of national telephone strike also looms.)
4. CHINA FIGHTING BEGINS AGAIN – CENTRAL GOV'T TROOPS CAPTURE THREE TOWNS (American-equipped Nationalist troops are driving to gain control of all important rail lines – Fighting breaks out in southern Manchuria.)

STATESIDE by A. Hamburger
```
OPINION
Uhl in NY's PM:
   We hate Franco, but Business is Business

   ..Every time you ask someone around the State
Department for policy on Spain you get the stock
answer that we think Franco stinks.

   ..Yet yesterday the State Dept. admitted, rath-
er shamefacedly, I think, that it had authorized
the sale of five C-47 transport planes from sur-
plus war material and a lot of equipment to fix up
the airport outside of Madrid.

   ..Which means that for all of our big words, we
are still doing business at the old stand.
```

```
    ..While  the  present  deal  involves  only  five
planes, there are reliable reports in Washington
that three planes were sold to the Spaniards be-
fore the present setup and that additional sales
of planes are in prospect.
```

(EDITOR'S NOTE: Well, that's a relief! It had seemed for the past few weeks that the old feisty <u>Honshu Pioneer</u> spirit had faded out completely. It's nice to see that Mr. Hamburger, one of the founding fathers of this paper, still has the guts to criticize pro-Fascist actions by his government, even if he has to do it by reprinting an op-ed piece from a New York publication. The "official" editorials continue at this point to be dry educational tracts about the G.I. Bill and readjustment to civilian life.)

HONSHU PIONEER – VOL I, NO. 142– WAKAMATSU, JAPAN – FEB. 20, 1946

HEADLINES:
1. NEW AND OLD LABOR DISPUTES STILL GO ON (250,000 telephone workers may strike soon – No wage offer made yet in Westinghouse strike.)
2. BOWLES CONDEMNS PRESSURE TO BREAK PRICE CONTROLS (Bowles to Congress: Pressure groups are causing inflation by lobbying for higher prices.)
3. ZAIBATSU BREAKING NEAR (Recommendations for breaking up Japanese monopolies to be on MacArthur's desk by the end of March.)
4. DOUGLAS MAY SUCCEED ICKES (Supreme Court Justice William Douglas appears to have the inside track to become the next Secretary of the Interior.)
5. NO ATOM SECRETS OUT (Sec'y of War Patterson: Despite reports, no atomic secrets have been revealed, and none will be.)

(EDITOR'S NOTE: Finally! A report about events in Japan [#3 above], or to be more accurate, the expectation of an event.)

HONSHU PIONEER – VOL I, NO. 143– WAKAMATSU, JAPAN – FEB. 21, 1946

HEADLINES:
1. PHONE OPERATORS VOTE STRIKE (41 of 50 affiliated unions vote to strike – No long distance calls will be possible – Union will meet company "more than half way".)
2. BYRNE REVEALS NO AMERICANS IN CANADIAN ROUNDUP (Recent spy ring arrests by the RCMP included no Americans.)
3. PERON FOLLOWERS FIRE ON MOB (Pre-election violence kills 2, wounds 25, as Peron supporters open fire on 30,000 gathered to hear opponent's speech.)
4. KEENAN SCORES JUSTICES (Justices Murphy & Rutledge dissent on Supreme Court's refusal to review the case of Lt. Gen. Homma, sentenced to be shot in Manila war crimes trial – Head Prosecutor Keenan: Opinions are "offensive to say the least".)
5. PEACE TIME WORK FOR JAP JOBLESS (Kyodo News Agency: Peace-time industries are the focus for finding jobs for 5,000,000 unemployed Japanese.)
6. TO TELEVISE A*BOMB TEST (Forthcoming atom bomb test against warships may be televised, but not to the public.)

(EDITOR'S NOTE: The Homma case [#4 above] was interesting for several reasons. He was the commanding Japanese general in the Philippines, and was heavily criticized by his superiors for his liberality and trying to befriend the Filipinos. However, he was also a poor administrator and a weak commander. His troops conducted the infamous Bataan Death March, where 76,000 Allied prisoners, many starving and sick with malaria, were marched 80 miles down the peninsula under the cruelest abuse imaginable. Thousands died along the way. It was unclear how much Homma

actually knew of this episode, because he had other problems to worry about at the time, but certainly his men were the perpetrators. After the surrender, MacArthur [who had something of a personal interest in these events, since the Bataan victims were his troops] ordered him extradited back to Manila, to be tried there by a military tribunal, instead of remaining in Japan to be tried by the Allied War Crimes Commission. He was quickly convicted and MacArthur ordered him shot. His defense attorney, John H. Skeen Jr., stated that it was a "highly irregular trial, conducted in an atmosphere that left no doubt as to what the ultimate outcome would be". What so offended Head Prosecutor Keenan were subsequent remarks by Associate Justice Frank Murphy of the U.S. Supreme Court: "Either we conduct such a trial as this in the noble spirit and atmosphere of our Constitution or we abandon all pretense to justice, let the ages slip away and descend to the level of revengeful blood purges.")

HONSHU PIONEER – VOL I, NO. 144– WAKAMATSU, JAPAN – FEB. 22, 1946

HEADLINES:
1. NEW STABILIZATION POLICY CAUSES: **STOCKS DROP** (Market closes 2 to 7 points lower on worries that new wage-price controls will squeeze firms too hard.)
2. PHONE STRIKE POSTPONED DAY (Waiting for government talks – Strike still likely.)
3. USSR CHARGES CANADA UNFRIENDLY (USSR charges recent spy arrests in Canada are part of a long-range anti-Russian campaign – Consul recalled to Moscow.)
4. POLISH JEWS MOVE CAUSED BY NAZIS (Thousands of Jews have fled Poland – "Reactionary Fascist gangsters" killed 353 Jews in Poland last year.)
5. RISE IN CLOTHES PRICES (As price relief to manufacturers, a 5% rise in the price of clothing and all cotton goods is expected.)

(EDITOR'S NOTE: Well, that's it – the last issue in my possession. Again, not a word about events in Japan. It seems that somebody decided a few weeks back that the function of this paper should be to keep the troops informed about events back in the U.S., and to prepare them for civilian life. Mostly pretty boring stuff if you ask me, compared to the early months of publication. I was born 27 days later. I doubt if even that historic event was reported in the <u>Honshu Pioneer</u>. I do not know exactly when they ceased publication, but it might as well have been back on the last day of January, in my opinion. The 97th Infantry Division itself was deactivated in March, so it is entirely possible that this was the last issue.)

FRED STARK CARTOONS AND MORE

(EDITOR'S NOTE: As previously mentioned, I think Fred Stark was probably my father's closest friend in Japan. He was a very talented artist and cartoonist with a great sense of humor, but he also contributed both prose and poetry to the paper. I did hear Fred's name mentioned a few times during my youth, but I don't believe they stayed in touch after the war. I had the impression that Fred was a bit of a rebel and an all-around wild man.

Apparently, Dad made a big impression on him during their time in San Luis Obispo, thanks to a crazy coincidence. Dad had a weekend pass and was away from the base, but had some kind of Jeep trouble or whatever, and was very late returning for Monday morning formation. He was the Platoon Leader of Fred's platoon, and as the whole company was standing at attention wearing fatigues, Dad zipped into place at the last possible instant to report his platoon "All present and accounted for, sir!", wearing his Olive Drab dress uniform. Fred was dazzled, and clearly saw Dad as a kindred spirit, not realizing how out of character this episode was for him.

We have seen a few of Fred's drawings and cartoons already, where they were important to illustrate the associated text, but he was a regular contributor to the Honshu Pioneer in his own right, both as a feature writer and especially as a cartoonist. He invented a few continuing characters to star in his cartoons: an American G.I. of the 97th Division named "Pvt. H. B. Twill", a little Japanese girl named "Cherry Blossom", and a more adult Japanese girl named "Rice Blossom". Collected below are a number of Fred's offerings, which I believe convey the feelings of the G.I.s in Japan better than anything else in this book.)

October 2, 1945

October 3, 1945

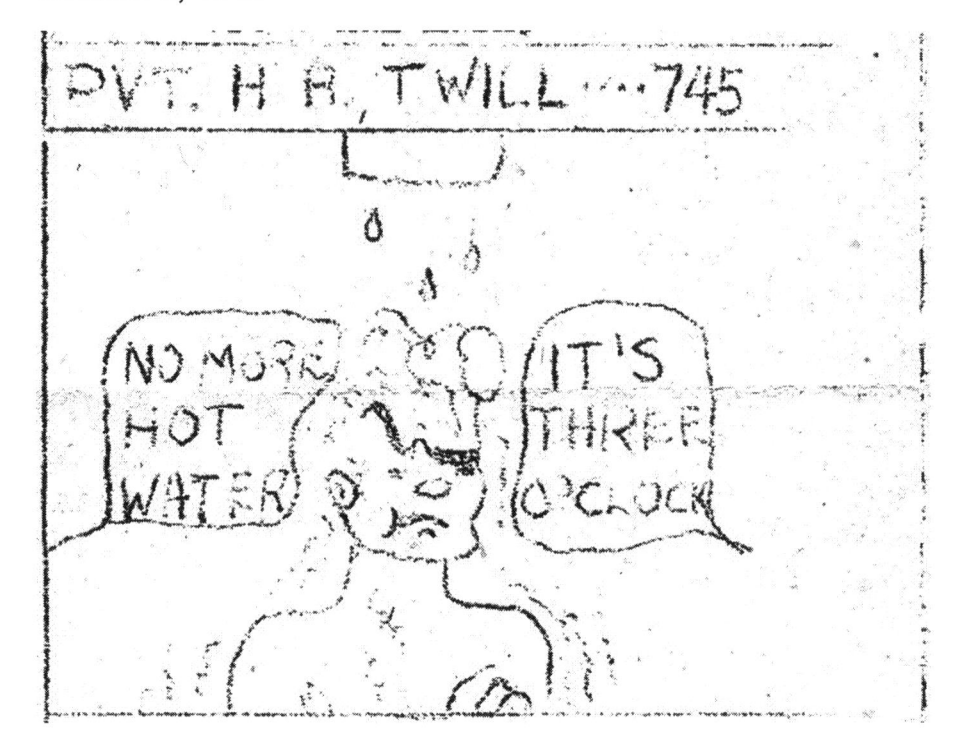

> PVT. H. R. TWILL ... 745
>
> NO MORE HOT WATER
>
> IT'S THREE O'CLOCK

(EDITOR'S NOTE: Clearly, Fred was still getting the hang of the stylus and stencil technique required by the Pioneer's mimeograph format. Trust me, the drawing quality is going to improve.)

October 4, 1945

"SURE GEORGE, TELL ME ABOUT THE POINT SYSTEM.... JUST ONCE!" [H.B. 'TWIL]

October 5, 1945

October 7, 1945

> PVT. H.B. TWILL ⌐ CAMP ARTHUR
>
> "WHAT ARE YA BUCKIN' FOR, CHERRY BLOSSOM, A 745 M.O.S?"

(EDITOR'S NOTE: A man who completed an official Army training program was given a Military Occupational Specialty, or M.O.S. 745 was the M.O.S. number for a rifleman.)

October 8, 1945

PVT. H.B. TWILL – CP. ART'R

"DAMMIT, CHERRY BLOS- SOM, I SAID INHALE!"

October 9, 1945

PVT. H.B. TWILL ~ CAMP ARTHUR

"THERE'S A YEN, CHERRY B. IT'S YER 10% CUT FER BRING-IN' ME LUCK IN THE CRAP GAME LAST NIGHT."

October 10, 1945

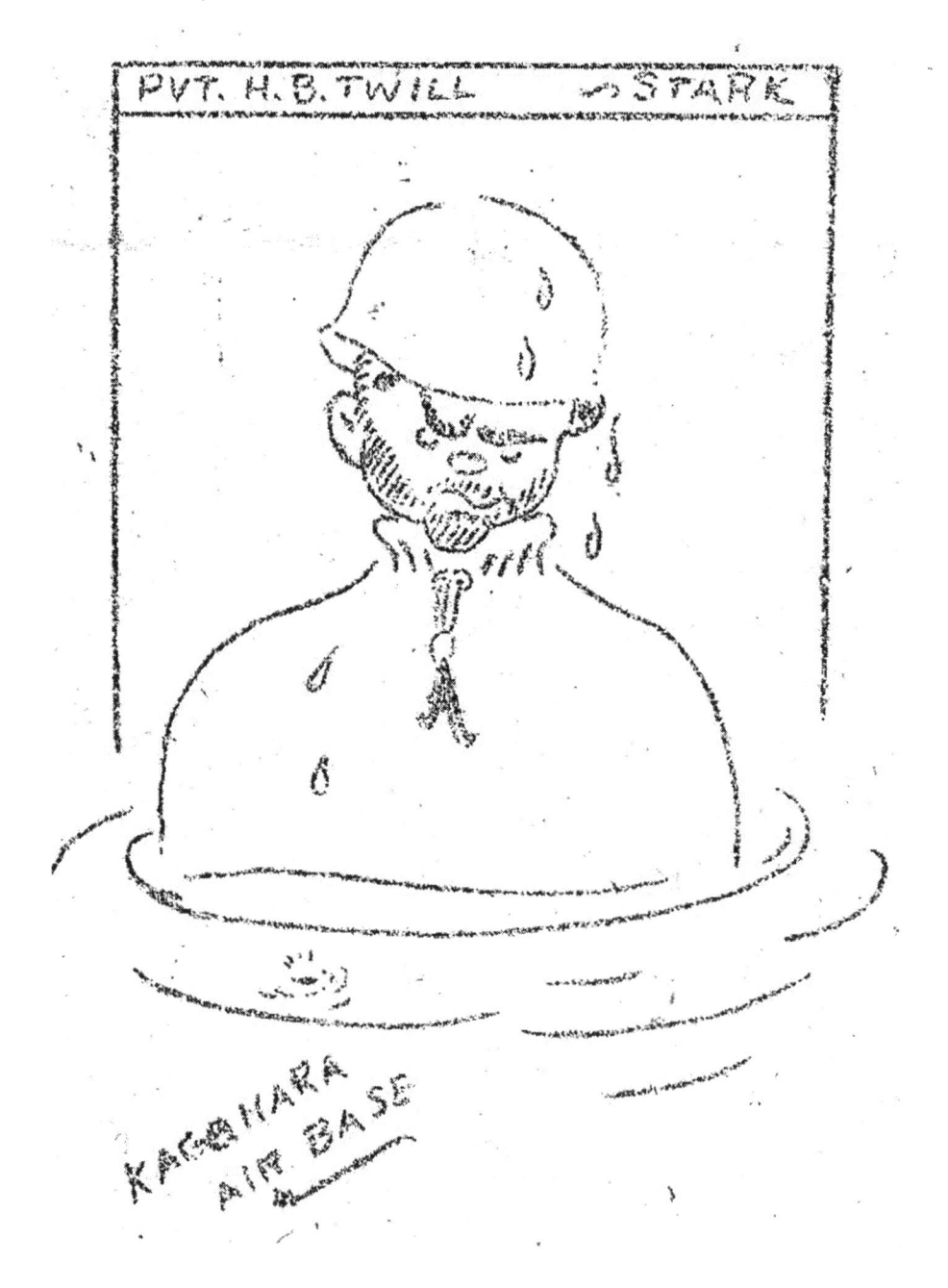

(EDITOR'S NOTE: Apparently conditions were rather damp when K Company arrived at the Kagohara Air Base, after leaving the relative comfort of Kazo.)

October 11, 1945

PVT. H.B. TWILL — TENT "X"

F.S.

"THERE'S A BUTT DOWN THERE, TOO, AND I'M GONNA GET IT BEFORE INSPECTION!"

October 12, 1945

> PVT. H.B. TWILL — KAGOHARA —
>
> "YA SHOULDA SEED ME IN A GREY PIN-STRIPE SUIT, CHERRY BLOSSOM"

(EDITOR'S NOTE: Again we see the Japanese indifference to bathroom privacy.)

October 14, 1945

PVT. H.B. TWILL — STARK

"JUST SEEN THE C.O."

October 15, 1945

> PVT. H. B. TWILL — STARK
>
> "AIN'T TELLIN' HER YER 6 YR. OLD, C.B."

(EDITOR'S NOTE: This might be my favorite Stark cartoon.)

October 16, 1945

[Cartoon: Two figures on ice — one seated reading "HONSHU PIONEER", another in heavy winter gear ice-fishing. Caption:] "I SEE THE 97th didn't GET ITS SECOND BATTLE STAR"

October 17, 1945

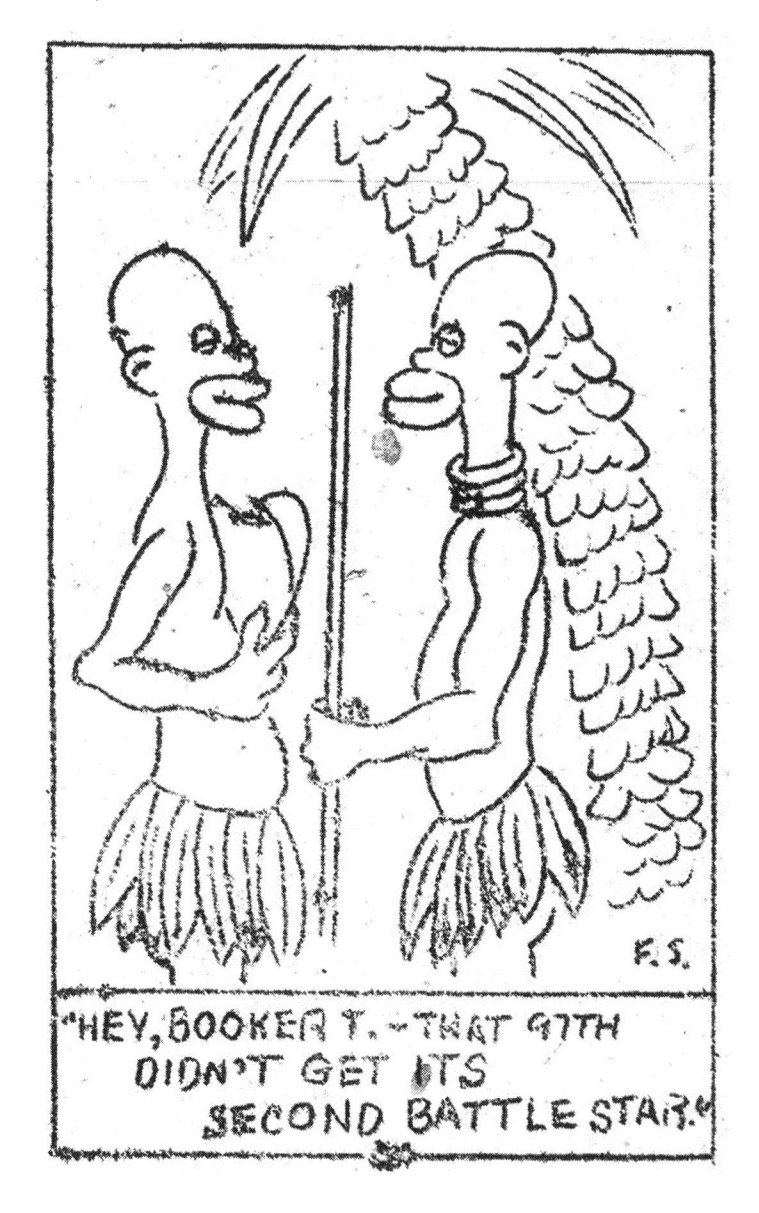

> "HEY, BOOKER T. — THAT 97TH DIDN'T GET ITS SECOND BATTLE STAR."

(EDITOR'S NOTE: "Battle Stars" were attached to campaign ribbons to indicate the number of specific actions during that campaign that the unit had participated in. Apparently there was some thought that the 97th should get another one, and Fred wanted to be sure that as many people as possible in all corners of the globe were aware of this.)

October 18, 1945

"MANUEL! MANUEL! THE 97TH DIDN'T GET ITS 2ND BATTLE STAR!"

October 19, 1945

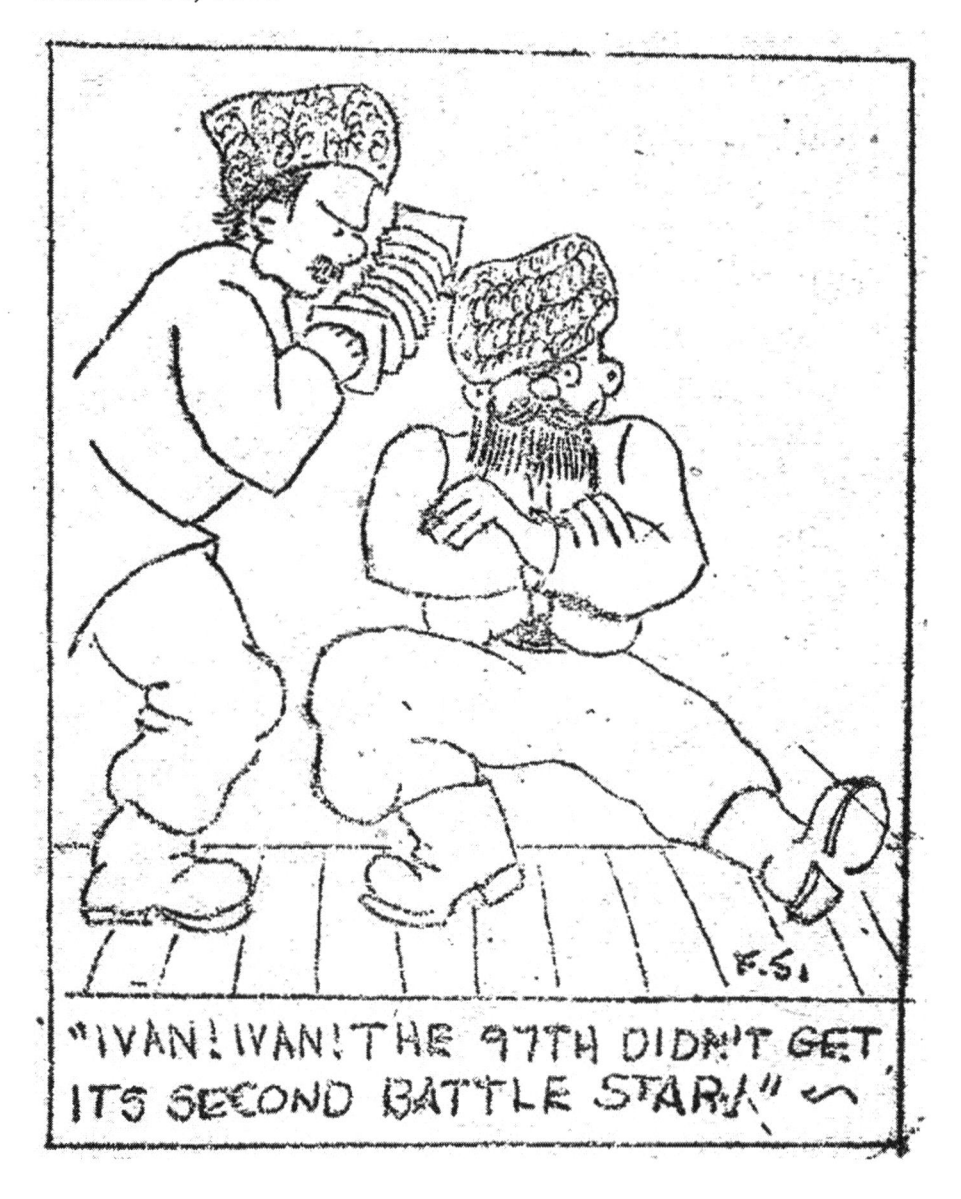

"IVAN! IVAN! THE 97TH DIDN'T GET ITS SECOND BATTLE STAR!"

October 20, 1945

(EDITOR'S NOTE: Ah! A new, more adult Japanese girl appears [her name is Rice Blossom], and Pvt. Twill seems not very interested in her. The Vienna sausage carton he is sitting on is a reference to the other protein source in the GI diet [other than canned salmon that is] that they soon grew heartily sick of.)

October 21, 1945

October 22, 1945

"PVT. H.S. TWILL — RICE BLOSSOM"

"I GUESS YOU KNOW I GOTTA SHAVE TONIGHT AN' CLEAN MY RIFLE AN' WRITE SOME LETTERS AN' GET MY LAUNDRY READY FER TOMORROW"

October 23, 1945

and the wounding of 200.
　　The present government pledges cooperation with the four Allied powers.

"YOU LOOK LIKE HELL WHEN YOU BIN DWINKIN' SHAKLRISHE BLOSSUM."

(EDITOR'S NOTE: I wish Fred would confine himself to drawing in the available space, instead of invading the surrounding copy. However, my guess is that he drew these on paper first, and then transferred them to the stencil at the last minute, and preserving a specific number of column-inches for him every day was difficult.)

October 24, 1945

(EDITOR'S NOTE: Notice the hash marks on his sleeve, the Trident patch, and the date – five years in the future. Get it?)

October 25, 1945

PVT. H.B. TWILL ⚭ PVT. STARK

"MIGHT AS WELL GET ACQUAINTED — WE'LL BE SEEING EACH OTHER A LOT."

October 26, 1945

PVT. H.B. TWILL and C.B.

GET THIS STRAIGHT, C.B.
ONLY ROOKIES GET HOMESICK
BUT DAMMIT — I WANNA GO
HOME!

October 27, 1945

> PVT. H.B. TWILL and RICE BLOSSOM
>
> "RICE BLOSSOM — I'LL GIVE YOU JUST 2 HOURS TO TAKE YOUR HAND OFF MY NEW PACIFIC THEATRE RIBBON."

(EDITOR'S NOTE: At last we see an indication of physical intimacy between Rice Blossom and Twill – two lit cigarettes in the dark. Up to now it seemed like he was trying to keep her at arm's length. It appears that the men of the 97th must have just received a new campaign ribbon for the Pacific Theater of Operations.)

October 28, 1945

PVT. H.B. TWILL vs STARK

"GEE – I DIDN'T KNOW IT WAS SO WARM, SARJINT."

October 28, 1945 – Sunday Supplement

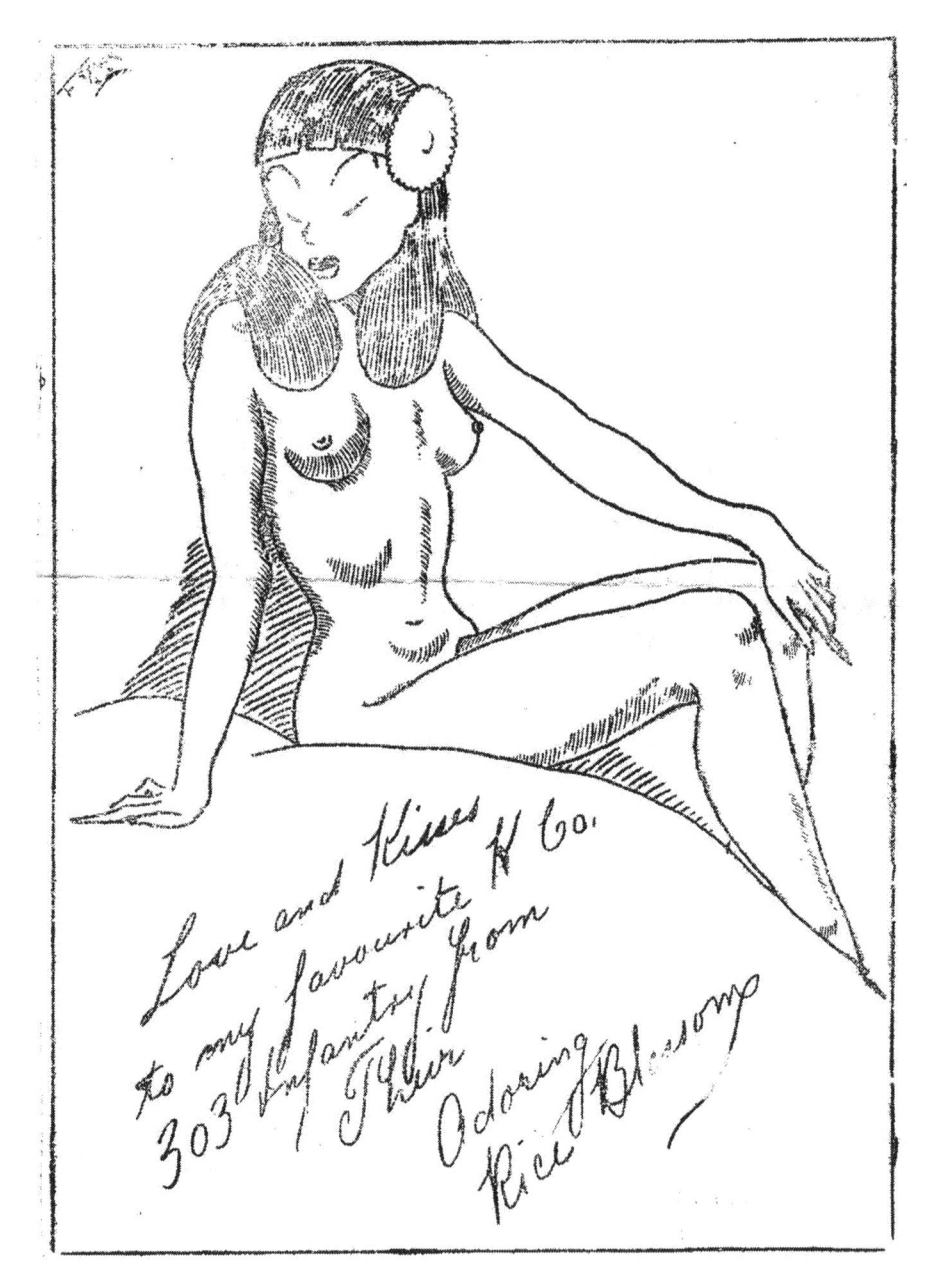

(EDITOR'S NOTE: Holy Moley! A Sunday gift from Fred to K Company! That Rice Blossom is getting sexier every day. This was a special insert sheet, suitable for pin-up purposes.)

October 28, 1945 – Sunday Supplement

    DAMN THE BACKSPACE, FULL SPEED AHEAD
Pencil shavings, fresh erasures,
  Pink-scrubbed cheeks on lotioned majors
      All create that certain smell
     Peculiar to Personnel.
Glory they have somehow missed in
Buildings with no heating system;
    Battling with the circular,
    Aren't you all tubercular?
Calloused fingers make keys stutter,
Blistered thumbs make space-bars flutter,
    Bullied, stepped-on Personnel –
   War is really worse 'n Hell.
                  – F.W.S. II

        THE RAT FROM URAWA

"I am the biggest ole rat in Urawa."

"What's that make me?"

"That makes you giving me another bottle of your ole sake."

"Stop saying 'ole'. It's Winnie the Pooh."

"Never you mind what's ole Winnie the Pooh."

"Nurse that bottle. I only got five more. And let me go back to sleep."

"I am the biggest ole rat in Urawa."

"I guess you think you gnaw everything."

"Even a ole rat can see that's a terrible pun. Even a ole Jap rat from Urawa."

"Stop sniveling and let me go back to sleep."

"Don't tell me what to do."

"You're being difficult, rat. Difficult and boring."

"Boy, do you sound like a ole school teacher."

"How did you get in here? I thought we had the place boarded up."

"You hate me, don't you?"

"Why not? You're always running around making a racket. And squeaking. And nibbling the woodwork."

"Never thought maybe I sleep during the day and run around at night, I suppose."

"You're sniveling again."

"There you go. Ole school-teacher again."

"If I give you another bottle of Sake will you let me go to sleep?"

"Maybe."

"You'll be running around again. Squeaking and nibbling."

"Biggest ole rat in Urawa."

— F.W.S. II

October 29, 1945

> PVT. H. B. TWILL & PVT. STARK
>
> "I'LL GIVE YOU 40 YEN FER A PACK OF BUTTS, BUDDY."

(EDITOR'S NOTE: Cigarettes were pretty scarce at this point. 40 yen was worth about $2.67 in 1945, but in 2013 dollars that would equate to more than $30! Apparently, the GI black market price to the Japanese was about 30 Yen per pack, so Twill is offering him a profit.)

October 30, 1945

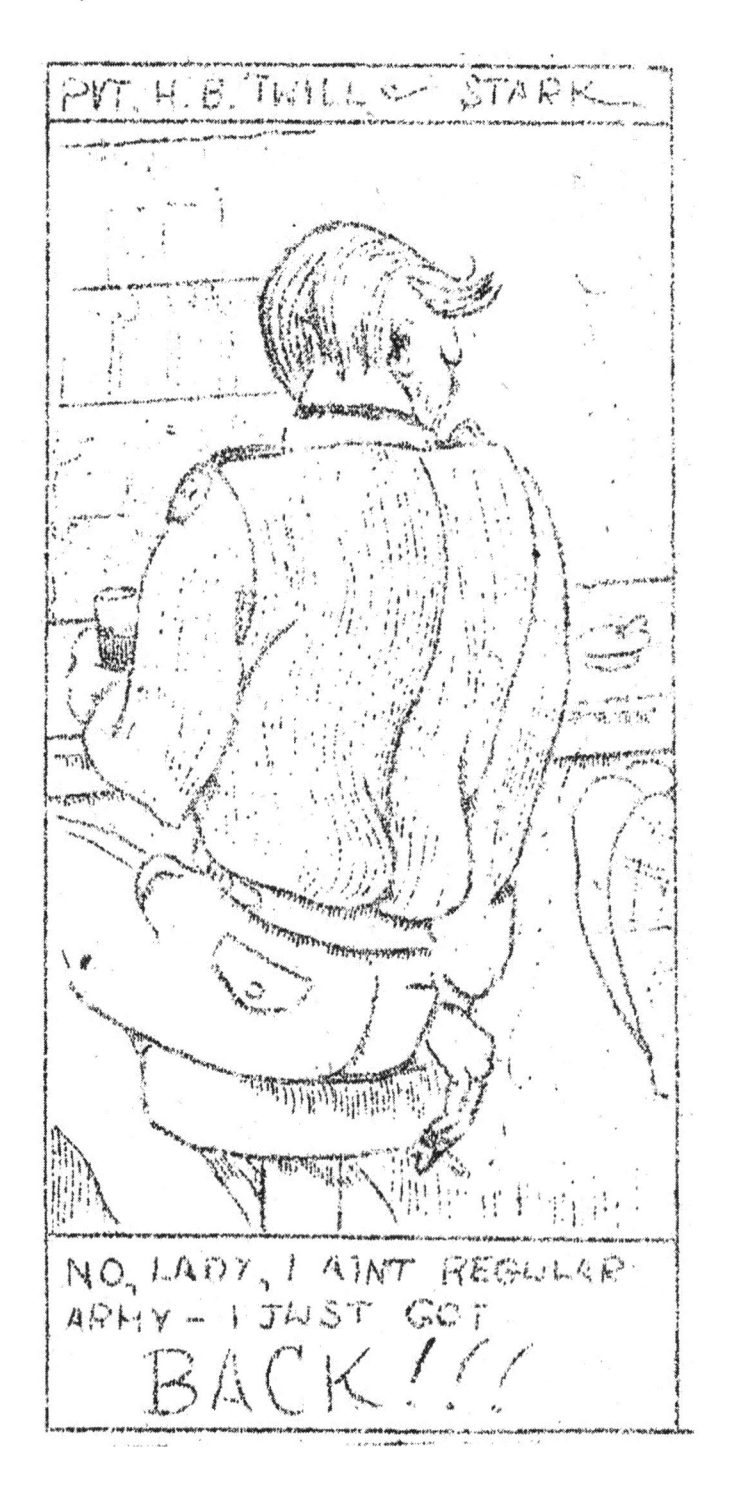

> PVT. H.B. TWILL — STARK
>
> NO, LADY, I AINT REGULAR ARMY — I JUST GOT BACK!!!

October 31, 1945

> PVT. H.B. TWILL ~ STARK
>
> "I DON'T KNOW WHERE THE SHORTSTOP IS ON CIGS, BUT BUDDY — I'M GONNA FIND OUT NOW!"

(EDITOR'S NOTE: As discussed in the Editorial for this date, the tobacco shortage, which was due primarily to GI black market sales to the Japanese, became acute at this time, and apparently Twill is ready to shoot those responsible.)

November 1, 1945

> PVT. H.B. TWILL
>
> "HELL, CHERRY BLOSSOM, I'LL WALK THIS GODDAM POST TH' REST OF MY LIFE—AIN'T NOBODY ELSE HIGHLY TRAINED ENOUGH BACK IN TH' STATES."
>
> —F.S.

(EDITOR'S NOTE: The bitterness of the men trapped in Japan by the lack of replacements [or so they were told] is obvious in this one.)

November 2, 1945

(EDITOR'S NOTE: November 2, 1945 marks the first appearance of Milton Caniff on the pages of the Honshu Pioneer. Milt was a very famous cartoonist in the U.S. at this time, known for his Terry and the Pirates and Steve Canyon comic strips, which were carried in almost every major U.S. paper. I remember reading both of them as a kid. Apparently, he must have decided to start a new strip for distribution to American military dailies, and the Honshu Pioneer was included. You can see how Fred Stark felt about this development in Pvt. Twill's reaction on the preceding page. I have no idea how Male Call was transferred to the mimeograph stencil, but the process left a lot to be desired. The Pioneer's small format and the mimeograph process itself made the text pretty much illegible, as you can see above. I don't blame Fred for feeling annoyed that this tiny little paper suddenly had room for a famous cartoonist to squeeze in and compete with him. I like Fred's poignant, thoughtful, descriptive cartoons a lot better than Male Call, anyway.)

November 3 1945

> PVT. H.B. TWILL ∞ PFC. (!) STARK
>
> "CIGARETTES AT LAST—HEBBE I'M GONNA DIE, BUT I'M GONNA DIE HAPPY!"

(EDITOR'S NOTE: It looks like Fred got promoted to Pfc! I had thought it was more than a decade after this before cigarettes were widely known to cause cancer, etc., but Fred seems to know about it already. Apparently the black market ring has been smashed, and tobacco is reaching the men again, but I didn't see any news of it.)

November 3 1945 – Sunday Supplement

PORTRAIT OF A LT GENERAL'S LT GENERAL

His name is Jasper Q. Frothingswithle... his friends (both of them) call him Jasp. He hails from Fort Riley, Kansas; was issued there fifty-eight years ago. "Family has been in the service since the French and Indian War." Probably have...

"Although my position in the Army means a few unpleasant things occasionally happen," he drawls pleasantly, "don't think I have an enemy in the world. Carry the .45 in my shoulder holster, though... kinda like the Old Army feel of her there." Hmmm...

The General's a short stocky man; almost – in his own rich words, "Sorta gittin a little wide around the old waist." Rear end, too...

In answer to that important question, the General says, "Course we all want to go home; everybody does. But," with a twinkle in his merry steel gray eyes, "till that happy day comes, we must all do that old job the Army gives us to the best of our old ability."

Sure thing, General Jasper Q. Frothingswithle... hope that old readjustment to first lieutenant won't be too much for that old ability. ...thanks for the interview...

– F.W.S. II

November 6, 1945

"HELL, RICE BLOSSOM, LET'S FERGET ABOUT MY BUDDY AND GO BACK TO URAWA."

(EDITOR'S NOTE: Sharp-eyed readers may note that we skipped a couple days. The 11/4/45 issue is one that I don't have, and the 11/5/45 issue did not have a Stark cartoon. It does have another episode of Male Call*, however. Did Fred go on strike to protest the inclusion of the new strip from Milton Caniff? I doubt it.)*

November 7, 1945

November 8, 1945

(EDITOR'S NOTE: Makes you wonder what kind of stuff might happen when they were on guard duty, doesn't it? This sort of thing could not have been encouraged.)

November 9, 1945

PVT. H. B. TWILL and CHERRY B.

"THE WAY THINGS ARE SHAPIN' UP IN THE WORLD, I FIGGER I'LL BE USING THIS DAM THING SOON."

November 10, 1945

> PVT. H.B. TWILL — STARK
>
> "SIR, HE SAYS HE AIN'T NEVER HEARD OF THE 97TH OR GRID SQUARES EITHER, AND THERE AIN'T NO ORDER HE HEARD OF COME DOWN ABOUT CARRYIN' SPEARS."

(EDITOR'S NOTE: This appears to be a reference to some of the fact-finding activities that GI's were assigned to in territory that had been conquered by the Japanese. I believe the consensus among the troops was that this was mostly a waste of time, or even a make-work project to keep them overseas.)

November 13, 1945

> **PVT. H. B. TWILL ∽ STARK**
>
> Twill couldn't be bitter today. Why hell, he's up in the clouds. He's been reading about U.S. ships carrying supplies for the Dutch to Indonesia——and Chinese Central Government troops to Manchuria.
>
> Twill doesn't want to go home on these ships. He wants to sit here on Honshu and wait for the next war. Of course, he won't have any idea what he's fighting for or against, but he's up in the clouds today. JUST HAPPY AS HELL!

(EDITOR'S NOTE: Again, it looks like Fred took a couple days off, but he returns with a vengeance. The level of sarcasm in this piece sheds some light on why he and my dad would have been such good friends. They saw the world pretty much the same way, and had very similar senses of humor.)

November 14, 1945

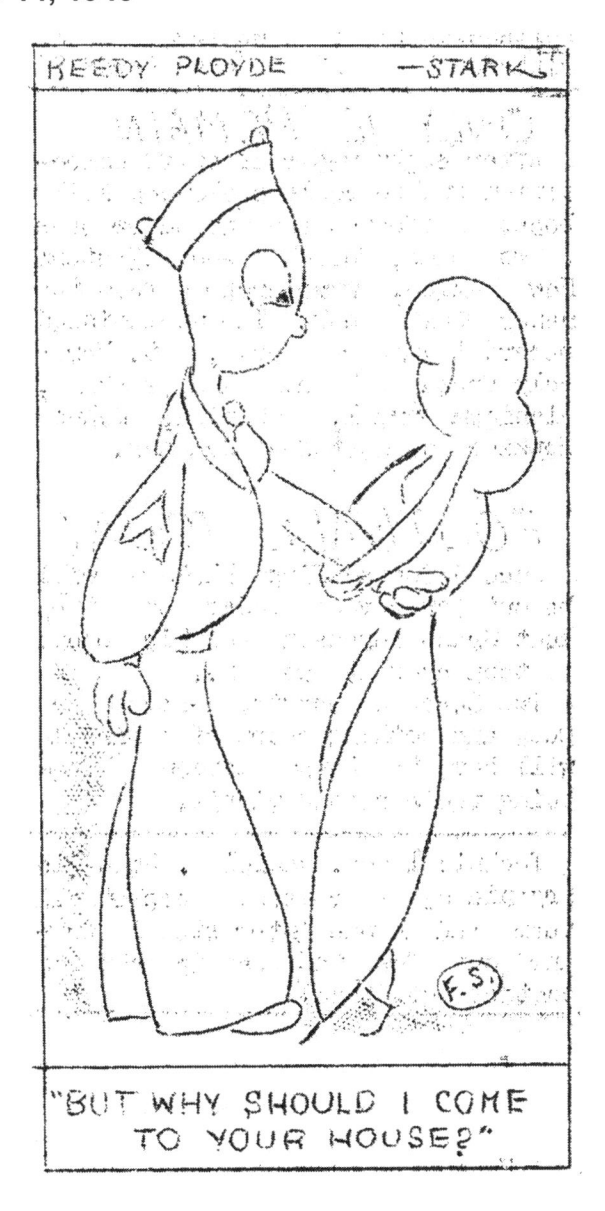

> REEDY PLOYDE — STARK
>
> "BUT WHY SHOULD I COME TO YOUR HOUSE?"

(EDITOR'S NOTE: "Reedy Ployde"? [For those of you who are half asleep, that means "redeployed", or in this case "Newly arrived in Japan".] I think it's a dirty trick for Fred to be introducing us to new characters after six weeks, but H. B. Twill – a seasoned veteran – would never be taken in by a Japanese hooker, so I guess a new face was needed.)

November 15, 1945

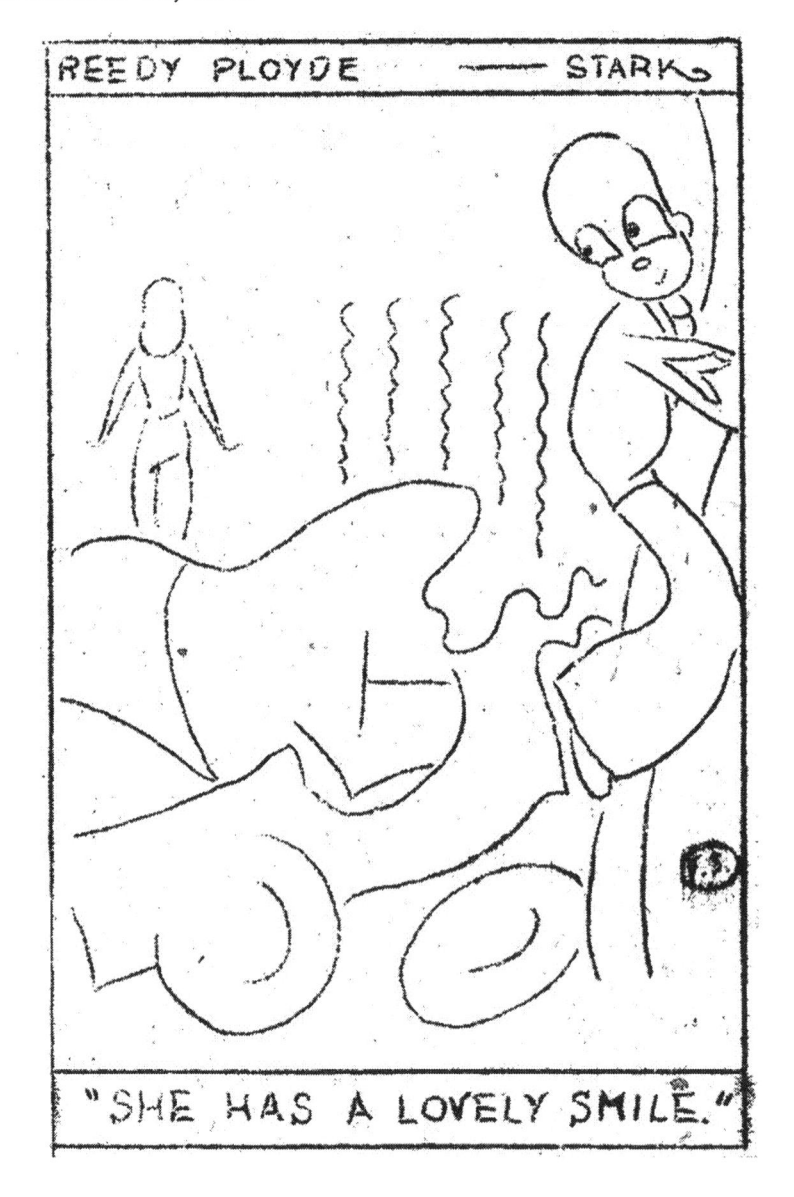

> REEDY PLOYDE — STARK
>
> "SHE HAS A LOVELY SMILE."

(EDITOR'S NOTE: Now I'm getting annoyed. Is he letting Cherry Blossom draw the cartoons now? Creativity and drawing quality have both taken a nose-dive in the last couple days. Has Fred been busy with other matters?)

November 16, 1945

REEDY PLOYDE — STARK

F.S.

("I CAN'T FIND IT, I CAN'T FIND 'NO' IN THIS PHRASE BOOK. OH GOSH! OH GOSH!")

November 19, 1945

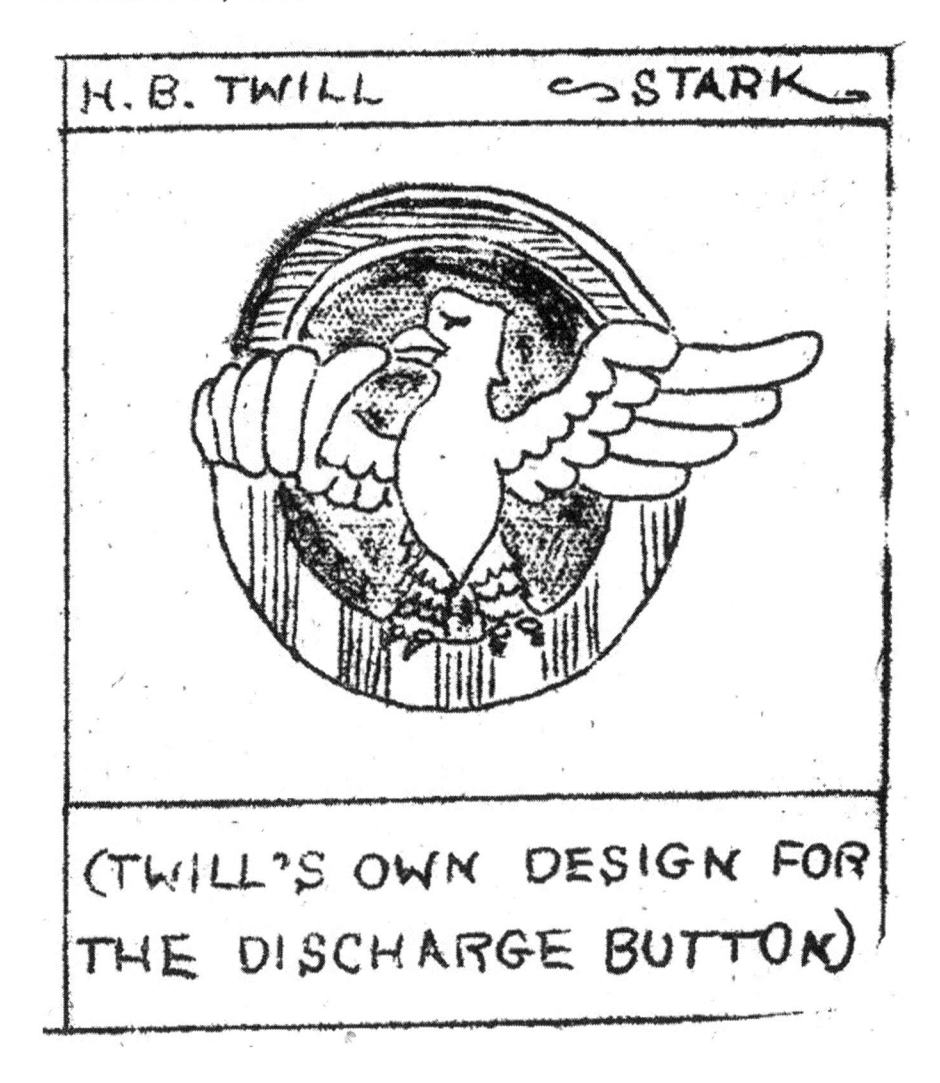

> H. B. TWILL — STARK
>
> (TWILL'S OWN DESIGN FOR THE DISCHARGE BUTTON)

(EDITOR'S NOTE: At least we see that Twill is still alive. Fred has been missing for a couple days. Since it was a weekend [this is Monday], I suspect a pass to Tokyo was involved.)

November 19, 1945

> PVT. H.B. TWILL ST. RK.
>
> "WHY SHOULD I B-B-BITCH— G-G-GOT MY C-CUBIC A-FEET OF AIR SP-P-PACE."

(EDITOR'S NOTE: It looks like cold weather has arrived in Urawa, not to mention bats. Still, it's good to see Pvt. Twill again.)

November 22, 1945

"I AIN'T IN LOVE WITH THE INFANTRY BUT I RESENT VERY STRONGLY THAT THESE GUYS SHOULD REQUEST I GET A HORSE."

(EDITOR'S NOTE: It appears that some Cavalry types have shown up in our area [perhaps for Thanksgiving dinner today], and Twill found them offensive. It looks like Cherry Blossom, wearing her Trident patch, managed to stay out of the mayhem.)

November 23, 1945

> PVT. H. B. TWILL — STARK
>
> "AN' PLEASE FERGIT ABOUT TH' CIGARETTES AN' CANDY AN' GIT ME JIST ONE BAR OF SOAP. AMEN."

(EDITOR'S NOTE: Soap was another black market item that pretty much disappeared at about this time. Dad wrote a limerick about it in his column.)

November 24, 1945

"WHERE'S THE SUNNAVABICH THAT POLICED UP THE BUTT I HAD HID UNDER MY BUNK."

November 25, 1945 – Sunday Supplement

Waldeck's Lonely Verse – Frederick W. Stark

COINCIDENCE MAKES THE WORLD GO ROUND. Coincidence also helps make a story interesting. Waldeck asked me to tell you this before I started in because he says too much coincidence in a story makes the reader feel like a sucker. You may consider yourself warned.

Now that I've told you that, I can tell you about Waldeck Riggs.

Waldeck Riggs was unfortunate enough to be sweating it out in the army of occupation in Japan for the saddening total of nine months. I know this is a saddening total because I was with Waldeck for all of those nine months plus six more in Europe before that. It's enough to drive strong men batty, and I personally think it did as good a job on Waldeck as anyone I know, including myself. Although Waldeck was a queer duck from the start.

Any guy everybody calls Waldeck instead of Wally has to be.

That's the reason I wasn't too surprised at the kid back in Kazo, Japan, when he started mumbling a verse from a poem – off and on for twenty-four hours a day. As a matter of fact I was proud of him when he told me he had made up this Verse. It didn't begin to get me (and the rest of the squad) down until the second week.

"Waldeck," I said, "maybe I can help you figure out the rest of that poem. Then you can send it to this babe and we can forget it all."

"What babe?" asked Waldeck. That had me for a minute. For two weeks he had been raving about the hair on this Irish wench named O'Rourke. That was Waldeck's little poem. When he told me he didn't know her I shut up. We had one more month before we were due back in the States. I didn't want to get into an argument with Waldeck and tell him that I thought writing poems that were about a girl he didn't know was kind of sappy. I didn't want Waldeck to lose his temper at me. Not when both of us were so close to going home.

If I hadn't shut up I might never have looked Wally up after we got out.

You know those little foreign shops at Rockefeller Center in New York? Imagine walking past them on a spring morning. About 10:30. It's very pleasant. It was so pleasant on this particular morning, I even gave old Waldeck a break.

"Waldeck," I said, "civilian clothes look almost as good on you as they do on me."

"Thank you," murmured Waldeck and stopped dead in his tracks. I never realized Waldeck took an interest in Norwegian pottery. But that's what he was staring at. I looked too. Then I saw it.

Wrapping up a little statue of a horse for an old lady. My heart started to play leapfrog with my Adam's apple and I saw that Waldeck was having the same difficulty plus a case of the shakes.

The next thing I knew he tore through the door up to the counter.

And then before me and the old lady and the little horse, if it could see through the wrapping paper, my buddy, my Waldeck Riggs, completely blew his top.

"You're Irish, aren't you?" panted Waldeck. "I mean that's a green dress you've got on. Like a shamrock. And those eyes. They're violet. I couldn't ever think of anything to rhyme with violet that would fit into the poem. I had to leave your eyes out. You don't really care, do you? We can figure something out though, can't we? Together I mean. We can get a whole bunch of verses right in swing with the one I've got now. Ha ha ha ha. It'll be a cinch. Brother, look at that hair. What a break. If your name's Patricia Maguire O'Rourke I'll die. Right here in this Norwegian pottery shop."

The old lady and I left. She seemed a little shocked. I was amazed. Anyway, it seemed like a private affair, and I never interrupt a friend's snow jobs.

Outside I lit up a butt and stared at the big bronze man holding the Earth on his back. Suddenly I had an idea. I caught the old lady with the package just before she climbed on the Madison Ave. bus.

"Excuse me, ma'am, but what's that babe's name? The one you bought the little horse from?"

"I believe that young lady's name," snorted the old gal as she tossed her frame on the bus, "is Maguire. Patricia Maguire."

Well. That's the Big Coincidence. The more I think about it the more I realize a person needs a lot of warning before they'll believe something like that. But it's true. I got a telegram from Waldeck right here on my desk. It says:

> "The glossy pelt
> Of the sultry Celt
> Mrs. Patricia
> Maguire
> Riggs."

The verse doesn't have the same melody to it that it did back in Kazo, Japan, but I don't think that's going to make any difference. Not after the way she looked at the jerk in the pottery shop. I think they'll live happily ever after.

Who knows? They might even get together, like Waldeck suggested, and write a poem to fit his verse.

-END-

(EDITOR'S NOTE: I suspect that Fred actually wrote quite a bit of stuff for the paper, but bylines were extremely rare, so attribution is difficult. Thank goodness he signed all his drawings.)

November 26, 1945

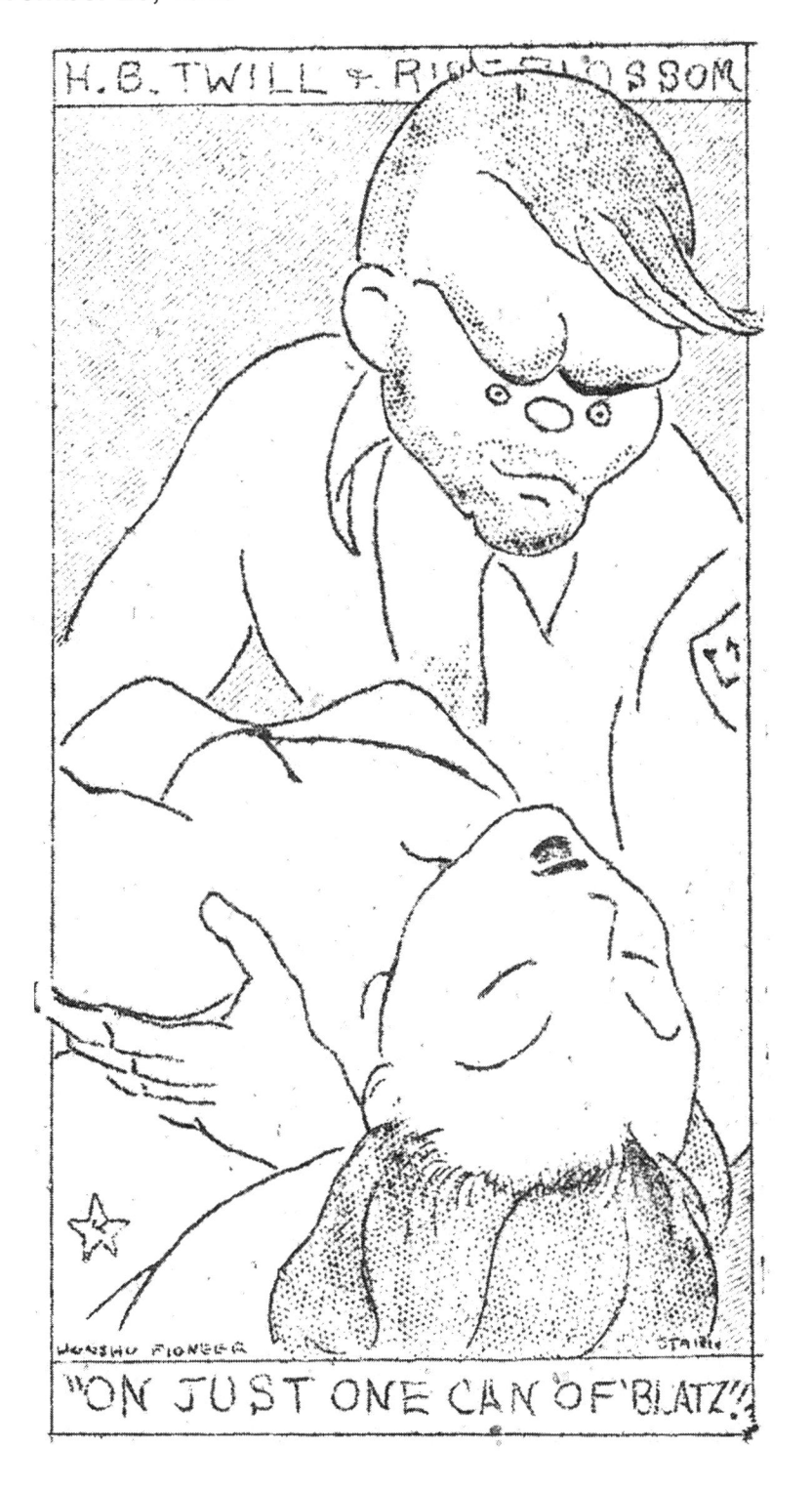

November 27, 1945

November 29, 1945

PVT. H.B. TWI[...] RATIONS

"5 WHOLE CHOCKLIT BARS, 6 BOTTLES OF BEER, AND A PACK OF BUTTS — WHY MAN, I DON'T NEVER WANNA GO HOME!"

December 2, 1945

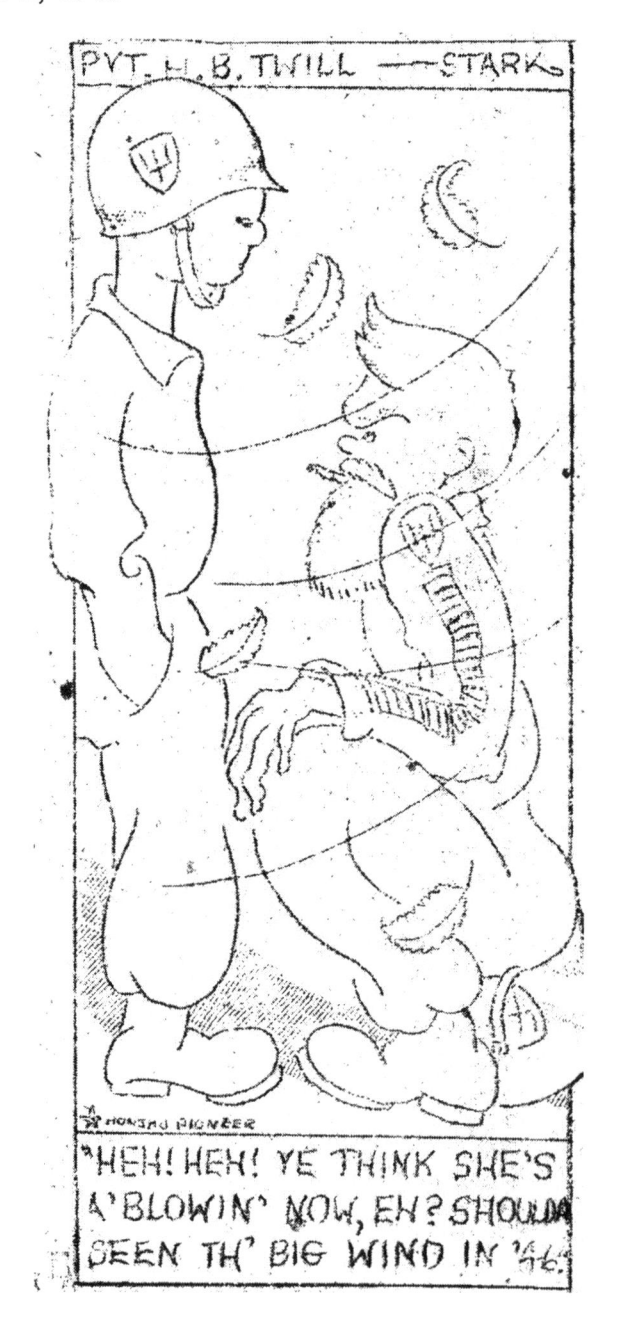

> "HEH! HEH! YE THINK SHE'S A'BLOWIN' NOW, EH? SHOULDA SEEN TH' BIG WIND IN '46."
>
> — PVT. H. B. TWILL — STARK

(EDITOR'S NOTE: A geriatric Twill with about a zillion hash marks on his sleeve is apparently still stuck in the Army, many decades hence – everybody's worst fear.)

December 4, 1945

December 5, 1945

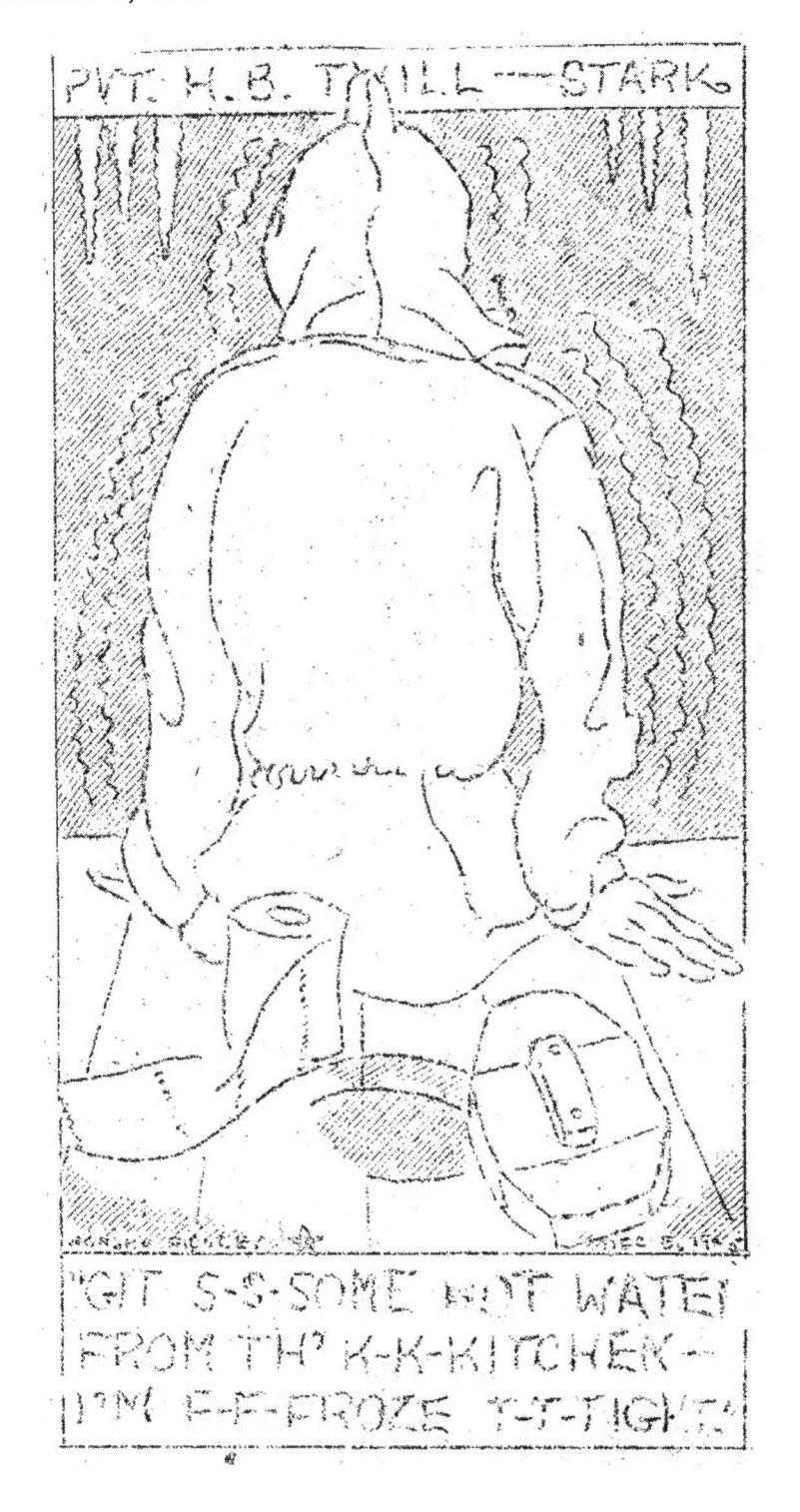

December 8, 1945

"HOW DO THEY TREAT YOU ARMY GUYS OVER HERE?"

(EDITOR'S NOTE: Apparently there was some thought that Navy guys had it better than their Army counterparts. Could this be related to the previous cartoon where Twill gets frozen to the latrine seat? By the way, cartoons are coming from several sources now, and Fred's work is seen less frequently, but he's still the only cartoonist on the masthead. The rest are from syndicates or other outside sources.)

December 10, 1945

> (TWILL ASKED US IF WE'D LIKE TO PRINT THIS PHOTO OF HIS COUSIN, JOE STACKINGSWIVEL, WHO JUST ENLISTED FOR 3 YEARS. TO PLEASE TWILL, WE PUT IT IN TODAY. ED.)

(EDITOR'S NOTE: I don't really need to explain Fred's implication that anyone who would enlist in the Army is a jackass, do I?)

December 12, 1945

> PVT. H.B. TWILL — STARK
>
> HERE LIES
> M/SGT
> H.B. TWILL
> LANDED JAPAN:
> SEPT. 26, 1945
> DIED JAPAN:
> AUG. 3, 1979
>
> HOUSING PIONEER DEC. 11 — STARK
>
> NEWS ITEM
> (Stars & Stripes: Dec. 11)
>
> "...There was no breakdown of figures available for the number of men shipping out of Japan and Korea."

(EDITOR'S NOTE: Things have gone from bad to worse for Twill, who never gets home, but dies in Japan after being stuck there for 34 years. I imagine Fred was feeling that his future might be the same. I'm sure many of them were hoping to be home for Christmas, but they now see that it isn't going to happen this year.)

December 13, 1945

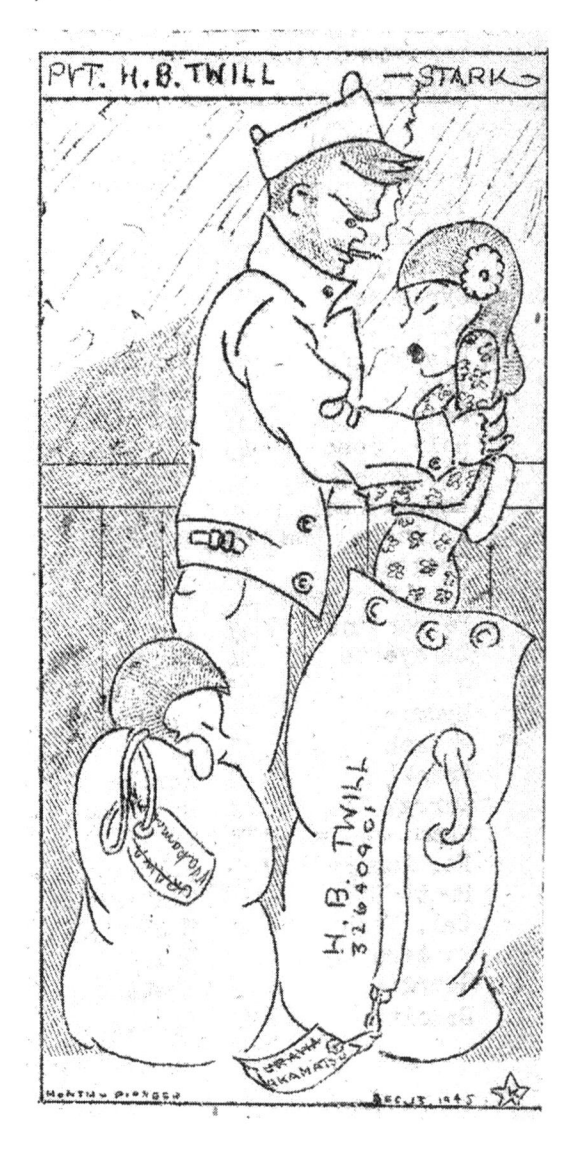

(EDITOR'S NOTE: If you look carefully at the tags, you might see that "Urawa" has been crossed out and "Wakamatsu" has been written in. This was the day that K Company moved from Urawa to Wakamatsu, and if you look back at my father's column for this date, it appears that some hearts may have been broken by the move. Twill has found a way to avoid this by smuggling Cherry Blossom and Rice Blossom along in his duffel bags.)

December 15, 1945

> PVT. H.B. TWILL — STAR
> I.G. ONE A.M.
>
> "THAT AIN'T NO EXTRA SOCK, CAPTIN — IT'S A GODDAM SOOVINEER!"

(EDITOR'S NOTE: Art's column for this date was also a diatribe against the new inspection protocols that were implemented upon their arrival in Wakamatsu. Apparently, someone up the ladder decided to start cracking the whip on these guys.)

December 18, 1945

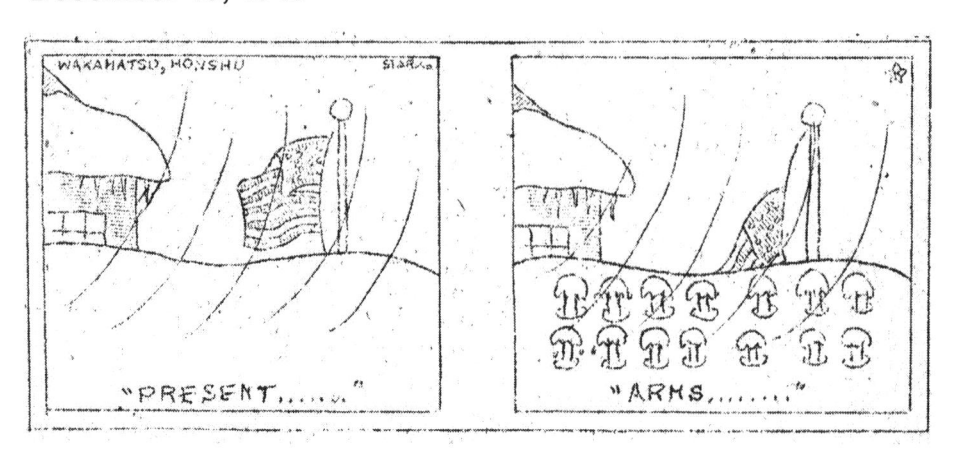

WAKAMATSU, HONSHU	
"PRESENT......"	"ARMS,......"

(EDITOR'S NOTE: Apparently, there was a bit of snow in Wakamatsu at this time.)

December 19, 1945

(EDITOR'S NOTE: Hey! Wait a minute! We've seen this cartoon before! It was just a couple of weeks ago, but before the Honshu Pioneer *became the official battalion paper, so maybe Fred wanted to share this one with a wider audience. It would seem to me that he would have to re-draw the whole thing to make a new stencil. I compared them side-by-side to see if they are actually different, and they are, very slightly. This might confirm my suspicion that he drew them on paper and then transferred them to the stencil.)*

December 20, 1945

(EDITOR'S NOTE: You may remember from the news coverage and editorials that fire was a terrible threat in these ancient wooden buildings that served as barracks in Japan. It was cold, and wood stoves were the only heat, but the buildings were not really built for them. This cartoon came four days after they had a major fire of their own in Wakamatsu. It looks as if a bunch of orders came down to try to reduce the danger.)

December 23, 1945 – Sunday Supplement

> Dear Sue: Spending a few mo. at Wakamatsu – all the rage this winter – my dear, it's simply swarming with eligible young men. Skiing, skating, dancing – Why don't you & Trish come down? I'm at the Hotel Wallace – Please come – Sal.

First in a series of full page illustrations depicting the gay life pursued by the Allied Occupation Forces on Honshu, Hokkaido, and Kyushu. Mr. Stark is now on detached service with the 1042nd Yak Pak Battalion in North-Western Tibet, where he is now preparing a second series of sketches, on the exciting life led by the men in this special unit.

(EDITOR'S NOTE: The drawing on the preceding page represents a new frontier in Fred's career at the Honshu Pioneer. A few comments are warranted:

1. *The word "gay" had a different meaning in 1945 than it does in 2013.*
2. *I do not believe that the U.S. Army had any Yak Pak Battalions deployed in North-Western Tibet at that time [or any other], but stay tuned – we may hear more of this.*
3. *The contrast between the words in the note and the illustration are worthy of a master of sarcasm like Fred, subtly pointing out the utter boredom and loneliness they were enduring in Wakamatsu.*
4. *Fred's artistic style reaches new heights in this drawing, which I would call an example of "pre-cubist Art Deco". I wonder what became of Fred after the war. Google seems to know nothing about him.*
5. *This was not the only art work that Fred contributed to this pre-Christmas Sunday Supplement. See next page.)*

December 23, 1945 – Sunday Supplement

(EDITOR'S NOTE: Fred's Christmas present to the men of the 303rd was another pin-up sheet of Rice Blossom, looking better than ever. Whatever else you might say about him, the guy could certainly draw.)

December 27, 1945

PVT. H. B. TWILL —STARK

"OVERSEAS? HELL, BABY— AIN'T THIS OVERSEAS?"

January 6, 1946 – Sunday Supplement

(EDITOR'S NOTE: The print quality of the following three pages was so good [relative to most of these relics], and the drawings so integral to the story, that I decided not to transcribe them, but to just let you see what they look like. This book will no doubt be printed without color, but in addition to improving its print quality, the <u>Honshu Pioneer</u> seems to have added a second color to its mimeograph process. The header block on Fred's feature was printed in red ink. You will still see a fair number of typos and misspellings, but remember, they only got one shot at typing that stencil – no spell check and no corrections.

You may remember that back on December 23 Fred reported that he had been transferred to a Yak Pack Battalion in Tibet, as a punishment for revealing how boring life was for G.I.'s in Japan. Apparently, he decided to follow up that story line.

This crazy report is so like my father's work that it's hard for me to believe he didn't have something to do with it. The drawings show off Fred's artistic talents at their highest level. Presumably, since it was for a Sunday Supplement, he had much more time to work on them.

As for the story, I hardly know what to say. The levels of fabricated detail and deadpan explanation of the most outrageous nonsense are as good as anything my father ever concocted. If Fred did this entire piece on his own, then I have to acknowledge him as Dad's equal in the story-telling line.)

Letter from Tibet

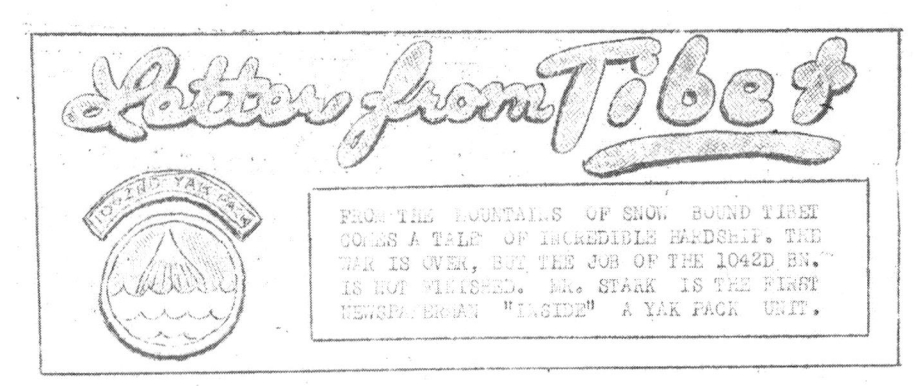

FROM THE MOUNTAINS OF SNOW BOUND TIBET COMES A TALE OF INCREDIBLE HARDSHIP. THE WAR IS OVER, BUT THE JOB OF THE 1042D BN. IS NOT FINISHED. MR. STARK IS THE FIRST NEWSPAPERMAN "INSIDE" A YAK PACK UNIT.

I AM WRITING BY THE LIGHT OF A Coleman lantern. My tent is approximately 15000 feet above sea-level, and the temperature is a good thirty-one degrees below zero.

Life in a Yak Pack Battalion is interesting, but it's no fun.

Major Borden, second in command of the 1042nd, mentioned last night that we are scheduled, weather permitting, to arrive in Chozahng the day after tomorrow. I'll find a warm billet there and work on the notes I've taken.

I'm sending this stuff back to Thring Lu by native runner. As for the second article, there is an Air Transport Command base twenty-seven miles from Chozahng and I'm sure everything will get to you on time.

ON THE MARCH

A Yak Pack Battalion on the march----it's something to see. If you can imagine a line of struggling humans and animals pushing slowly through a driving snow up an impossible incline, you have a vague idea of what I'm talking about.

We get a break every hour, and it's during these breaks that a man starts to do a little thinking. He wonders how it is possible that three Yak Pack units in the United States Army have received so little publicity from the War Department. Activated in 1927, the 1042d Yak Pack Battalion and the 17th and 18th Amphibious Yak Pack Companies are almost unknown to both soldiers and civilians.

I spoke to Maj. Borden about this tonight and he mentioned the surprise element. "The use of Yaks in forward echelon supply work, with an emphasis on mountain warfare, has, with the exception of (see YAKS, next page)

WEST POINTER F. BOSWELL BORDEN, WHO ENTERED 1042D BN. IN 1929.

> Donald. A fine specimen of bull yak who has been in the 1042nd since 1939. Used in the States for breeding, he still carries full equipment with his squad.
>
> (AT STATION NO. #4 19 MILES EAST OF NILANG ON THE PUNJAB-TIBET BORDER - 12/21/45)

> Third platoon of the 1042nd Yak Pack on our second day out of Tiring Mu. Notice the second Yak from left, whose hind foot has slipped into an ermine hole hidden by the snow. The weight of his pack caused him to lose his balance, and he rolled over and over before regaining his footing at the bottom of the incline. The Yak in the foreground wears no pack; two yaks from a squad of six are held in reserve each day and carry no equipment. -----

our 1042nd, been completely neglected since Hannibal crossed the Alps. The Yak used amphibiously was unheard of prior to the inception of the 17th and 18th. Of course, now that the war's over, there's no reason our eighteen year old ban on information should not be lifted. That's why Col. Bessamer suggested we bring one of you newspaper fellows along."

Well, the ban might just as well be lifted, because all of the Yak Pack outfits saw enough combat in World War II to make their story indelible forever, in the minds of Hun and Jap.

Maj. Borden has already cabled to Capt. Swenson of L2, Records Division, Yak command, Special troops, Ft. McGooley, Utah, for complete data on the combat participation of these outfits.

This information on the 1042nd I have already. The Battalion, now doing practical field research with new Quartermaster equipment here in Tibet, went into action near Oro-Mio, Italy on Thanksgiving Day, in 1943. They served throughout the Italian Campaign as a frontline supply route maintenance group, attached to the 4th Alpine Chausseurs of de Poussigny's French 7th Division. Although the 1042nd's casualties were kept down to three percent, the rugged climactic conditions took a good deal out of men and yak alike, and the entire battalion bivouaced near Rome on V-E plus six for a well deserved rest. It was not until July that the outfit received alert orders for its new destination---Skinner Barracks, Rompur.

"It was quite a trip," said Maj. Borden dreamily. "We were carried in LST's through the Suez Canal as far as Karachi. There they loaded us on British lorries for the dusty overland route through Rajputana. I guess most of the men have forgotten how many pup tents we pitched before we hit the Punjab-Tibet frontier. It was quite a trip."

Col. Bessamer, who wears the Croix de Guerre (one palm) and the Medaille Militaire underneath his heavy parka, told Maj. Borden at Skinner Barracks that all of the men in the 1042nd had elected to stay with the unit.

"I don't mind telling you it was a relief to the Colonel," Maj. Borden continued. "All these men are highly trained and it's damned near impossible to get replacements. Besides, a yak gets to know his Packmaster as well as he knows the other Yaks in the squad. A Yak would be rather unnerved to wake up and find a green fellow waiting to strap on his pack."

Major Borden was unable to help me out on the 17th and 18th Amphibious, because both these companies served in the Pacific theatre. They caught a bit of the old Dickens at Nawiyoto Atoll. I read about it in the Infantry Journal. You'll have to wait until Swensen gets that cable back to me before I can tell you anything about the Amphibs. We took most of our training in the States in Utah and Colorado, while they spent most of their time in Florida and Mississippi."

The glare from my Coleman lantern is beginning to annoy the Yaks tethered outside. Anyway, it's late and my bones ache.

We travelled over thirty miles today in an effort to prove that our combination alpine snow boots (spiked), lower pant leg and double sock combined, will not become moist during an eleven hour exposure period. They did.

To Be Continued

January 8, 1946

PVT. H.B. TWILL — STARK

"I WONDER COULD A 81MM MORTAR SHELL GIT FROM HERE TO THE PENTAGON..."

Headline on newspaper: DEMOBILIZATION SLOWED DOWN

January 12, 1946

(EDITOR'S NOTE: Fred had a cartoon in his regular spot in the January 12 issue. Apparently, it was still pretty cold in that damn latrine.)

January 13, 1946

PVT. H.B. TWILL—STARK

"HERE'S MY RIFLE, BUDDY— LET'S SEE YER PISTOL."

January 20, 1946 – Sunday Supplement

(EDITOR'S NOTE: This was the cover of the Sunday Supplement insert for January 20, 1946, called "MR." Although he does not mention her name, Fred's exquisite portrait of his beloved Cherry Blossom is as good as it gets. I can't help wondering if she was totally a creature of his imagination, or a real Japanese girl [my bet]. This was the issue that also contained Dad's article on the Bushido suicides, which Fred illustrated, as you may remember.)

January 20, 1946 – Sunday Supplement

CAVALRY CHARGES

by

FREDERIC WAGNER STARK II

There's something I'd like to know:
Were cavalry charges really as
Glamorous
As movies and paintings and books
Make them out to be?

When the bullet from a Prussian needlepoint
Pierced the breastplate of a cuirassier
Did it sting less
Than a buzzing piece of lead from a Nazi burp gun
Ripping through a doughboy's OD shirt?

Did a guy from the 27th lancers or
The 10th Hussars look just as
Silly
Bleeding in two separate portions at Balaclava
As a bisected GI from the 1st Division at St. Malc?

I wonder if a disemboweled Kuban Kossack
Riding a saddle on his backbone was
Happier
Than a US Marine who suddenly finds he's
Going to have trouble
Sitting down – for the rest of his life?

Were cavalry charges really as glamorous
As movies
And paintings
And books
Make them out to be?

(EDITOR'S NOTE: You must remember that the 97th saw heavy action in Europe, with 80% casualties, before their relatively peaceful sojourn in Japan. Fred's powerfully anti-war poem indicates that he hasn't forgotten, and he hopes nobody else will, either.)

January 23, 1946

"MACARTHUR'S REALLY KNOCKING HIMSELF OUT GETTING REPLACEMENTS"

(EDITOR'S NOTE: The headline from a few days earlier indicated that the Army, desperate for replacement troops, had decided to take men who had previously been rejected as unfit for service, or 4-F. Apparently the seasoned veterans in Japan were a bit skeptical about the quality of the newcomers. On the other hand, they should have welcomed them with open arms, since the arrival of replacements hastened their own departure for home.)

Well, that's it. That's all I have of Fred's amazing work. My father's last column was published six days later, on January 29. I would like to think that the two of them got to ride home on the same boat, after working so closely together all this time, but, of course, I have no idea what actually happened.

I have a hard time believing that a person of Fred's talent did not leave a record of himself somewhere that Google would be able to find, but he probably would have been retired by the time the Internet came along, so I guess it's not that surprising.

I did manage to turn up a copy of his enlistment form, thanks to Ancestry.com, and learned that he was born in Pennsylvania in 1926, but enlisted in Boston in 1944. That means he was just

19 years old when all this was going on. It appears that he died in Palm Beach, Florida in 1994.

I wish I had seen these papers when my dad was still alive, because I would have loved to learn more about Fred, and their time working together on the Honshu Pioneer.

EPILOGUE

It took me over five months to transcribe, scan in and format all this content, and during that time my idea of what this book was going to be about changed several times. I started out just to collect my father's writings as a family keepsake, but then I got interested in the actual history that was going on at the time, so I started summarizing the headlines from each issue, as well. This eventually led me to start reading more of the editorials, and many of them knocked my socks off, so they had to be included, too. Lastly, I started to actually look at Fred Stark's work, and slowly came to the realization that he was a truly exceptional talent – a genius, really. So then I had to go back through everything again and collect his work, almost as a separate book, and quite possibly the most entertaining part. So what started out to be a collection of my dad's writings actually ended up as a history of the entire enterprise.

In the meantime, a friend recommended that I read <u>Occupation</u> by John Toland, a historical novel that focuses on the War Crimes trials in Tokyo. That book happens to be out of print, but my devoted daughter Tracy managed to track down a copy for me, and it was certainly very illuminating. As historical fiction, it is heavy on the history and light on the fiction. To say it is meticulously researched would be an understatement. I did some research of my own to get familiar with events of the time, and Toland had every detail nailed exactly, plus a whole lot more information that I would never have found.

In the process of assembling all this I learned a lot about history, Japan, World War II and the international politics of the early post-war period. I learned a lot of things about my father – many of them pretty surprising. Most importantly I learned a whole lot about the feelings, beliefs, standards, hopes and fears of the guys who fought that war. They were indeed "The Greatest Generation", as Tom Brokaw dubbed them.

Over the years of my adult life I have occasionally met people who knew my dad, not in the war, but through work or church or other activities. When they realized I was Art's son, every one of them went out of their way to let me know how much they admired and loved him. That goes for me too. He really was an amazing guy.

Well, I have enjoyed doing this very much, and I hope a few of you managed to read this far and actually enjoyed it too.

Printed in Germany
by Amazon Distribution
GmbH, Leipzig